VACATION & SECOND HOMES

NEW REVISED EDITION

Design VH4061

345 Designs For Recreation, Retirement and Leisure Living

480 to 4,136 square feet

HOME PLANNERS

Published by Home Planners
A Division of Hanley-Wood, Inc.
Editorial and Corporate Offices:
3275 West Ina Road, Suite 110
Tucson, Arizona 85741

Distribution Center:
29333 Lorie Lane
Wixom, Michigan 48393

Rickard D. Bailey, CEO and Publisher
Cindy Coatsworth Lewis, Publications Manager
Paulette Mulvin, Senior Editor
Amanda Kaufmann, Project Editor
Paul D. Fitzgerald, Book Designer

Photo Credits

Front Cover: Andrew D. Lautman
Back Cover: Andrew D. Lautman
First Printing, January 1995

10 9   8   7   6   5   4   3

On the front cover: For lake-side leisure, this comfortable country
home, Design VH4061, offers all the best. See page 91 for floor
plans and details. Front cover photo is shown in reverse.

On the back cover: Get away from it all in this heart-warming
retreat, Design VH2488. Page 191 takes a closer look.

TABLE OF CONTENTS

In addition to the many planning and construction aids available to help you successfully build your home, Home Planners offers Quote One®, an exclusive service designed to help you estimate the costs involved in building your home, based on your individual zip code. The Quote One® service is available for many of the homes shown in this collection. Please see page 300 for more information regarding this valuable tool.

Design VH3658

ABOUT THE DESIGNERS

The Blue Ribbon Designer Series™ is a collection of books featuring the home plans of a diverse group of outstanding home designers and architects known as the Blue Ribbon Network of Designers. This group of companies is dedicated to creating and marketing the finest possible plans for home construction on a regional and national basis. Each of the companies exhibits superior work and integrity in all phases of the stock-plan business including modern, trendsetting floor planning, a professionally executed blueprint package and a strong sense of service and commitment to the consumer.

Design Basics, Inc.

For nearly a decade, Design Basics, a nationally recognized home design service located in Omaha, has been developing plans for custom home builders. Since 1987, the firm has consistently appeared in *Builder* magazine, the official magazine of the National Association of Home Builders, as the top-selling designer. The company's plans also regularly appear in numerous other shelter magazines such as *Better Homes and Gardens, House Beautiful* and *Home Planner.*

Stephen Fuller/Design Traditions

Design Traditions was established by Stephen S. Fuller with the tenets of innovation, quality, originality and uncompromising architectural techniques in traditional and European homes. Especially popular throughout the Southeast, Design Traditions' plans are known for their extensive detail and thoughtful design. They are widely published in such shelter magazines as *Southern Living* magazine and *Better Homes and Gardens.*

Alan Mascord Design Associates, Inc.

Founded in 1983 as a local supplier to the building community, Mascord Design Associates of Portland, Oregon began to successfully publish plans nationally in 1985. With plans now drawn exclusively on computer, Mascord Design Associates quickly received a reputation for homes that are easy to build yet meet the rigorous demands of the buyers' market, winning local and national awards. The company's trademark is creating floor plans that work well and exhibit excellent traffic patterns. Their motto is: "Drawn to build, designed to sell."

Larry E. Belk Designs

Through the years, Larry E. Belk has worked with individuals and builders alike to provide a quality product. After listening to over 4,000 dreams and watching them become reality all across America, Larry's design philosophy today combines traditional exteriors with upscale interiors designed for contemporary lifestyles. Flowing, open spaces and interesting angles define his interiors. Great emphasis is placed on providing views that showcase the natural environment. Dynamic exteriors reflect Larry's extensive home construction experience, painstaking research and talent as a fine artist.

Larry W. Garnett & Associates, Inc.

Starting as a designer of homes for Houston-area residents, Garnett & Associates has been marketing designs nationally for the past ten years. A well-respected design firm, the company's plans are regularly featured in *House Beautiful, Country Living, Home* and *Professional Builder.* Numerous accolades, including several from the Texas Institute of Building Design and the American Institute of Building Design, have been awarded to the company for excellence in architecture.

Home Planners

Headquartered in Tucson, Arizona, with additional offices in Detroit, Home Planners is one of the longest-running and most successful home design firms in the United States. With over 2,500 designs in its portfolio, the company provides a wide range of styles, sizes and types of homes for the residential builder. All of Home Planners' designs are created with the care and professional expertise that fifty years of experience in the home-planning business affords. Their homes are designed to be built, lived in and enjoyed for years to come.

Donald A. Gardner, Architects, Inc.

The South Carolina firm of Donald A. Gardner was established in response to a growing demand for residential designs that reflect constantly changing lifestyles. The company's specialty is providing homes with refined, custom-style details and unique features such as passive-solar designs and open floor plans. Computer-aided design and drafting technology resulting in trouble-free construction documents places the firm at the leading edge of the home plan industry.

The Sater Design Collection

The Sater Design Collection has a long established tradition of providing South Florida's most diverse and extraordinary custom designed homes. Their goal is to fulfill each client's particular need for an exciting approach to design by merging creative vision with elements that satisfy a desire for a distinctive lifestyle. This philosophy is proven, as exemplified by over 50 national design awards, numerous magazine features and, most important, satisfied clients. The result is an elegant statement of lasting beauty and value.

Home Design Services, Inc.

For the past fifteen years, Home Design Services of Longwood, Florida, has been formulating plans for the sun-country lifestyle. At the forefront of design innovation and imagination, the company has developed award winning designs that are consistently praised for their highly detailed, free-flowing floor plans, imaginative and exciting interior architecture and elevations which have gained international appeal.

EDITOR'S NOTE

Lucky you! Building a second or vacation home is an exciting venture! With over 345 plans to choose from, *Vacation & Second Homes* is the perfect guide to a successful home-building experience. What can you expect to find in this book? Because it includes designs from the nine designers in the Blue Ribbon Network of Designers, the most important thing you'll notice is variety. That is, variety in style, size, applications, amenities—you name it. The homes featured in this collection range from 400-square-foot lake-side cottages to elaborate second homes. Styled after rustic dwellings of the past, some provide the rudimentary comforts of home. Others, with the most contemporary looks, find room for spas, two-story gathering rooms and gourmet kitchens for pure pampering.

Vacation homes may run smaller, but, as less elaborate versions of permanent residences, they also tend to mimic many of the same styles, from Tudor to Bungalow. Or you might view building a vacation home as a unique opportunity to explore a different housing style. One very popular style that was developed for vacation living is the A-frame. The style actually came about as a sort of joke by architect Rudolph Schindler. Faced with designing something for an exclusive area at Lake Arrowhead with a "Norman Style"-only rule, Schindler, a one-time draftsman for Frank Lloyd Wright, contemplated how to bring in the modern style he was so adept at. It came about in the A-frame, which he declared "Norman" and which no one bothered to challenge as such. Nowadays, the A-frame remains one of the most popular vacation-home styles.

Another very remarkable style has been named "Florida Contemporary." Pier-style homes, built largely along Southern waterways and beaches, offer character and livability. This leads to one of the most important factors in vacation-home design—floor plans that accommodate leisure lifestyles. One aspect of this is larger-sized rooms with few interior walls

for open living spaces. And, as today's home builder wants as many amenities as possible, many of the designs contained in this collection carry the favorites—full kitchens, luxury baths, volume looks.

Sleeping areas may take on different configurations as well. Instead of two or three large, private bedrooms, a vacation home may function nicely with one private master suite and a large loft bunk area for children. Or there might be several smaller bedrooms that offer some degree of privacy but don't demand a great percentage of the overall square footage.

Great and abundant outdoor living areas are essential to a vacation home. There are many choices: decks, patios, balconies and terraces to name a few. A large main deck is a natural gathering place for general relaxation, dining and conversation. A master suite terrace allows space for more private encounters. A children's deck provides an activity center for boisterous play.

Other components exist to make the perfect vacation home. A fireplace in the main living area cheers and warms on a cold winter evening. Built-in storage spaces keep the home from becoming crowded and cluttered and a small laundry area accommodates quick clean-ups.

If you envision something a little more substantial as a second home, many of the plans in this collection fill the bill. With square footages topping out at over 4,000 square feet, there's room enough for your most elaborate fancy. Sweeping master bedroom suites, great entertaining spaces and ample sleeping zones for family and friends are a few items to look for. Before you finish planning, select one of the "Outdoor Projects"—featured at the end of the book—to extend livability.

No matter what your building situation, as a final ingredient, add plenty of windows and skylights to fill interior spaces with light and the scenic views beyond!

Design VH3442

One-Story Traditionals

Photo by Andrew D. Lautman

Design by
Home Planners,
Inc.

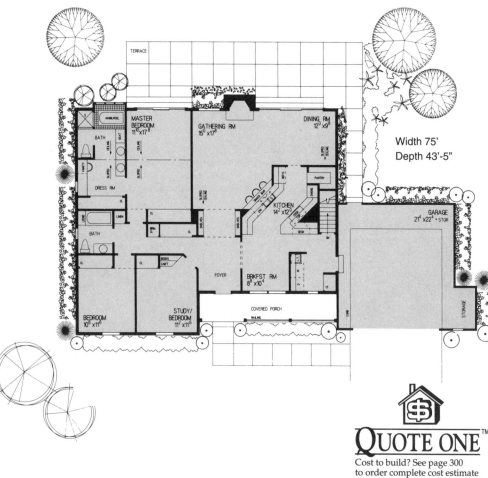

Width 75'
Depth 43'-5"

Design VH2947

Square Footage: 1,830

L **D**

● This charming one-story traditional home greets visitors with a covered porch. A galley-style kitchen shares a snack bar with the spacious gathering room, where a fireplace is the focal point. An ample master suite includes a luxury bath with a whirlpool tub and a separate dressing room. Two additional bedrooms, with one that could double as a study, are located at the front of the home.

California Engineered Plans and California Stock Plans are available for this home. Call 1-800-521-6797 for more information.

Quote One™

Cost to build? See page 300
to order complete cost estimate
to build this house in your area!

Design VH3600/VH3601

Square Footage: 2,258/2,424

L

● This unique one-story plan seems tailor-made for a small family or for empty-nesters. Formal areas are situated well for entertaining—living room to the right and formal dining room to the left. A large family room is found to the rear. It has access to a rear wood deck and is warmed by a welcome hearth. The U-shaped kitchen features an attached morning room for casual meals. It is near the laundry and a washroom. Bedrooms are split. The master suite sits to the right of the plan and has a walk-in closet and a fine bath. A nearby study has a private porch. One family bedroom is on the other side of the home and also has a private bath. If needed, the plan can also be built with a third bedroom sharing the bath.

Design by
Home Planners,
Inc.

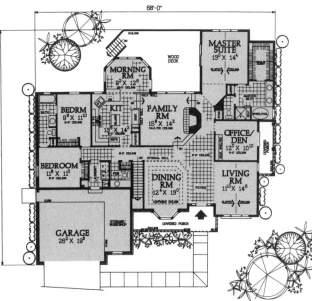

VH3601

QUOTE ONE™

Cost to build? See page 300 to order complete cost estimate to build this house in your area!

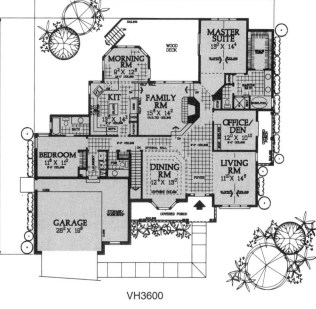

VH3600

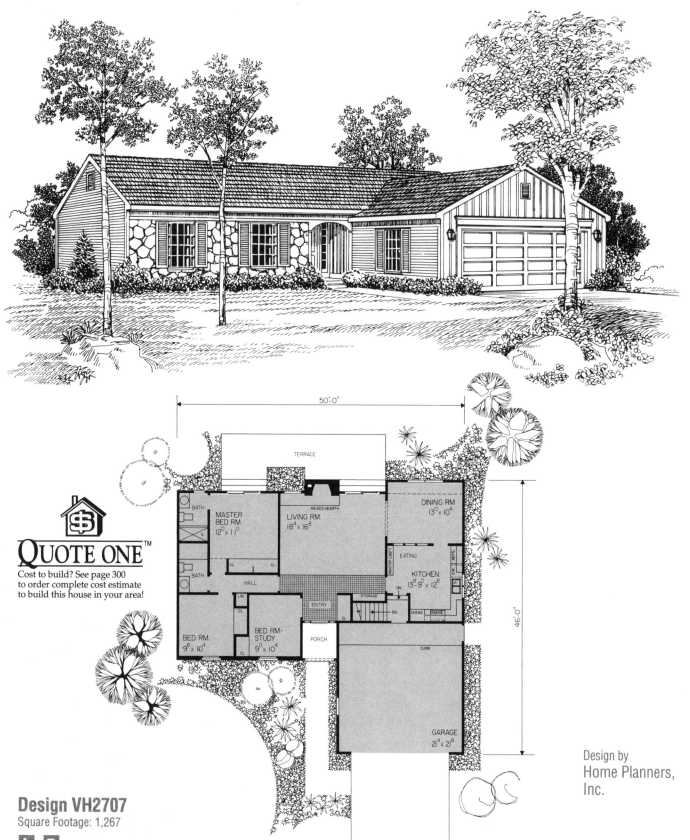

TERRACE

BATH

MASTER
BED RM.
12⁰ x 11⁰

LIVING RM.
18⁴ x 16⁸

RAISED HEARTH

DINING RM.
13⁰ x 10⁴

EATING

PANTRY CAB'T

BATH

CL CL

HALL

LIN.

CL

BED RM.
9⁸ x 10⁴

BED RM-
STUDY
9⁰ x 10⁴

CL

ENTRY

STORAGE

DN.

CL

DN.

KITCHEN
13'-9" x 12⁸

REFR.

DW

OVENS

RANGE

PORCH

CURB

GARAGE
21⁴ x 21⁸

50'-0"

46'-0"

Design by
Home Planners,
Inc.

Design VH2707
Square Footage: 1,267

L **D**

● Here is a charming Early American adaptation that will serve as a picturesque and practical retirement home. Also, it will serve admirably those with a small family in search of an efficient, economically built home. The living area, highlighted by the raised hearth fireplace, is spacious. The kitchen features eating space and easy access to the garage and basement. The dining room is adjacent to the kitchen and views the rear yard. Then, there is the basement for recreation and hobby pursuits. The bedroom wing offers three bedrooms and two full baths. Don't miss the sliding doors to the terrace from the living room and the master bedroom. Storage units are plentiful including a pantry cabinet in the eating area of the kitchen. This plan will be efficient and livable.

Design by
Home Planners,
Inc.

Design VH2505

Square Footage: 1,366

L D

● This design offers you a choice of three distinctively different exteriors. Which is your favorite? Blueprints show details for all three optional elevations. A study of the floor plan reveals a fine measure of livability. In less than 1,400 square feet there are features galore. An excellent return on your construction dollar. In addition to the two eating areas and the open planning of the gathering room, the indoor-outdoor relationships are of great interest. The basement may be developed for recreational activities. Be sure to note the storage potential, particularly the linen closet, the pantry, the china cabinet and the broom closet.

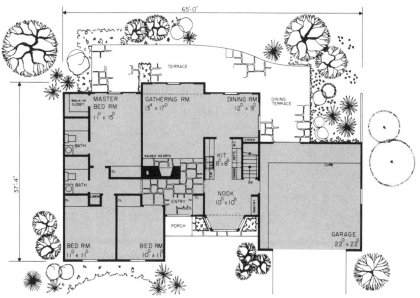

Design VH2878

Square Footage: 1,521

L **D**

● This charming one-story traditional design offers plenty of living space in a compact size. Thoughtful zoning puts all bedroom sleeping apart from household activities in the living and service areas. The home includes a spacious gathering room with a sloped ceiling, a formal dining room and a separate breakfast room. There's also a handy pass-through between the breakfast room and the large, efficient kitchen. The master bedroom suite has a private bath and a walk-in closet. A third bedroom can double as a sizable study just off the central foyer. This design offers the elegance of traditional styling with the comforts of a modern lifestyle.

California Engineered Plans and California Stock Plans are available for this home. Call 1-800-521-6797 for more information.

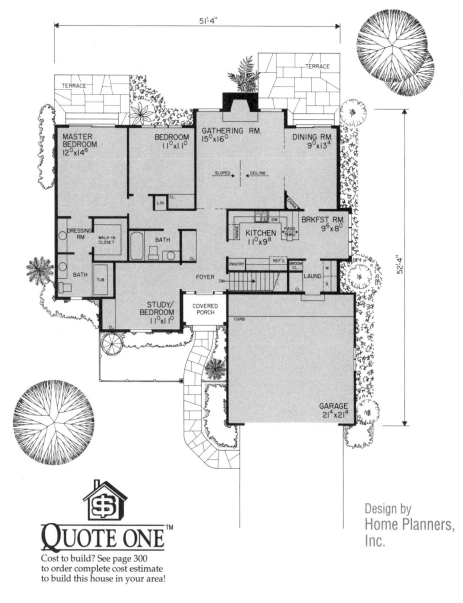

QUOTE ONE™

Cost to build? See page 300
to order complete cost estimate
to build this house in your area!

Design by
Home Planners, Inc.

VH9529

Design VH9529/VH9530/VH9531
Square Footage: 1,420

● This efficient floor plan carries three different exterior elevations for just the right look. Inside, a living room or den opens to the right of the entry. It offers an optional built-in or closet. In the kitchen, an abundance of counter space and an accommodating layout make meal preparations simple. A great room and dining room connect to this area and will conform to everyday living. Two bedrooms include a master suite with a private bath and ample closet space. The master bedroom also accesses the outdoors for an added treat.

Design by
Alan Mascord
Design Associates, Inc.

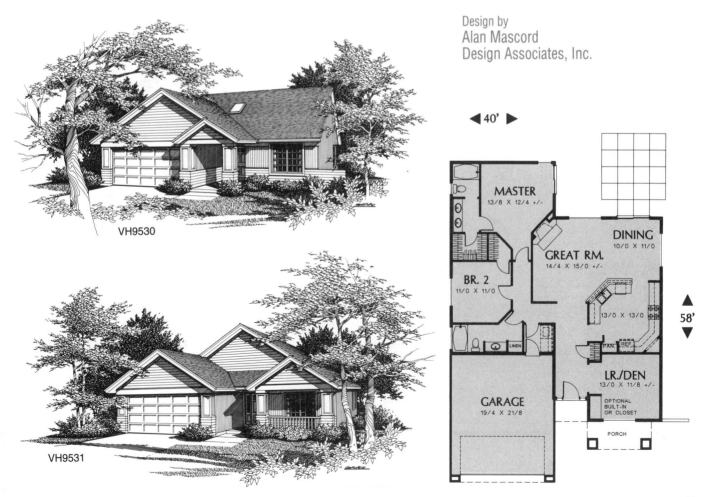

VH9530

VH9531

◀ 40' ▶

58'

MASTER
13/8 X 12/4 +/-

DINING
10/0 X 11/0

GREAT RM.
14/4 X 15/0 +/-

BR. 2
11/0 X 11/0

13/0 X 13/0

PAN. REF.

LINEN

GARAGE
19/4 X 21/8

LR./DEN
13/0 X 11/8 +/-

OPTIONAL
BUILT-IN
OR CLOSET

PORCH

Design VH9528

Square Footage: 1,843

● The vaulted living room of this design makes a grand first impression. A niche in the entry hall further accentuates this area. On the right, a dining room accommodates formal meals well. In the kitchen, an island cooktop will please cooks of any caliber. A sunny nook opens to the vaulted family room with its warming fireplace. Nearby, two secondary bedrooms—or a bedroom and a den—offer ample closet space. A full hall bath features interesting angles. In the master bedroom suite, a bathroom with a spa tub, a large walk-in closet and outdoor access all command attention.

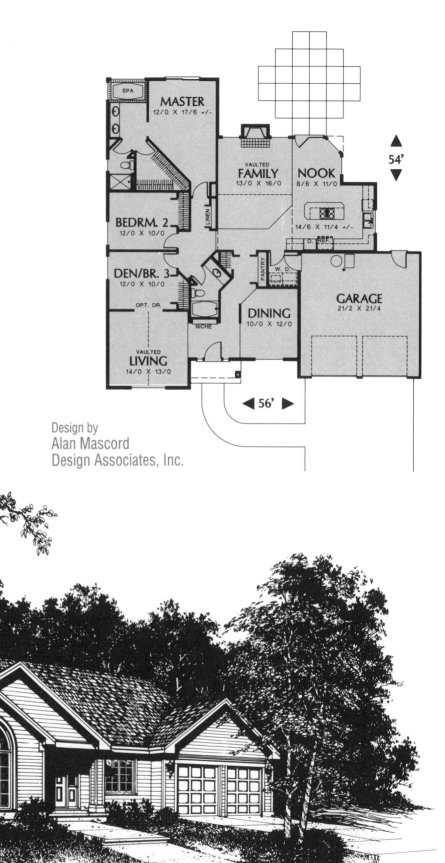

Design by
Alan Mascord
Design Associates, Inc.

Design by
LifeStyle
HomeDesigns

Width 52'-4"
Depth 57'-4"

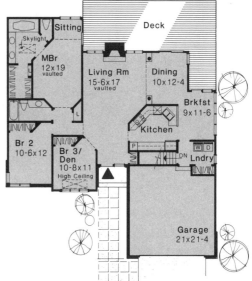

Design VH8890

Square Footage: 1,630

● This home design effectively separates living and sleeping zones for added comfort. A vaulted living room offers a fireplace flanked by bright windows. Columns define the dining room, which accesses a rear wraparound deck. The well-designed kitchen handily serves the airy breakfast room. A nearby laundry room makes chores a breeze. In the sleeping wing, the master bedroom suite impresses with its vaulted ceiling, sitting room and skylit bathroom. Bedroom 3 could also be used as a den or a home office.

Design VH9611

Square Footage: 1,817

Design by
Donald A.
Gardner,
Architects, Inc.

● This inviting ranch offers many special features uncommon to the typical house this size. A large entrance foyer leads to the spacious great room with cathedral ceiling, fireplace, and operable skylights that allow for natural ventilation. A bedroom just off the foyer doubles nicely as a study. The large master suite contains a walk-in closet and a pampering master bath with double-bowl vanity, shower and whirlpool tub. For outdoor living, look to the open deck with spa at the great room and kitchen, as well as the covered deck at the master suite.

Width 58'-10"
Depth 62'-8"

13

© The Sater Group, Inc.

JenKing

Design VH6600

Square Footage: 1,795

● This engaging three-bedroom split plan promotes casual living both inside and out, offering contemporary amenities for convenient living. The foyer opens to the formal dining room on the right, and straight ahead, the great room complete with a fireplace and a built-in entertainment center. Double French doors unfold onto a large veranda. The kitchen includes a large walk-in pantry, an eating bar and a bayed breakfast nook. The relaxing master suite enjoys access to a screened porch, His and Hers walk-in closets and a private bath with a glass-enclosed shower. Two secondary bedrooms offer privacy and plenty of storage.

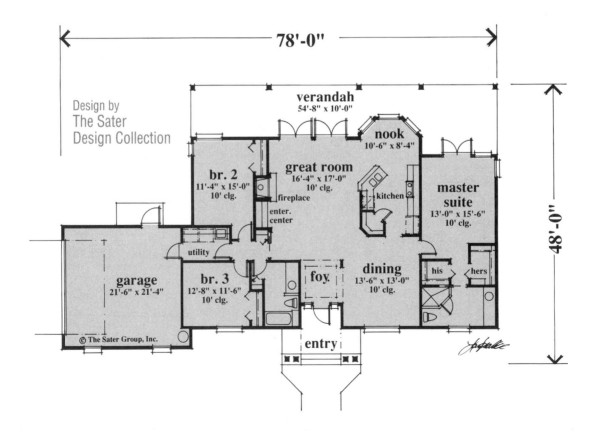

78'-0"

48'-0"

Design by
The Sater
Design Collection

verandah
54'-8" x 10'-0"

nook
10'-6" x 8'-4"

br. 2
11'-4" x 15'-0"
10' clg.

great room
16'-4" x 17'-0"
10' clg.

fireplace

kitchen

master
suite
13'-0" x 15'-6"
10' clg.

enter.
center

utility

garage
21'-6" x 21'-4"

br. 3
12'-8" x 11'-6"
10' clg.

foy.

dining
13'-6" x 13'-0"
10' clg.

his

hers

© The Sater Group, Inc.

entry

Design by
Larry E. Belk
Designs

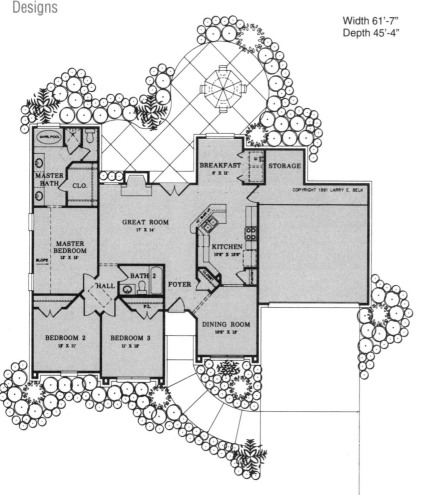

Width 61'-7"
Depth 45'-4"

Design VH8061
Square Footage: 1,553

● Two dominating brick gables give a unique look to this lovely starter home. Inside, the foyer opens to a great room with ten-foot ceilings. A dining room for formal entertaining is located to the right. Ten-foot ceilings contin-ue throughout the kitchen and breakfast room and give the home an open, spacious feel. An angled kitchen sink and a 42"-high bar open the kitchen to the great room and the breakfast room, thus allowing the cook to be part of all family gatherings. As an added bonus, the angled design brings the fireplace into view from the kitchen. The master suite features a master bath loaded with all the amenities including double vanities with knee space, a whirlpool tub and a separate shower. Bedrooms 2 and 3 and the second bath are located close by. Please specify crawlspace or slab foundation when ordering.

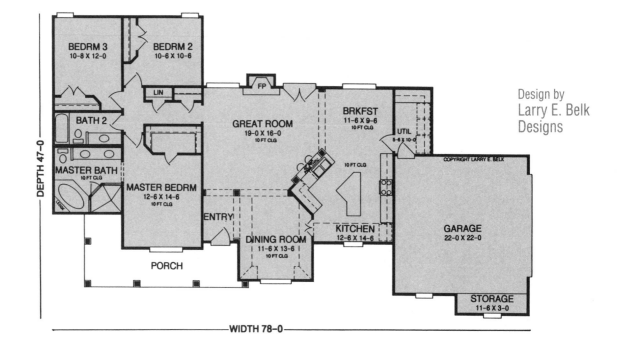

Design by
Larry E. Belk
Designs

BEDRM 3
10-8 X 12-0

BEDRM 2
10-6 X 10-6

LIN

BATH 2

MASTER BATH
10 FT CLG

MASTER BEDRM
12-6 X 14-6
10 FT CLG

ENTRY

GREAT ROOM
19-0 X 16-0
10 FT CLG

FP

BRKFST
11-6 X 9-6
10 FT CLG

UTIL
5-6 X 10-0

10 FT CLG

KITCHEN
12-6 X 14-6

DINING ROOM
11-6 X 13-6
10 FT CLG

PORCH

GARAGE
22-0 X 22-0

STORAGE
11-6 X 3-0

DEPTH 47-0

WIDTH 78-0

Design VH8063

Square Footage: 1,789

● A traditional brick and siding elevation with a lovely wraparound porch sets the stage for a plan that incorporates features demanded by today's lifestyle. The entry opens to the great room and dining room. The use of square columns to define the areas gives the plan the look and feel of a much larger home. The kitchen features loads of counter space and a large work island. The sink is angled toward the great room and features a 42" pass-through bar above. Washer, dryer and freezer space are available in the utility room along with cabinets for storage and countertops for work area. The master bedroom includes a walk-in closet with ample space for two. The master bath features all the amenities: a corner whirlpool, a shower and His and Hers vanities. Bedrooms 2 and 3 are located nearby and complete the plan. Please specify slab or crawlspace when ordering.

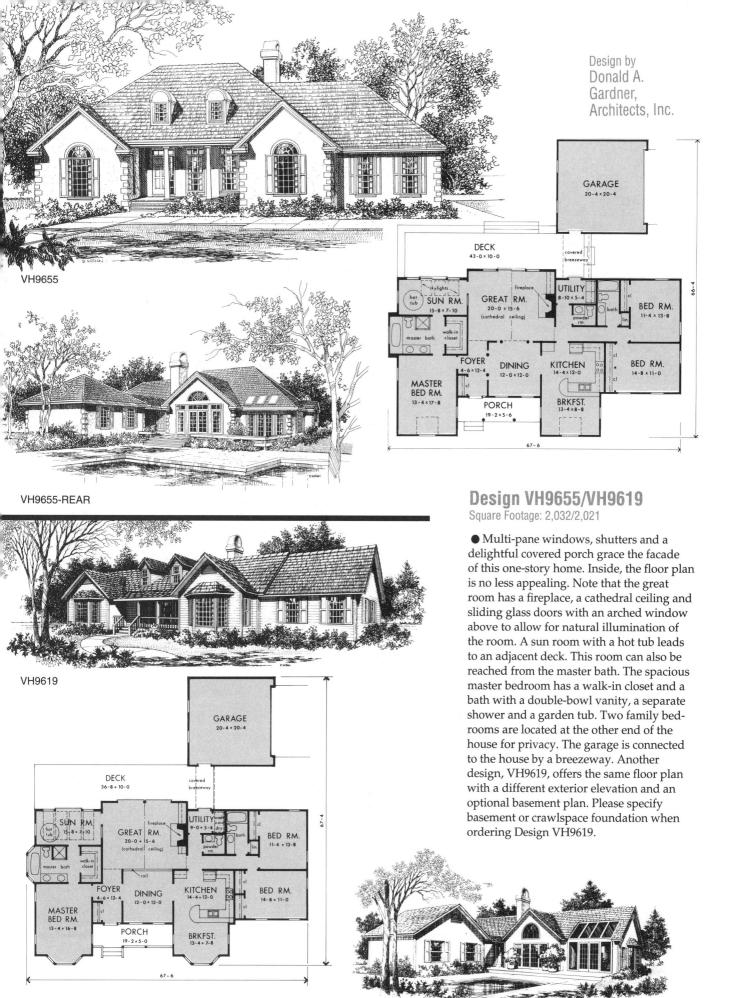

Design by
Donald A.
Gardner,
Architects, Inc.

VH9655

VH9655-REAR

VH9619

GARAGE
20-4 × 20-4

DECK
43-0 × 10-0

covered
breezeway

hot tub
SUN RM.
15-8 × 7-10
skylights

GREAT RM.
20-0 × 15-6
(cathedral ceiling)

fireplace

UTILITY
8-10 × 5-4

powder rm.

bath

lin.

BED RM.
11-4 × 13-8

master bath

walk-in closet

FOYER
4-6 × 12-4

DINING
12-0 × 12-0

KITCHEN
14-4 × 12-0

BED RM.
14-8 × 11-0

MASTER BED RM.
13-4 × 17-8

cl

PORCH
19-2 × 5-6

BRKFST.
13-4 × 8-8

67-6

66-4

GARAGE
20-4 × 20-4

DECK
36-8 × 10-0

covered
breezeway

hot tub
SUN RM.
15-8 × 7-10

GREAT RM.
20-0 × 15-6
(cathedral ceiling)

fireplace

UTILITY
9-0 × 5-4
wash/dry

powder rm.

bath

cl

BED RM.
11-4 × 13-8

master bath

walk-in closet

rail

FOYER
4-6 × 12-4

DINING
12-0 × 12-0

KITCHEN
14-4 × 12-0

BED RM.
14-8 × 11-0

MASTER BED RM.
13-4 × 16-8

PORCH
19-2 × 5-0

BRKFST.
13-4 × 7-8

67-6

67-4

Design VH9655/VH9619
Square Footage: 2,032/2,021

● Multi-pane windows, shutters and a delightful covered porch grace the facade of this one-story home. Inside, the floor plan is no less appealing. Note that the great room has a fireplace, a cathedral ceiling and sliding glass doors with an arched window above to allow for natural illumination of the room. A sun room with a hot tub leads to an adjacent deck. This room can also be reached from the master bath. The spacious master bedroom has a walk-in closet and a bath with a double-bowl vanity, a separate shower and a garden tub. Two family bedrooms are located at the other end of the house for privacy. The garage is connected to the house by a breezeway. Another design, VH9619, offers the same floor plan with a different exterior elevation and an optional basement plan. Please specify basement or crawlspace foundation when ordering Design VH9619.

VH9619-REAR

17

Design by
Design
Basics,
Inc.

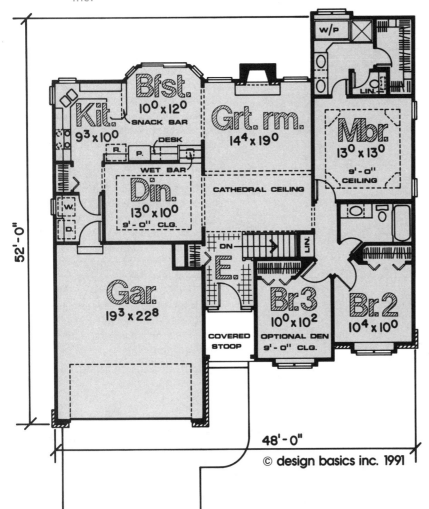

Design VH9328
Square Footage: 1,496

● Sleek roof lines, lap siding and brick accents highlight the exterior of this three-bedroom ranch home. A tiled entry views the spacious great room featuring a sloping cathedral ceiling and window-framed fireplace. Note the strategic location of the dining room (with nine-foot boxed ceiling and wet bar/servery) which accommodates formal entertaining and family gatherings. Natural light and warmth add comfort to the bayed breakfast area with pantry, handy planning desk and the peninsula kitchen. Well-segregated sleeping quarters add to the flexibility of this modern floor plan. Both secondary bedrooms share a full bath and linen closet. Bedroom 3 is easily converted to a den or home office. With the nine-foot-high boxed ceiling, walk-in closet, sunlit whirlpool tub and double vanities, the master suite is soothing and luxurious.

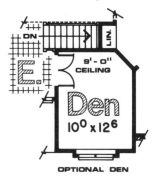

OPTIONAL DEN

© design basics inc. 1991

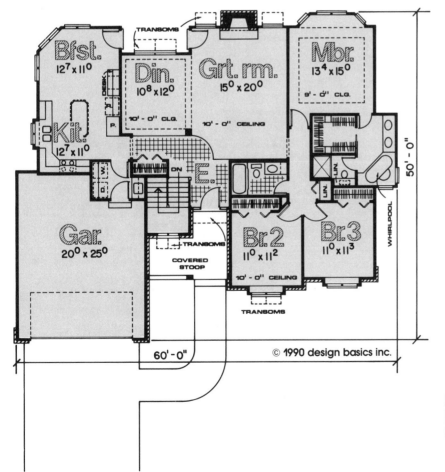

Design VH9257
Square Footage: 1,735

● A covered porch at the entry to this home welcomes family and guests alike. Ten-foot ceilings at the entry foyer, great room and dining room give a feeling of open spaciousness to living areas. The formal dining room sits between the kitchen area and great room—a perfect spot for entertaining. Note service entrance with laundry just off the kitchen en route to the garage. Three bedrooms include two secondary bedrooms with shared bath and a master suite with elegant bayed window and bath with angled whirlpool, double vanity and walk-in closet. An open staircase in the entry allows for the possibility of a finished basement area in the future.

Design by
Design
Basics,
Inc.

Design VH7221
Square Footage: 1,580

● Brick wing walls provide a visually expansive front elevation. From the entry, traffic flows into the bright great room with an impressive two-sided fireplace. The dining room opens to the great room, offering a view of the fireplace. French doors off the entry open into the kitchen. Here, a large pantry, a planning desk and a snack bar are appreciated amenities. The breakfast nook accesses a large, comfortable screened porch. The laundry room is strategically located off the kitchen and provides direct access to the garage. French doors access the master suite with its formal ceiling and pampering bath. Two secondary bedrooms could be one bedroom and a den.

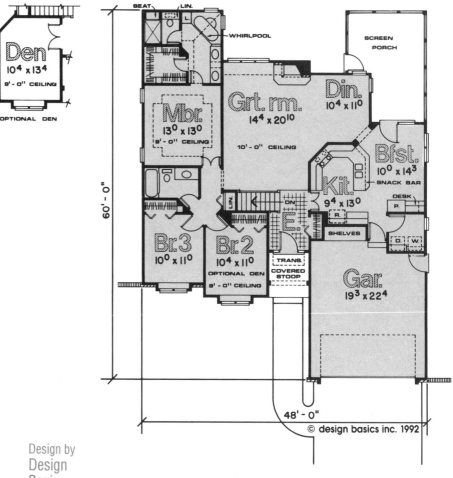

Den
10⁴ x 13⁴
9'-0'' CEILING

OPTIONAL DEN

SEAT   LIN.

WHIRLPOOL

SCREEN PORCH

Mbr.
13⁰ x 13⁰
9'-0'' CEILING

Grt. rm.
14⁴ x 20¹⁰
10'-0'' CEILING

Din.
10⁴ x 11⁰

Bfst.
10⁰ x 14³

SNACK BAR

Kit.
9⁴ x 13⁰

DESK

P.

SHELVES

Br. 3
10⁰ x 11⁰

Br. 2
10⁴ x 11⁰
OPTIONAL DEN
9'-0'' CEILING

LIN.

DN

TRANS.
COVERED
STOOP

Gar.
19³ x 22⁴

D   W

60'-0''

48'-0''

© design basics inc. 1992

Design by
Design Basics, Inc.

G. McDONALD

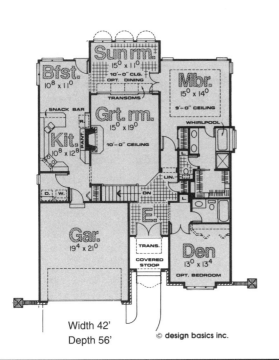

Width 42'
Depth 56'

© design basics inc.

Design VH7214
Square Footage: 1,658

● The prominent entry of this home enhances a captivating elevation. Inside, the entry captures fantastic views from the great room to the sun room with its arched windows. A peninsula kitchen features a corner sink and a snack bar that opens to the breakfast area. The sun room offers access to the breakfast area, the great room and the master suite; or use it as a lovely dining room. The spacious master suite includes a whirlpool bath with dual lavs and a walk-in closet. The den off the entry has a bedroom option.

Design VH7213
Square Footage: 1,422

● This small ranch home makes a grand statement with its prominent entry. A twelve-foot ceiling integrates the great room, the semi-formal dining room and the kitchen. Arched openings to the kitchen, with built-in bookcases, provide a dramatic backdrop for the dining area. The efficient kitchen features two Lazy Susans, a plant shelf above the upper cabinets and an airy window. The spacious covered porch opens off the dining room. The master suite features a boxed nine-foot ceiling, a whirlpool bath and a walk-in closet. A hall bath serves the secondary bedrooms. Bedroom 3 can easily convert to a den.

Width 50'
Depth 58'

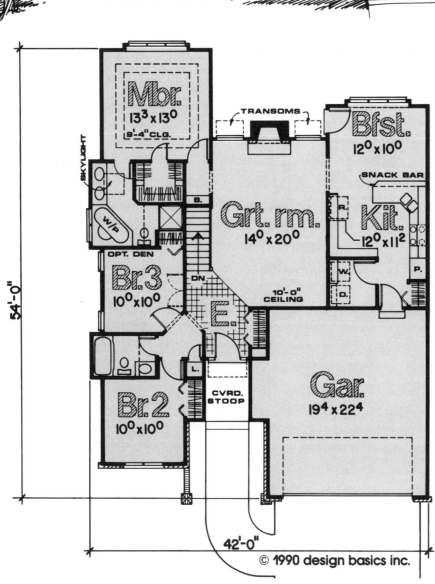

Design VH9256
Square Footage: 1,347

● Though it may appear oversized, this plan is really quite compact and economical. From the ten-foot ceiling in the entry to the spacious great room with fireplace, it has an open feeling. A snack bar and pantry in the kitchen complement the work area. Bright windows light up the entire breakfast area. To the left side of the plan are three bedrooms, two of which share a full bath. The master suite has a boxed window, built-in bookcase and tiered ceiling. The skylit dressing area features a double vanity and there's a whirlpool in the bath.

Design by
Design
Basics,
Inc.

Design VH9371
Square Footage: 1,205

● At only 1,205 square feet in size, this home feels considerably larger. The angled entry of this design features two plant shelves and a roomy closet. Straight ahead, the vaulted great room provides a window-flanked fireplace, a built-in bookcase and easy access to the kitchen and dinette. This area offers a snack bar, a wrapping counter and a pantry. The secondary bedroom extends privacy for guests or it could easily serve as a den. The master bedroom is highlighted by a box ceiling and a bath with a whirlpool and dual sinks.

Design by
Design
Basics,
Inc.

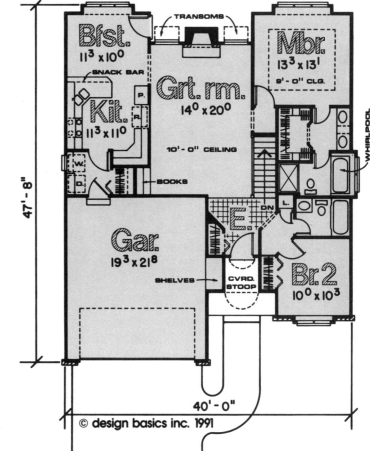

© design basics inc. 1991

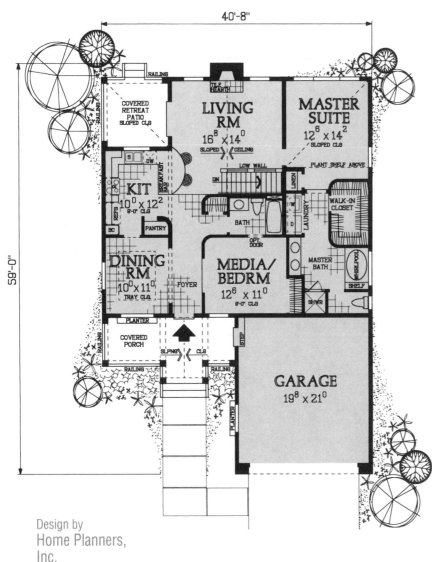

Design VH3442

Square Footage: 1,273

L D

● For those just starting out or the empty-nester, this unique one-story plan is sure to delight. A covered-porch introduces a dining room with a tray ceiling and views out two sides of the house. The kitchen is just off this room and is most efficient with a double sink, dishwasher and pantry. The living room gains attention with a volume ceiling, fireplace and access to a covered patio. The master bedroom also features a volume ceiling while enjoying the luxury of a private bath. In it, a walk-in closet, washer/dryer, double-bowl vanity, garden tub, separate shower and compartmented toilet comprise the amenities. Not to be overlooked, a second bedroom may easily convert to a media room or study—the choice is yours.

Cost to build? See page 300
to order complete cost estimate
to build this house in your area!

Design by
Home Planners,
Inc.

Design VH3481A

Square Footage: 1,901

L

Width 42'
Depth 63'-6"

● In just under 2,000 square feet, this pleasing one-story home bears all the livability of houses twice its size. A combined living and dining room offers elegance for entertaining; with two elevations to choose from, the living room can either support an octagonal bay or a bumped-out nook. The U-shaped kitchen finds easy access to the rear family room; sliding glass doors lead from the family room to a back stoop. The master bedroom has a quaint pot-shelf and a private bath with a spa tub, a double-bowl vanity, a walk-in closet and a compartmented toilet. With two additional family bedrooms—one may serve as a den if desired—and a hall bath with dual lavatories, this plan offers the best in accommodations. Both elevations come with the blueprint package.

Design by
Home Planners,
Inc.

Design VH3481B

Square Footage: 1,908

L

Width 42'-4"
Depth 63'-10"

Quote One™

Cost to build? See page 300
to order complete cost estimate
to build this house in your area!

25

Design VH8064

Square Footage: 1,742

● This traditional elevation fronts a compact layout with all the frills normally found in a larger home. Ten-foot ceilings in all major living areas give the home an open, spacious feel. The kitchen features an angled eating bar, a pantry and lots of cabinet and counter space. The master suite is highlighted by a luxury bath. Standard features include His and Hers vanities with knee space, a corner whirlpool tub and a separate shower with a seat. An enormous walk-in closet with a window for natural light completes this owner's retreat. Bedrooms 2 and 3 and a large linen closet are nearby. Bedroom 2 is notable for its oversized walk-in closet. Please specify slab or crawlspace foundation when ordering.

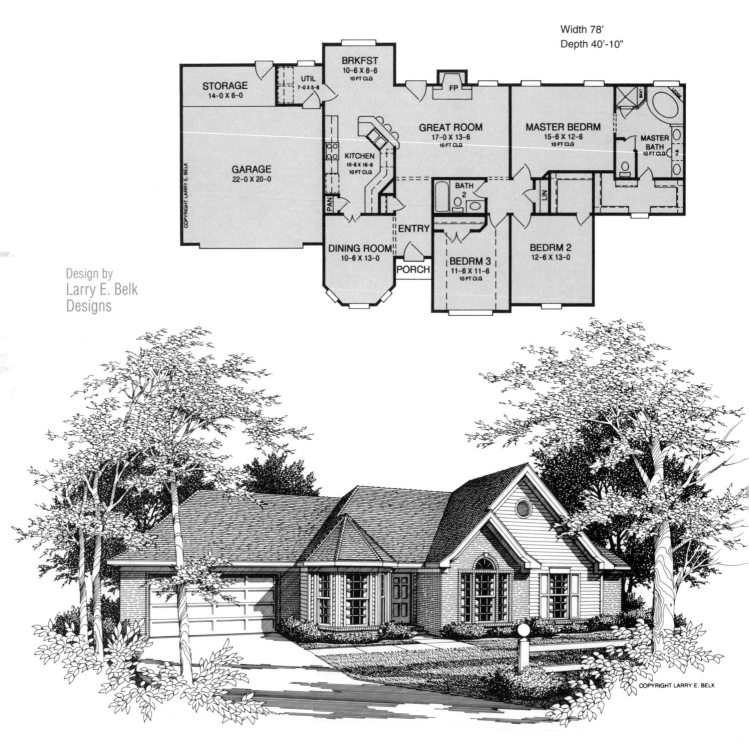

Width 78'
Depth 40'-10"

Design by
Larry E. Belk
Designs

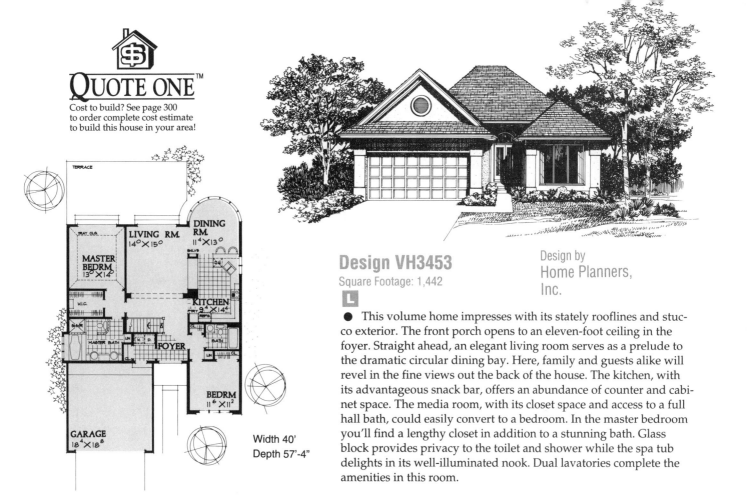

TERRACE

LIVING RM.
14⁰ × 15⁰

DINING RM.
11⁴ × 13⁰

TRAY CLG.

MASTER BEDRM.
13⁰ × 14⁰

W.I.C.

KITCHEN
9⁴ × 14⁴

MASTER BATH

FOYER

BATH

GARAGE
18⁴ × 18⁸

BEDRM.
11⁶ × 11²

Width 40'
Depth 57'-4"

Design VH3453

Square Footage: 1,442

L

Design by
Home Planners, Inc.

● This volume home impresses with its stately rooflines and stucco exterior. The front porch opens to an eleven-foot ceiling in the foyer. Straight ahead, an elegant living room serves as a prelude to the dramatic circular dining bay. Here, family and guests alike will revel in the fine views out the back of the house. The kitchen, with its advantageous snack bar, offers an abundance of counter and cabinet space. The media room, with its closet space and access to a full hall bath, could easily convert to a bedroom. In the master bedroom you'll find a lengthy closet in addition to a stunning bath. Glass block provides privacy to the toilet and shower while the spa tub delights in its well-illuminated nook. Dual lavatories complete the amenities in this room.

Width 46'-4"
Depth 55'-8"

TERRACE

DINING
13⁶ × 10⁴

MASTER SUITE
18⁸ × 19⁰

GATHERING ROOM
13⁸ × 15²

KIT
11⁸ × 10⁰

MASTER BATH

BATH

FOYER

LAUND.

ENTRY

PORCH

BED/STUDY
14⁸ × 13⁸

GARAGE
19⁸ × 19⁸

Design VH3451 Square Footage: 1,560

L

● This split-bedroom plan includes two bedrooms in only 1,560 square feet. The master bedroom is to the rear of the home and includes a private bath. A family bedroom or study is to the left of the home with a full bath. The washer and dryer are placed within easy reach of both bedrooms. A spacious gathering room provides space for relaxing or entertaining guests. A formal dining room adjacent to the kitchen offers access to a terrace for evening meals outside.

Design VH3569

Square Footage: 1,981

L **D**

● A graceful entry opens
this impressive one-story
design; the foyer introduces
an open gathering room/din-
ing room combination. A
front-facing study could easily convert into a bedroom for
guests—a full bath is directly
accessible from the rear of
the room. In the kitchen,
such features as an island
cooktop and a built-in desk
add to livability. A corner
bedroom takes advantage of
front and side views. The
master bedroom accesses the
rear terrace and also sports a
bath with dual lavatories and
a whirlpool. Other special
features of the house include
multi-pane windows, a
warming fireplace, a cozy
covered dining porch and a
two-car garage. Note the
handy storage closet in the
laundry area.

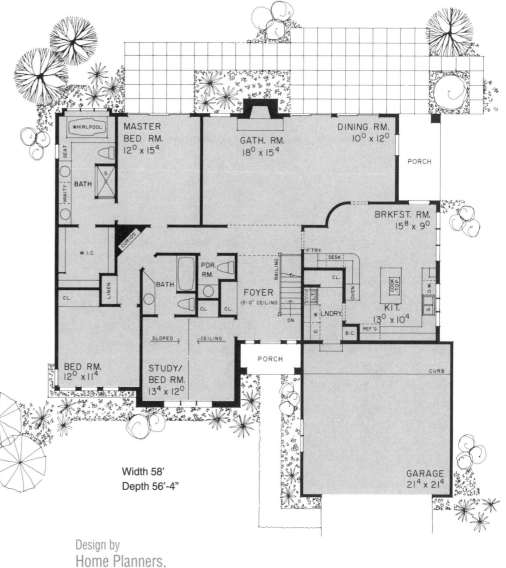

Width 58'
Depth 56'-4"

Cost to build? See page 300
to order complete cost estimate
to build this house in your area!

Design by
**Home Planners,
Inc.**

Design VH3560

Square Footage: 2,189

L

● Simplicity is the key to the stylish good looks of this home's facade. Inside, the kitchen contains a work counter with eating space on the living area side. A sloped ceiling, a fireplace and sliding glass doors to the rear terrace are highlights in the living area. The master bedroom also sports sliding glass doors to the terrace and a dressing area with double walk-in closets and lavatories; two family bedrooms are found on the opposite side.

California Engineered Plans and California Stock Plans are available for this home. Call 1-800-521-6797 for more information.

Design by
Home Planners,
Inc.

QUOTE ONE™

Cost to build? See page 300 to order complete cost estimate to build this house in your area!

Width 56'
Depth 72'

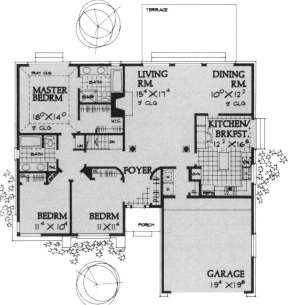

QUOTE ONE™

Cost to build? See page 300 to order complete cost estimate to build this house in your area!

Width 52'-8"
Depth 49'

Design VH3454

Square Footage: 1,699

L D

Design by
Home Planners,
Inc.

● An efficient, spacious interior comes through in this compact floor plan. Through a pair of columns, an open living and dining room area creates a warm space for all sorts of living pursuits. Sliding glass doors guarantee a bright, cheerful interior while providing easy access to outdoor living. The L-shaped kitchen has an island work surface, a practical planning desk and an informal eating space. The breakfast area has access to an outdoor living area—perfect for enjoying a morning cup of coffee. Sleeping arrangements are emphasized by the master suite with its tray ceiling and sliding glass doors to the yard.

Copyright 1992 Stephen S. Fuller, Inc.

Design by
Design Traditions

Design VH9950
Square Footage: 2,095

● This special cottage design carries a fully modern floor plan. The entry leads to open living areas with a dining room and a living room flanking the foyer. The family room—with a fireplace and built-in bookcases—is nearby the bright breakfast room with deck access. The efficiently patterned kitchen provides a helpful lead-in to the dining room. Two secondary bedrooms make up the left side of the plan. A full, compartmented bath connects them. In the master bedroom suite, a tiered ceiling and a bath with dual lavatories, a whirlpool tub, a separate shower, a compartmented toilet and a walk-in closet are sure to please. The two-car, side-load garage opens to the laundry room. This home is designed with a basement foundation.

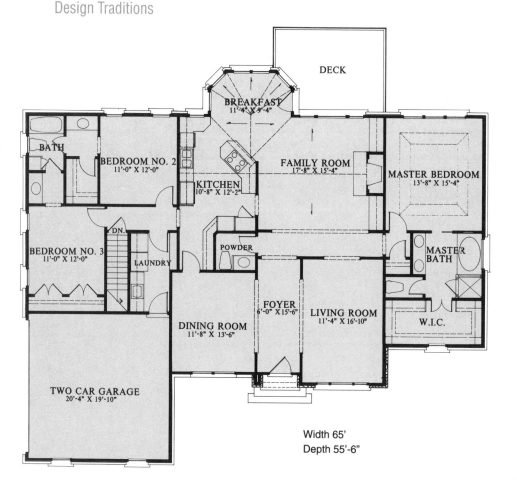

Width 65'
Depth 55'-6"

Design VH9914
Square Footage: 1,770

● Perfect for sloping lots, this European-style plan includes living areas on one level and bedrooms on another. The great room contains a fireplace and access to the rear deck. Close by are the U-shaped kitchen and breakfast room with a boxed window. The formal dining room completes the living areas and is open to the entry foyer. Bedrooms are a few steps up from the living areas and include a master suite with two walk-in closets and a sumptuous bath with a compartmented toilet. Secondary bedrooms share a full bath with a double-bowl vanity. On the lower level is garage space and bonus space that may be used later for additional bedrooms or casual gathering areas. This home is designed with a basement foundation.

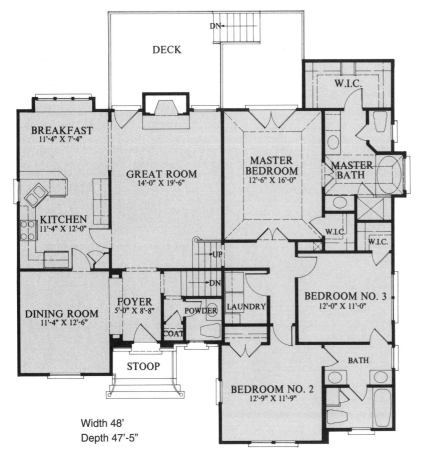

DN

DECK

W.I.C.

BREAKFAST
11'-4" X 7'-4"

GREAT ROOM
14'-0" X 19'-6"

MASTER
BEDROOM
12'-6" X 16'-0"

MASTER
BATH

KITCHEN
11'-4" X 12'-0"

W.I.C.

W.I.C.

UP

BEDROOM NO. 3
12'-0" X 11'-0"

DN

DINING ROOM
11'-4" X 12'-6"

FOYER
5'-0" X 8'-8"

POWDER

LAUNDRY

COAT

STOOP

BATH

BEDROOM NO. 2
12'-9" X 11'-9"

Width 48'
Depth 47'-5"

Design by
Design Traditions

31

Design VH9821

First Floor: 2,070 square feet
Second Floor: 790 square feet
Total: 2,860 square feet

Design by
Design Traditions

● The striking combination of wood frame, shingles and glass creates the exterior of this classic cottage. The foyer opens to the main level layout. To the left of the foyer is a study with a warming hearth and a vaulted ceiling. To the right is the formal dining room. A great room with an attached breakfast area is to the rear near the kitchen. A guest room is nestled in the rear of the plan for privacy. The master suite provides an expansive tray ceiling, a glass sitting area and easy passage to the outside deck. Upstairs, two bedrooms are accompanied by a loft for a quiet getaway. This home is designed with a basement foundation.

Width 58'-4"
Depth 54'-10"

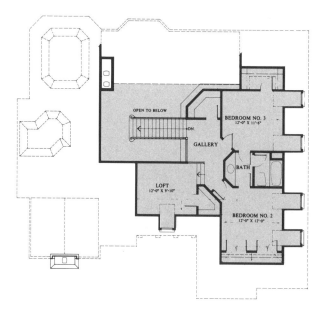

Design by
Design Traditions

PORCH

MASTER
BATH

MASTER BEDRDOOM
16'-4" X 13'-6"

BREAKFAST
13'-4" X 9'-0"

BEDROOM/
OFFICE
10'-4" X 11'-0"

GREAT ROOM
17'-0" X 17'-8"

KITCHEN
13'-4" X 10'-6"

BEDROOM NO. 2
10'-4" X 12'-0"

BATH

LAUNDRY

DN.

BATH

TWO CAR GARAGE
20'-6" X 19'-6"

DINING ROOM
11'-4" X 12'-10"

FOYER
5'-4" X
12'-10"

BEDROOM/
STUDY
11'-2" X 12'-0"

PORCH

Width 61'
Depth 70'-6"

Design VH9853
Square Footage: 2,090

● This traditional home features board-and-batten and cedar shingles in an attractively proportioned exterior. Finishing touches include a covered entrance and porch with column detailing and an arched transom, flower boxes and shuttered windows. The foyer opens to both the dining room and great room beyond with French doors opening onto the porch. Through the double doors to the right of the foyer is the combination bedroom/study. A short hallway leads to a full bath and a secondary bedroom with ample closet space. The master bedroom is spacious, with walk-in closets on both sides of the entrance to the master bath. With separate vanities, a shower and a toilet, the master bath forms a private retreat at the rear of the home. Convenient to both the great room and dining room, the kitchen opens to an attractive breakfast area featuring a bay window. An additional room is remotely located off the kitchen, providing a retreat for today's at-home office or guest. This home is designed with a basement foundation.

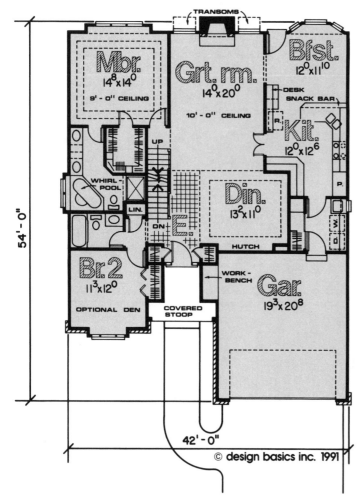

Design VH9339

First Floor: 1,517 square feet
Second Floor: 234 square feet
Total: 1,751 square feet

● Attractive brick and wood siding and a covered front porch make this a beautiful design—even for narrower lots. The entry gives way to a dining room with hutch space and then further opens to a bright, airy great room. The kitchen is highlighted by a French door entry, ample counters, and a roomy pantry. The first floor holds two bedrooms—a secondary bedroom with bath and the master suite with roomy walk-in closet, corner whirlpool, and dual lavs. On the second floor is a totally private third bedroom with its own bath.

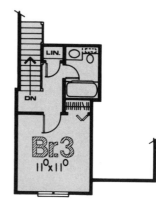

Design by
**Design
Basics,
Inc.**

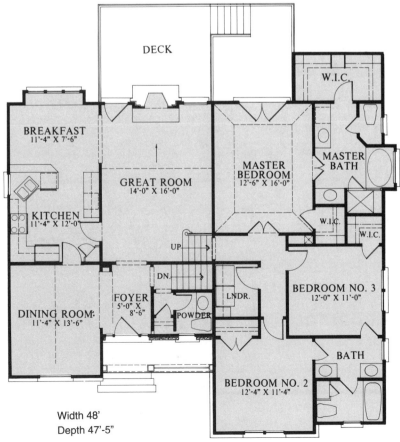

DECK

BREAKFAST
11'-4" X 7'-6"

GREAT ROOM
14'-0" X 16'-0"

MASTER
BEDROOM
12'-6" X 16'-0"

W.I.C.

MASTER
BATH

KITCHEN
11'-4" X 12'-0"

W.I.C.

W.I.C.

UP

DN.

FOYER
5'-0" X
8'-6"

LNDR.

POWDER

BEDROOM NO. 3
12'-0" X 11'-0"

DINING ROOM
11'-4" X 13'-6"

BATH

BEDROOM NO. 2
12'-4" X 11'-4"

Width 48'
Depth 47'-5"

Design by
Design Traditions

Design VH9949
Square Footage: 1,770

● Wood frame, weatherboard siding and stacked stone give this home its country cottage appeal. The concept is reinforced by the double elliptical-arched front porch, the Colonial balustrade and the roof-vent dormer. Inside, the foyer leads to the great room and the dining room. The well-planned kitchen easily services the breakfast room. A rear deck makes outdoor living extra enjoyable. Three bedrooms include a master suite with a tray ceiling and a luxurious bath. The two secondary bedrooms share a compartmented bath. This home is designed with a basement foundation.

Design VH9855
Square Footage: 2,935

● A one-story plan for even a large family, this home provides all the necessities and many luxuries as well. For formal occasions, there's a grand dining room just off the entry foyer. It has a vaulted ceiling and is just across the hall from the gourmet kitchen. The great room has beautiful ceiling treatment and access to the rear deck. For more casual times, the breakfast nook and adjoining keeping room with a fireplace fill the bill. The master suite is huge and contains every amenity. Its sitting room allows access to the rear deck. Note the gigantic walk-in closet here. Two family bedrooms share a full bath. Each of these bedrooms has its own lavatory. This home is designed with a basement foundation.

Design by
Design Traditions

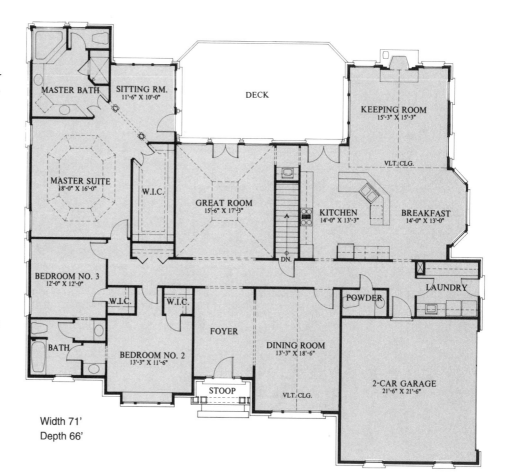

Width 71'
Depth 66'

Design by
Larry E. Belk
Designs

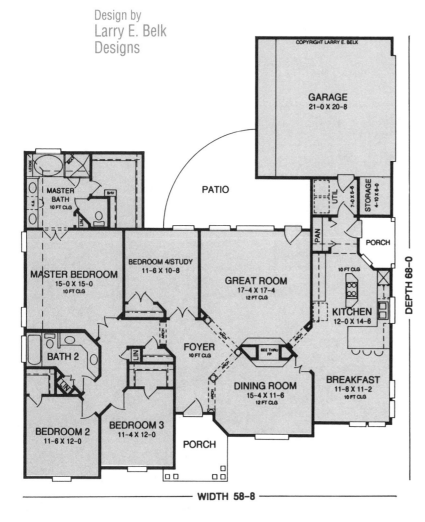

COPYRIGHT LARRY E. BELK

GARAGE
21-0 X 20-8

PATIO

MASTER
BATH
10 FT CLG

MASTER BEDROOM
15-0 X 15-0
10 FT CLG

BEDROOM 4/STUDY
11-6 X 10-8

GREAT ROOM
17-4 X 17-4
12 FT CLG

UTIL
7-0 X 6-8

STORAGE
4-10 X 6-0

PORCH

10 FT CLG

BATH 2

FOYER
10 FT CLG

SEE THRU
FP

KITCHEN
12-0 X 14-6

BEDROOM 2
11-6 X 12-0

BEDROOM 3
11-4 X 12-0

PORCH

DINING ROOM
15-4 X 11-6
12 FT CLG

BREAKFAST
11-8 X 11-2
10 FT CLG

PAN

LIN

LIN

DEPTH 68-0

WIDTH 58-8

Design VH8066
Square Footage: 2,237

● Brick, siding and an accent of wood shingles give this one-story home its distinctive appearance. The foyer leads through a series of columns with graceful, connecting arches to the formal dining room and great room that share a see-through fireplace. An L-shaped kitchen sports an eating bar, a large pantry and a cooktop work island for added convenience. Outdoor dining is easy thanks to an adjacent covered porch. Thoughtful planning makes the master suite a relaxing retreat. Indulge yourself in the soothing whirlpool tub. Other amenities include His and Hers vanities, a separate shower with a seat and an extra-large walk-in closet. Bedrooms 2 and 3 have walk-in closets and share a full bath. Bedroom 4 serves as a study, opening from the foyer through double French doors. However, by interchanging the position of the closet and doors, the study becomes a fourth bedroom with access from the hall. This plan is available with either a crawlspace or slab foundation. Please specify when ordering.

Design VH8629

First Floor: 1,782 square feet
Loft: 264 square feet
Total: 2,046 square feet

● This delightful 1½-story plan has a formal living and dining area for evening entertainment and boasts a huge family gathering space. Designed for efficiency, the two secondary bedrooms have private entrances off the formal living area. The master bedroom has all of the features of a larger home including a soaking tub, large walk-in shower and private toilet area. The kitchen is at the heart of the home with a bay-windowed breakfast area adjacent to the efficient laundry room. A loft area on the second floor provides additional space for the growing family. Included in the blueprints are details for two different exteriors.

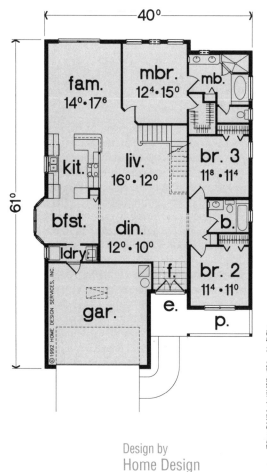

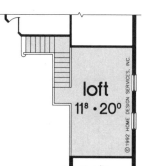

Design by
Home Design
Services, Inc.

Design VH9734

Square Footage: 1,977
Bonus Room: 430 square feet

● A two-story foyer with a Palladian window above sets the tone for this sunlit home. Columns mark the passage from the foyer to the great room, where a centered fireplace and built-in cabinets are found. A screened porch with four skylights above and a wet bar provides a pleasant place to start the day or wind down after work. The kitchen is flanked by the formal dining room and the breakfast room with sliding glass doors to the large, rear deck. Hidden quietly in the rear, the master suite includes a bath with dual vanities and skylights. Two family bedrooms (one an optional study) share a bath with twin sinks.

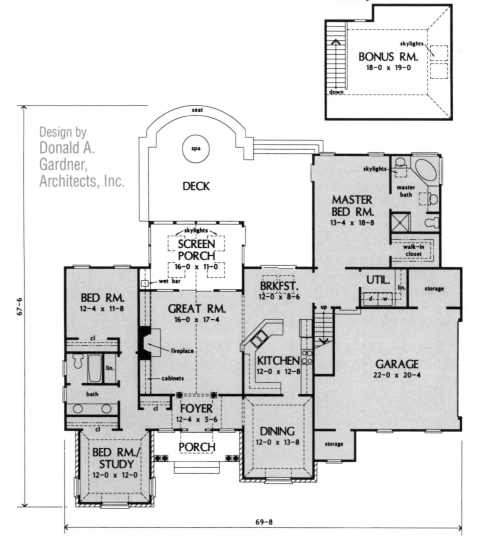

Design by
Donald A.
Gardner,
Architects, Inc.

Design VH9873
Square Footage: 2,078

● A porch with column detailing covers the entry to this single-story American classic. Once inside, the foyer opens to the living room with a wall of windows and French doors that lead outside. A splendid colonnade defines the banquet-sized dining room. To the right, the spacious kitchen with work island opens to a sunlit breakfast area and great room featuring a warming hearth and doors to the rear deck. A hallway just off the foyer leads to the double doors of the master suite. Inside, the special shape of the suite and the mirrored ceiling detail make this room unique. The bath accommodates every need with His and Hers vanities, a garden tub and a walk-in closet. Two additional bedrooms, with spacious closets and a common bath with dual vanities and an individual tub, complete the main level. This home is designed with a basement foundation.

GREAT ROOM
13'-0" X 17'-0"

MASTER BATH
16'-0" X 8'-0"

MASTER BEDROOM
12'-0" X 15'-0"

LIVING ROOM
14'-0" X 17'-0"

KITCHEN
8'-0" X 13'-0"

BREAKFAST
12'-0" X 8'-0"

BEDROOM NO.2
11'-6" X 12'-0"

DINING ROOM
11'-0" X 12'-6"

FOYER
5'-0" X 12'-0"

BEDROOM NO.3
12'-0" X 11'-0"

TWO CAR GARAGE
21'-6" X 19'-6"

Design by
Design Traditions

Width 66'
Depth 54'

Copyright 1992 Stephen S. Fuller, Inc.

Design VH9868

First Floor: 1,725 square feet
Second Floor: 650 square feet
Total: 2,375 square feet

● This example of classic American architecture features a columned front porch and wood framing. Bay window detailing and an arched dormer above the porch complete the picture. The foyer includes a closet and an open staircase to the upper level. Straight ahead, the great room is largely glass, and opens to the vaulted breakfast area which leads outdoors to the patio. The octagonal kitchen is designed for ease of movement and to promote the flow of family traffic. The dining room and living room share a hearth and an open design with bay window treatments

for interest and natural light. The master bedroom at the right rear of the home features a tray ceiling and a large bay window. The master bath, with dual vanities, an individual shower and walk-in closets, completes the master suite. The upper level is comprised of a gallery and a loft open to the great room and foyer below. Beyond the loft are two bedrooms that share a bath and an unfinished bonus room. This home is designed with a basement foundation.

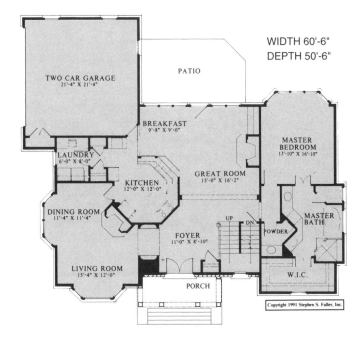

WIDTH 60'-6"
DEPTH 50'-6"

TWO CAR GARAGE
21'-4" X 21'-4"

PATIO

BREAKFAST
9'-8" X 9'-0"

LAUNDRY
6'-0" X 8'-0"

MASTER BEDROOM
13'-10" X 16'-10"

KITCHEN
12'-0" X 12'-0"

GREAT ROOM
15'-0" X 16'-2"

DINING ROOM
11'-4" X 11'-4"

UP   DN

MASTER BATH

FOYER
11'-0" X 8'-10"

POWDER

LIVING ROOM
15'-4" X 12'-0"

W.I.C.

PORCH

Copyright 1991 Stephen S. Fuller, Inc.

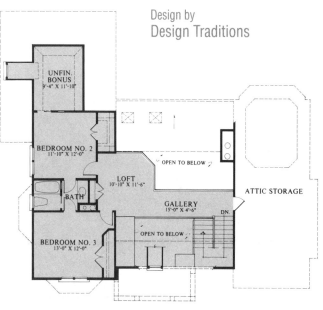

Design by
Design Traditions

UNFIN. BONUS
9'-4" X 11'-10"

BEDROOM NO. 2
11'-10" X 12'-0"

OPEN TO BELOW

LOFT
10'-0" X 11'-6"

BATH

ATTIC STORAGE

GALLERY
15'-0" X 4'-6"

DN

BEDROOM NO. 3
13'-0" X 12'-0"

OPEN TO BELOW

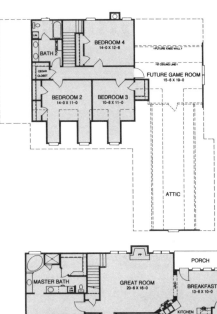

Design VH8072 First Floor: 1,638 square feet
Second Floor: 877 square feet; Total: 2,515 square feet

● A charming elevation welcomes visitors to this compact, four-bedroom home. A roomy front porch provides a great place for relaxing during hot summer evenings. The small porch off the garage is added for decoration and makes a great place for displaying hanging baskets full of blooming flowers. Inside, the entry leads to an oversized great room and a formal dining room with an entrance flanked by square columns. The kitchen features a large breakfast room. The master suite is located downstairs and includes a roomy master bath with a corner whirlpool, a shower, a sitting area and a walk-in closet. Upstairs, Bedrooms 2 and 3 are located at the front of the house. A future game room is shown with access to attic space for later expansion. Please specify crawlspace or slab foundation when ordering.

Width 60'-10"
Depth 61'-4"

Design by
Larry E. Belk
Designs

Design VH8050

First Floor: 1,844 square feet
Second Floor: 841 square feet
Total: 2,685 square feet

● Two shed dormers and a front porch, perfect for evening relaxation, evoke the charm of the country farmhouse in a home designed for the constraints of a suburban lot. Inside, impact is created at the front door with a dining room defined by columns and connecting arched openings. The conveniently designed kitchen features a work island and an eating bar. The family room, with a corner fireplace, has access to a rear covered porch. Three bedrooms and a bath are located on the second floor. A large area—perfect for a game room or a craft room—is located over the garage and makes this plan a great pick for the growing family.

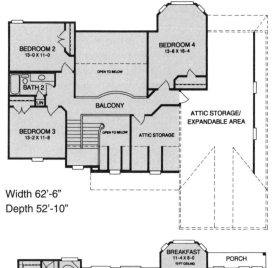

Width 62'-6"
Depth 52'-10"

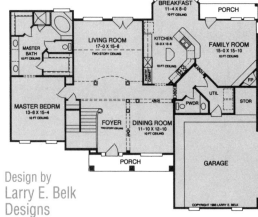

Design by
Larry E. Belk
Designs

42

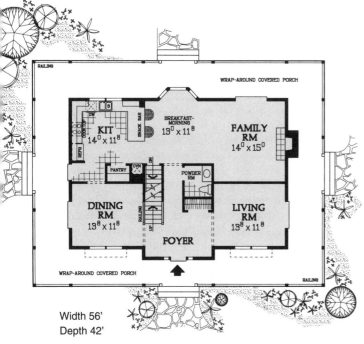

Width 56'
Depth 42'

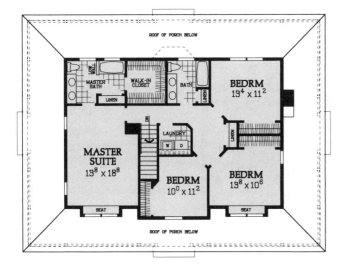

Design VH3653

First Floor: 1,216 square feet
Second Floor: 1,191 square feet
Total: 2,407 square feet

L D

● This home has captured the heart of tradition and will wrap you in its comfort.
From the wraparound covered porch, the
foyer introduces formal entertaining space
furnished by the living room to the right
and the dining room to the left. The open,
casual living area located at the rear claims
the length of the floor plan. Here, a cheerful
fireplace warms a family room that combines with a bay-windowed breakfast-
morning room. The U-shaped kitchen provides maximum efficiency and sports a
snack bar for on-the-go meals. The second
floor contains three family bedrooms that
share a full bath. The relaxing master suite
features a large walk-in closet and an inviting master bath. For added convenience, the
second-floor laundry room is centrally
located.

Design by
Home Planners,
Inc.

Cost to build? See page 300
to order complete cost estimate
to build this house in your area!

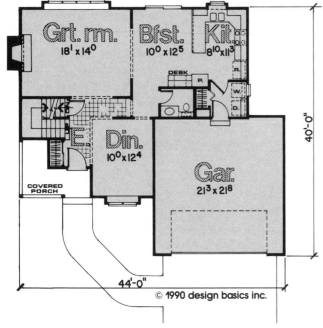

© 1990 design basics inc.

Design VH9260

First Floor: 891 square feet
Second Floor: 759 square feet
Total: 1,650 square feet

● A quaint covered porch leads to a volume entry with decorator plant ledge above the closet in this home. The formal dining room has a boxed window that can be seen from the entry. A fireplace in the large great room adds warmth and coziness to the attached breakfast room and well-planned kitchen. Notice the nearby powder room for guests. Upstairs are three bedrooms. Bedroom 3 has a beautiful arched window under a volume ceiling. The master bedroom has a walk-in closet and pampering dressing area with double vanity and a whirlpool under a window. The upstairs landing overlooks the entry below.

Design by
Design
Basics,
Inc.

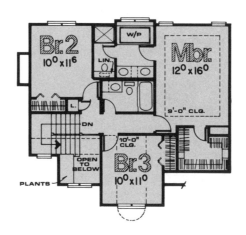

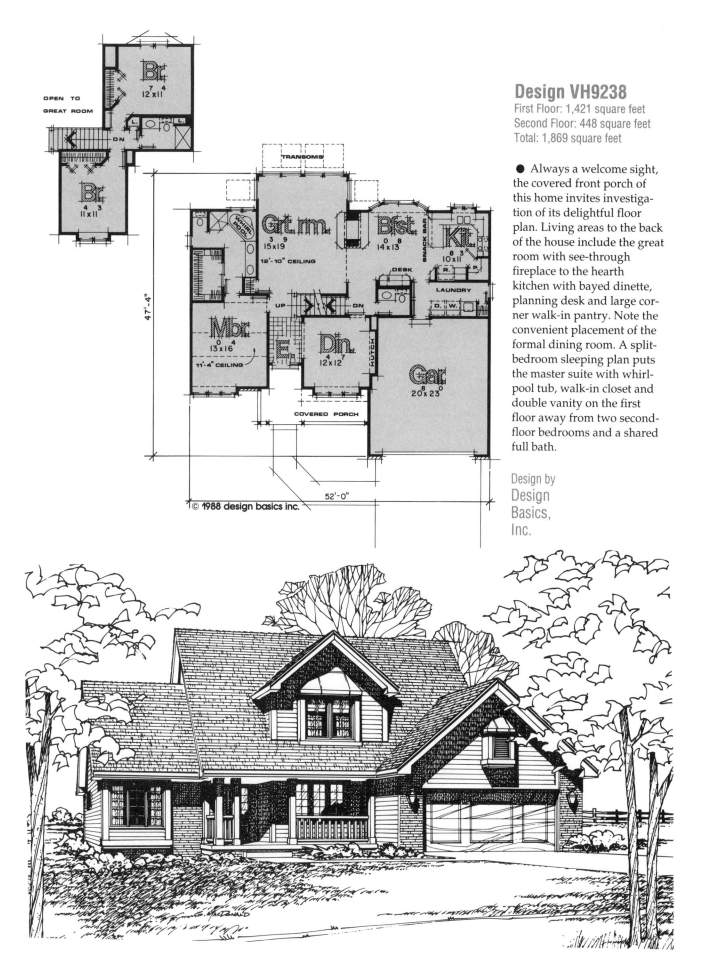

Design VH9238

First Floor: 1,421 square feet
Second Floor: 448 square feet
Total: 1,869 square feet

● Always a welcome sight, the covered front porch of this home invites investigation of its delightful floor plan. Living areas to the back of the house include the great room with see-through fireplace to the hearth kitchen with bayed dinette, planning desk and large corner walk-in pantry. Note the convenient placement of the formal dining room. A split-bedroom sleeping plan puts the master suite with whirlpool tub, walk-in closet and double vanity on the first floor away from two second-floor bedrooms and a shared full bath.

Design by
Design Basics, Inc.

OPEN TO GREAT ROOM

Br.
12 x 11

Br.
11 x 11

DN

TRANSOMS

Gr. rm.
15 x 19
12'-10" CEILING

WHIRL POOL

Bst.
14 x 13

SNACK BAR

Kit.
10 x 11

DESK

LAUNDRY

D. W.

Mbr.
13 x 16
11'-4" CEILING

UP

DN

Dn.
12 x 12

HUTCH

Gar.
20 x 23

COVERED PORCH

47'-4"

52'-0"

© 1988 design basics inc.

Design VH9420

First Floor: 1,587 square feet
Second Floor: 716 square feet
Bonus Room: 427 square feet
Total: 2,730 square feet

Design by
Alan Mascord
Design Associates, Inc.

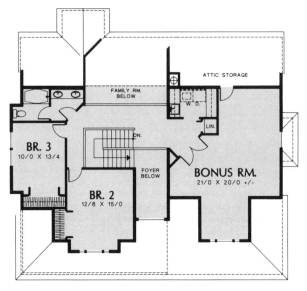

◀ 54' ▶

▲
49'
▼

● This compact Victorian home has its fully featured master bedroom on the main floor. A wraparound porch with a pair of French doors leading from the dining room complements the facade. The upper hallway overlooks the vaulted family room on one side and the two-story foyer on the other. A bonus room over the garage allows some expansion space to either add another bedroom or a game room.

Design VH7220

First Floor: 905 square feet
Second Floor: 863 square feet
Total: 1,768 square feet

● A covered porch and Victorian accents create a classical elevation. Double doors to the entry open to a spacious great room and an elegant dining room. In the gourmet kitchen, features include an island snack bar and a large pantry. French doors lead to the breakfast area which also enjoys access to a covered porch. Cathedral ceilings in the master bedroom and dressing area add an exquisite touch. His and Hers walk-in closets, a large dressing area with dual lavs and a whirlpool complement the master bedroom. A vaulted ceiling in Bedroom 2 accents a window seat and an arched transom window.

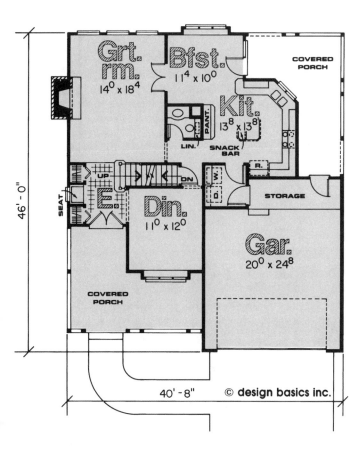

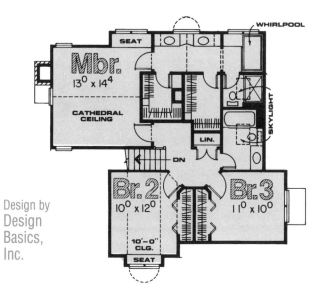

Design by
Design
Basics,
Inc.

Design by
Home Planners,
Inc.

QUOTE ONE™

Cost to build? See page 300
to order complete cost estimate
to build this house in your area!

Design VH3331

First Floor: 1,115 square feet
Second Floor: 690 square feet
Total: 1,805 square feet

L

● Who could guess that this compact design contains three bedrooms and two full baths? The kitchen has indoor eating space in the dining room and outdoor eating space in an attached deck. A fireplace in the two-story gathering room welcomes company.

California Engineered Plans and California Stock Plans are available for this home. Call 1-800-521-6797 for more information.

BATH

LINEN   LINEN

DINING
10¹⁰ x 11⁶

DECK

KITCHEN
9⁰ x 12⁶

GATHERING RM
15⁴ x 15⁰

MASTER
BEDROOM
11⁴ x 16⁶

FOYER

COVERED PORCH

UP

Width 43'
Depth 32'

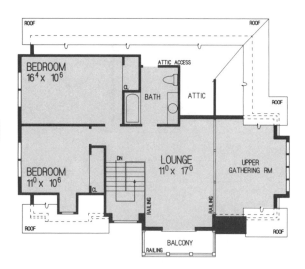

ROOF

BEDROOM
16⁴ x 10⁶

ATTIC ACCESS

BATH

ATTIC

ROOF

BEDROOM
11⁰ x 10⁶

LOUNGE
11⁰ x 17⁰

UPPER
GATHERING RM

ROOF

BALCONY

RAILING

Design VH2491

First Floor: 1,060 square feet
Second Floor: 580 square feet
Total: 1,640 square feet

● This modest-looking plan surprises
everyone with its wealth of amenities inside. Look for a U-shaped kitchen with
snack bar, morning room, sunken gathering
room (note fireplace with wood box), and
abundant built-ins. The master suite on the
second floor is a true eye-catcher.

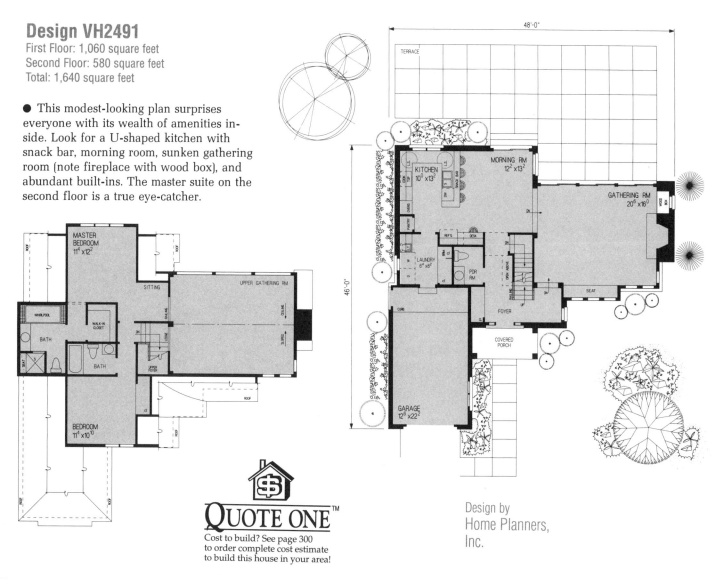

Quote One™
Cost to build? See page 300
to order complete cost estimate
to build this house in your area!

Design by
Home Planners,
Inc.

Design VH8044

First Floor: 1,897 square feet
Second Floor: 1,219 square feet
Total: 3,116 square feet
Bonus Room: 451 square feet

Design VH8045

First Floor: 1,844 square feet
Second Floor: 1,103 square feet
Total: 2,947 square feet

● A stucco finish and a front porch with a metal roof dress up a more traditional farmhouse in this home designed for the growing family. A large kitchen, breakfast room and family room are open and adjacent to one another to provide a big area for family gatherings. The family room features a corner fireplace with a raised hearth and provides access to the covered porch in the rear. The living and dining rooms are available for more formal entertaining. Visual impact is created at the front door by opening both rooms from the foyer. The master bedroom is located downstairs. The luxuriously appointed master bath includes His and Hers walk-in closets, a seating area at the double vanity, a separate shower and a corner whirlpool tub. Either a three- (Design VH8044) or four-bedroom (Design VH8045) upstairs is available. Please specify crawlspace or slab foundation when ordering.

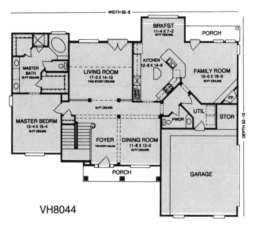

VH8044

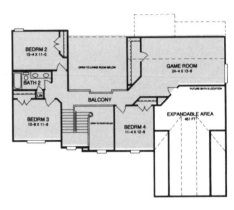

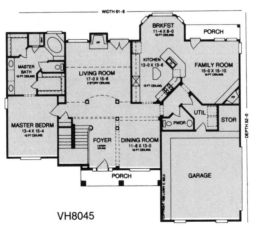

VH8045

Design by
Larry E. Belk
Designs

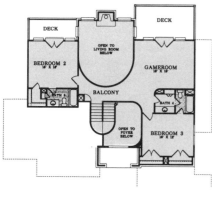

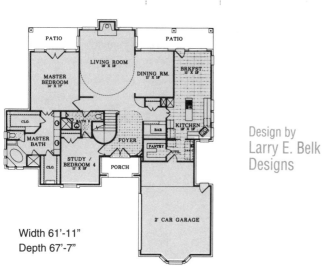

Width 61'-11"
Depth 67'-7"

Design by
Larry E. Belk
Designs

Design VH8023
First Floor: 2,109 square feet
Second Floor: 1,060 square feet
Total: 3,169 square feet

● Old-world charm blends a warm, inviting exterior with a traditional, efficient floor plan. The kitchen is a delight with its large cooktop island, walk-in pantry and sunlit sink with a corner grouping of windows. The pampering master suite offers access through French doors to a covered patio and includes a relaxing master bath with His and Hers walk-in closets, a corner whirlpool tub surrounded by windows and dual vanities. Bedroom 4 may be used as a study or would be ideal used as an office. Upstairs, a curved balcony overlooks the two-story living room. Bedroom 2 features a full bath, a walk-in closet and access to an upper deck. Bedroom 3 enjoys access to its own full bath. A game room with French doors opening to an upper deck completes the second floor.

Design VH8065
First Floor: 1,482 square feet
Second Floor: 631 square feet
Total: 2,113 square feet

● Four-square design reminiscent of the 1940s gives this home its landmark look. An inviting porch opens to a two-story foyer. Straight ahead, the living room is visible through two columns mounted on pedestals and connected by a graceful arch. Dormers located in the living room's vaulted ceiling flood the area with natural light. The dining room is situated nearby and entered through another arched opening. A large kitchen and a sunny breakfast room invite casual conversations and unhurried meals. The master bedroom includes a luxurious master bath with His and Hers walk-in closets, a soothing whirlpool tub and a separate shower. Two additional bedrooms (one with a balcony) and a full bath share the second floor. This plan is available with either a crawlspace or slab foundation. Please specify when ordering.

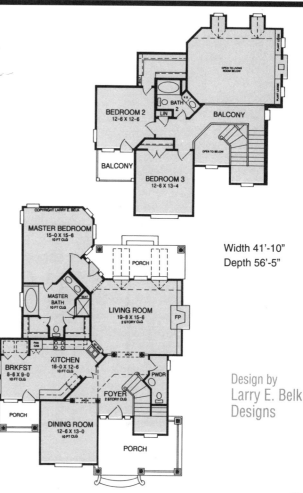

Width 41'-10"
Depth 56'-5"

Design by
Larry E. Belk
Designs

51

Design VH9848
First Floor: 915 square feet
Second Floor: 935 square feet; Total: 1,850 square feet

● The appearance of this home at once suggests classic values. On entry, the foyer opens to a hallway leading to the kitchen and main-level powder room and to a generous family room with a fireplace and double doors to a large deck. The dining room is adjacent to the family room and is framed by columns. In the kitchen, the design maximizes convenience. The staircase off the foyer leads to the upper level where the master suite and two family bedrooms are found. A bonus room completes the second floor. This home is designed with a basement foundation.

Design by
Design Traditions

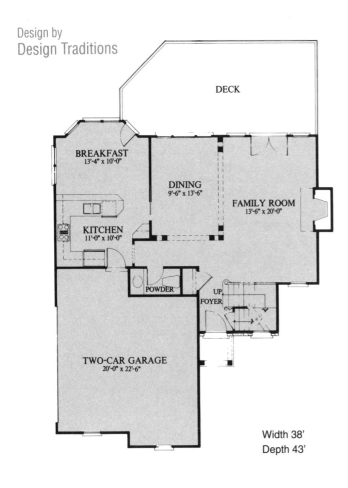

DECK

BREAKFAST
13'-4" x 10'-0"

DINING
9'-6" x 13'-6"

FAMILY ROOM
13'-6" x 20'-0"

KITCHEN
11'-0" x 10'-0"

POWDER

UP
FOYER

TWO-CAR GARAGE
20'-0" x 22'-6"

Width 38'
Depth 43'

W.I.C.

M.BATH

BEDROOM No.2
11'-8" x 10'-0"

BATH

W.I.C.

MASTER SUITE
13'-0" x 15'-0"

BEDROOM No.3
10'-8" x 10'-0"

LAUN.

DN

BONUS

Design VH9907 First Floor: 1,720 square feet
Second Floor: 545 square feet; Total: 2,265 square feet

● Even a large family will be easily
accommodated in this gorgeous stucco and brick, two-story home. The
volume rooflines make the home seem
estate-sized, though in only just over
2,200 square feet a completely livable
floor plan is found. The first floor
contains all the living areas: a family
room with a fireplace, formal living
and dining rooms and a generous
kitchen with an attached breakfast
nook. The master suite is also located
on the first floor and is well-appointed
with a tray ceiling, a walk-in closet
and a double-bowl vanity in the bath.
Upstairs are three bedrooms and two
full baths. This home is designed with
a basement foundation.

Design by
Design Traditions

Width 50'
Depth 53'-6"

Design by
Design Traditions

Design VH9875 First Floor: 1,475 square feet
Second Floor: 545 square feet; Total: 2,020 square feet

● This quaint country manor combines stucco and stone
to create unrivaled warmth and charm. The two-story foyer
is highlighted by the beautiful, open-railed staircase and a
view of the living and dining rooms. The kitchen, equipped
with ample space and a work island, makes preparations
a breeze. The luxurious master suite, with a sitting area
and a private bath, guarantees satisfaction. Upstairs, two
secondary bedrooms and a bonus room share access to a
centrally located hall bath. This home is designed with a
basement foundation.

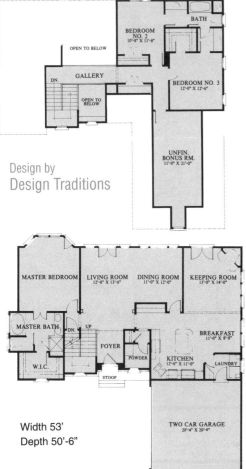

Width 53'
Depth 50'-6"

53

Design VH9849 First Floor: 780 square feet
Second Floor: 915 square feet; Total: 1,695 square feet

● The lines of this home are very clean, as well as traditional. Inside, contemporary priorities reign. To the left of the foyer is the powder room. Opposite is a formal dining room with passage to the kitchen, which is open to the breakfast area and the great room. This area is particularly well-suited to entertaining both formally and informally, with an open, airy design to the kitchen. The large fireplace is well-placed and framed by glass and light. Opening from the great room is a two-car garage and a staircase to the second level. The master suite's double-door entrance, tray ceiling and fireplace are of special interest. The adjoining master bath and walk-in closet complement this area well. The laundry room is found on this level and is convenient to any of the bedrooms. Bedrooms 2 and 3 complete the second floor with a shared bath. This home is designed with a basement foundation.

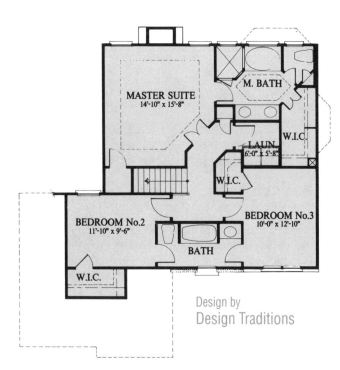

Design by
Design Traditions

Design by
Design Traditions

Design VH9948

First Floor: 915 square feet
Second Floor: 935 square feet
Total: 1,850 square feet

● Brick and clapboard siding
with pairs of double gables
establish the Georgian character
of this home. The front porch,
with a Colonial balustrade and
a Palladian window above, completes this elegant presentation
of an Early American home.
Indoors, the foyer leads to a
great room with a fireplace and
a columned dining room. A deck
opens through double doors. In
the kitchen, an island cooktop
sets the pace. A breakfast/keep-
ing room makes this a pleasant
gathering area. Upstairs, three
bedrooms include an elegant
master suite with a pampering
bath. Two bedrooms share a
bath. This home is designed
with a basement foundation.

MASTER BEDROOM
17'-2" X 13'-6"

BEDROOM NO. 2
12'-0" X 10'-0"

BATH

BEDROOM NO. 3
11'-2" X 10'-0"

MASTER BATH

LAUNDRY

DN

W.I.C.

UNFIN.
BONUS

DECK

BREAKFAST/
KEEPING
13'-4" X 13'-0"

DINING ROOM
10'-0" X 13'-6"

GREAT ROOM
13'-6" X 20'-0"

KITCHEN
10'-8" X 10'-6"

POWDER

UP

FOYER

DN

STOOP

TWO CAR GARAGE
20'-0" X 18'-6"

Width 38'
Depth 43'

Design VH9902

First Floor: 830 square feet
Second Floor: 1,060 square feet
Total: 1,890 square feet

● The pleasing character of this house does not stop behind its facade. The foyer opens up into a large space encompassing the great room with a fireplace and the kitchen/breakfast room. Stairs lead from the great room to the second floor—and here's where you'll find the laundry! The master suite spares none of the amenities: full bath with double vanity, shower and tub, walk-in closet. Bedrooms 2 and 3 share a full bath. This home is designed with a basement foundation.

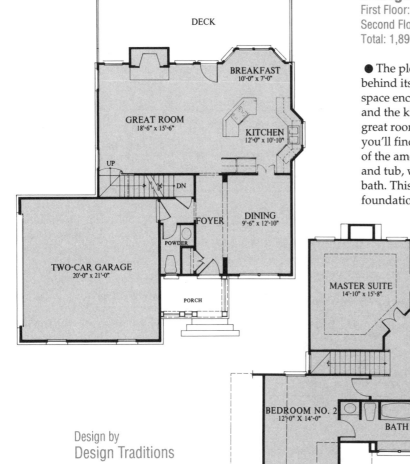

Width 41'
Depth 40'-6"

Design by
Design Traditions

Copyright 1992 Stephen S. Fuller, Inc.

FAMILY ROOM
15'-6" x 17'-0"

BREAKFAST
11'-0" x 6'-0"

LAUNDRY

KITCHEN
10'-0" X 13'-8"

PWDR.

COAT

PAN.

FOYER
7'-10" x 12'-4"

DN

UP

LIVING ROOM
10'-2" x 13'-0"

DINING ROOM
10'-2" x 12'-0"

TWO-CAR GARAGE
20'-0" x 25'-8"

STOOP

WIDTH 54'
DEPTH 39'

MASTER SUITE
15'-6" x 15'-0"

BEDROOM No.2
11'-6" x 12'-6"

BEDROOM No.4
10'-0" x 10'-0"

M. BATH

DN

OPEN TO BELOW

BATH

BEDROOM No.3
13'-0" x 13'-0"

MASTER CLOSET

Design VH9905

First Floor: 1,020 square feet
Second Floor: 1,175 square feet
Total: 2,195 square feet

● This handsome Colonial home will serve the family well for generations to come. Interesting window treatments add to livability—many of the rooms expand into bays. The living and dining rooms define the front of the house while the family room with its fireplace, the breakfast nook and the kitchen with its abundant counter space all define the back of the house. A deck serves the rear of the house and may be accessed from the family room. The second floor does not lack in livability: three bedrooms share a full bath with a double-bowl vanity; the master suite features two walk-in closets and a compartmented bath. Both the master suite and Bedroom 2 feature bay windows. This home is designed with a basement foundation.

Design by
Design Traditions

Design VH2923

First Floor: 1,100 square feet
Second Floor: 970 square feet
Total: 2,070 square feet

Design by
Home Planners,
Inc.

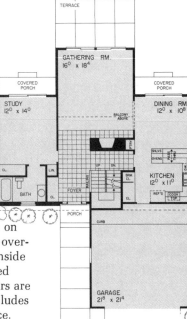

● This Trend Home is as charming on the outside as it is comfortable on the inside. Note the Early American window treatments, second-story overhang, central fireplace, and textured look of stone and board siding. Inside one finds a large rear gathering room with fireplace, efficient U-shaped kitchen, formal dining room, study, and foyer on the first floor. Upstairs are three bedrooms plus an upper gathering room. The two-car garage includes storage space. Note the view windows and covered porch in the rear.

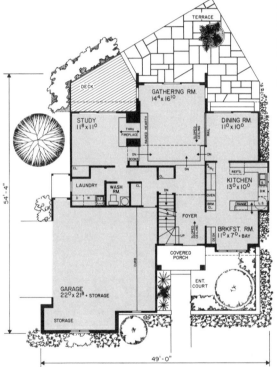

Design VH2826

First Floor: 1,112 square feet
Second Floor: 881 square feet
Total: 1,993 square feet

D

ALTERNATE KITCHEN / DINING RM./
BREAKFAST RM. FLOOR PLAN

● This is an outstanding example of the type of informal, traditional-style architecture that has captured the modern imagination. The interior plan houses all of the features that people want most - a spacious gathering room, formal and informal dining areas, efficient, U-shaped kitchen, master bedroom, two children's bedrooms, second floor lounge, entrance court and rear terrace and deck. Study all areas of this plan carefully.

QUOTE ONE™

Cost to build? See page 300
to order complete cost estimate
to build this house in your area!

Design by
Home Planners,
Inc.

Design VH9259

First Floor: 1,224 square feet
Second Floor: 950 square feet
Total: 2,174 square feet

● Abundant windows throughout this home add light and a feeling of openness. The front entry separates formal from informal living patterns: living room and dining room on the left, den and family room on the right. If desired, the den can be made to open up to the family room with French doors. To the rear is the kitchen which opens to the bayed breakfast room. Notice the fireplace in the family room. Upstairs there are four bedrooms. Three secondary bedrooms share a full bath. Bedroom 2 has a volume ceiling and half-round window. The master suite features a plant shelf, whirlpool, skylight above the vanity and a walk-in closet.

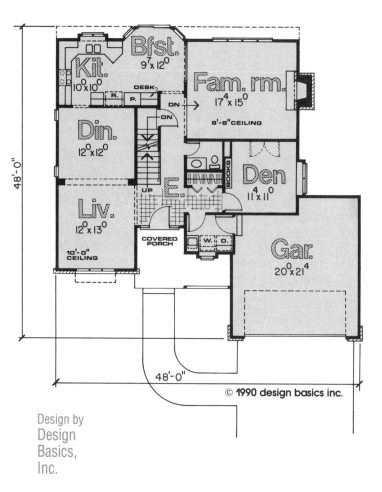

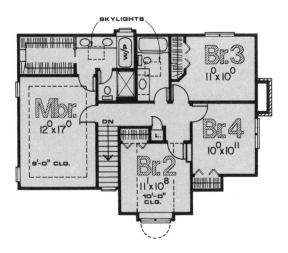

Design by
Design
Basics,
Inc.

© 1990 design basics inc.

60

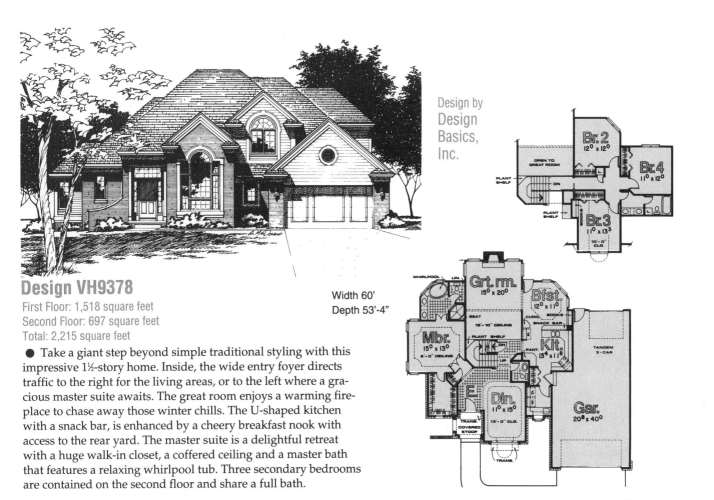

Design by
Design
Basics,
Inc.

Design VH9378

First Floor: 1,518 square feet

Second Floor: 697 square feet

Total: 2,215 square feet

Width 60'

Depth 53'-4"

● Take a giant step beyond simple traditional styling with this impressive 1½-story home. Inside, the wide entry foyer directs traffic to the right for the living areas, or to the left where a gracious master suite awaits. The great room enjoys a warming fireplace to chase away those winter chills. The U-shaped kitchen with a snack bar, is enhanced by a cheery breakfast nook with access to the rear yard. The master suite is a delightful retreat with a huge walk-in closet, a coffered ceiling and a master bath that features a relaxing whirlpool tub. Three secondary bedrooms are contained on the second floor and share a full bath.

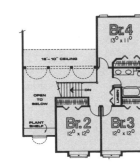

Design by
Design
Basics,
Inc.

Width 60'

Depth 59'-4"

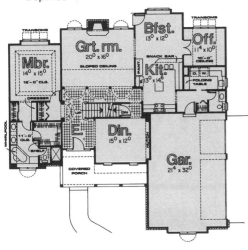

Design VH7219

First Floor: 1,875 square feet

Second Floor: 687 square feet

Total: 2,562 square feet

● The front porch and arched windows provide a country feel for this attractive two-story home. Fifteen-foot arched openings to the great room will dazzle guests. The formal dining room is easily accessible from the large island kitchen. French doors in the breakfast room open to a versatile office with a sloping ten-foot ceiling. A convenient utility area off the kitchen features access to the garage, a half bath and a generous laundry room complete with a folding table. A private entrance into the master suite reveals a pleasing interior. A volume ceiling, a built-in dresser and linen storage area, two closets and a beautiful corner whirlpool with dramatic window treatment are ample endowments. On the second level, three large secondary bedrooms share a bath with dual lavs.

Design VH9516 First Floor: 1,396 square feet
Second Floor: 523 square feet; Total: 1,919 square feet

Width 44'
Depth 51'

● A covered porch flanked with double columns provides special interest for this lovely traditional home. Separate entry through the den creates a perfect opportunity for use as an office or home-operated business. The foyer leads to all areas of the house, maximizing livability. The kitchen combines with the dining area and great room to make the most of this open space. The split bedrooms with the master suite on the first floor and two secondary bedrooms upstairs make this an ideal design for empty-nesters or active retired couples.

Design by
Alan Mascord
Design Associates, Inc.

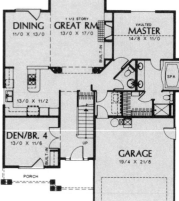

Design VH9532

First Floor: 663 square feet
Second Floor: 740 square feet
Total: 1,403 square feet

● This traditional home bespeaks comfort with a two-story great room that features a fireplace and back-yard access and a roomy kitchen that directly serves the bayed dining area. A laundry room and a powder room complete the first floor. Upstairs, three bedrooms include a master bedroom with a walk-in closet and a bath with dual lavatories. The secondary bed-rooms each enjoy ample closet space. With a two-car garage and a wrap-ping front porch, this design is sure to please.

Design by
Alan Mascord
Design Associates, Inc.

Width 36'
Depth 40'-6"

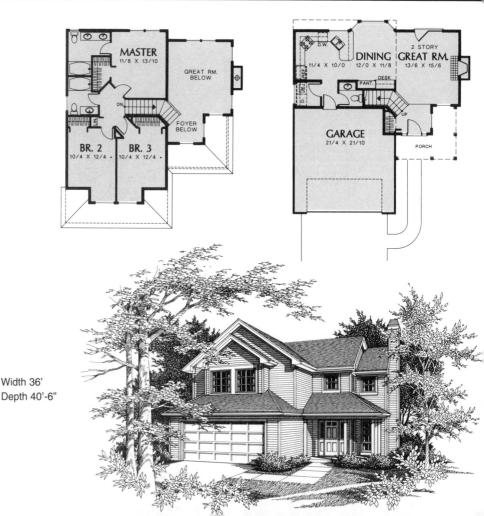

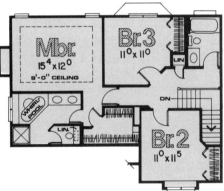

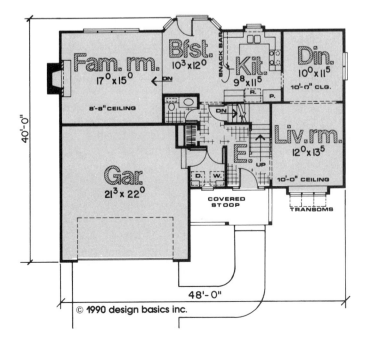

Design VH9282

First Floor: 1,042 square feet
Second Floor: 803 square feet
Total: 1,845 square feet

● At 1,845 square feet, this classic two-story home is perfect for a variety of lifestyles. Upon entry from the covered front porch, the thoughtful floor plan is immediately evident. To the right of the entry is a formal volume living room with ten-foot ceiling. Nearby is the formal dining room with bright window. Serving the dining room and bright bayed dinette, the kitchen features a pantry, Lazy Susan and window sink. Off the breakfast area, step down into the family room with a handsome fireplace and wall of windows. Upstairs, two secondary bedrooms share a hall bath. The private master bedroom has a boxed ceiling, walk-in closet and a pampering dressing area with double vanity and whirlpool.

Design by
Design
Basics,
Inc.

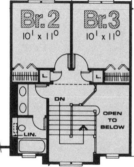

Design by
Design
Basics,
Inc.

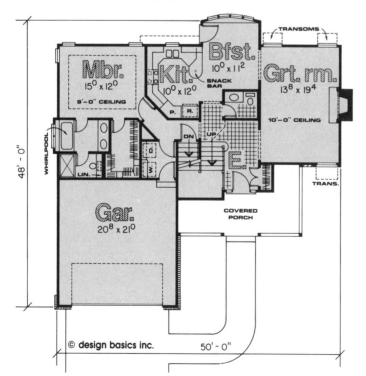

© design basics inc.

Design VH7215

First Floor: 1,191 square feet
Second Floor: 405 square feet
Total: 1,596 square feet

● This charming country-style elevation features a wrapping porch and oval window accents. The spacious great room, directly accessible from the two-story entry and the bowed breakfast area, has a warming fireplace and transom windows. An angled wall adds drama to the peninsula kitchen and creates a private entry to the master suite. In the master suite, a boxed, nine-foot ceiling, a compartmented whirlpool bath and a spacious walk-in closet assure modern livability. The second-level balcony overlooks the U-stairs and entry. Twin linen closets just outside the upstairs bedrooms serve a compartmented bath with natural light.

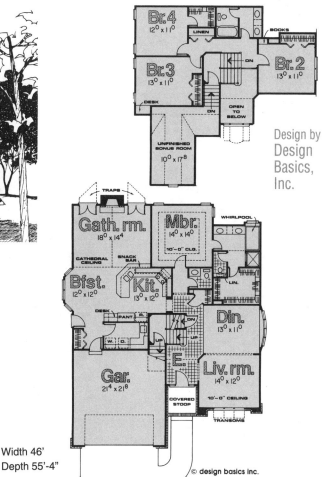

Design VH7218

First Floor: 1,688 square feet
Second Floor: 715 square feet
Total: 2,403 square feet

● A powerful entry and brick accents enhance this beautiful elevation. Inside, a volume living room and U-shaped stairs create elegant first impressions. French doors, a brick fireplace and a cathedral ceiling in the gathering room are sure to please. In the well-organized kitchen, an angled sink, a large pantry and a wraparound snack bar make mealtimes a cinch. The master suite features a whirlpool tub, dual lavs, an open shower and an extensive walk-in closet. Secondary bedrooms share a large compartmented bath with dual lavs.

Width 46'
Depth 55'-4"

© design basics inc.

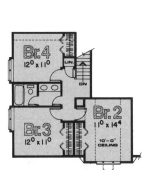

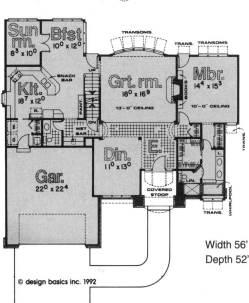

Width 56'
Depth 52'

© design basics inc. 1992

Design VH7217

First Floor: 1,654 square feet
Second Floor: 654 square feet
Total: 2,308 square feet

● Brick accents and bright windows highlight this appealing front elevation. The entry provides a wide, dramatic view of the formal dining room and the spacious great room. An extra-tall bowed window complements the thirteen-foot ceiling in the great room. French doors connect the delightful sun room to the kitchen/dinette area. A wet bar conveniently serves the dining and great rooms. A dramatic master suite with dual bookcases features a deluxe bath, abundant windows, outdoor access and generous closet space.

Design VH9324

First Floor: 1,519 square feet
Second Floor: 594 square feet
Total: 2,113 square feet

● Sophisticated styling and comfortable living define this 1½-story home both inside and out. To the right of the volume entry is a formal living room with a 10-foot ceiling. Boxed windows brighten the formal dining room. In the kitchen/breakfast area, practical features include two Lazy Susans, a snack bar and planning desk. Nearby, the casual family room offers a sloped ceiling and cozy fireplace. The secluded main-floor master bedroom sports a 10-foot ceiling. Study the dressing area with dual lavs, a pampering whirlpool and large walk-in closet. Each secondary bedroom has convenient access to a hall bath complete with a linen closet. A loft area, open to the family room, easily converts to an optional bedroom.

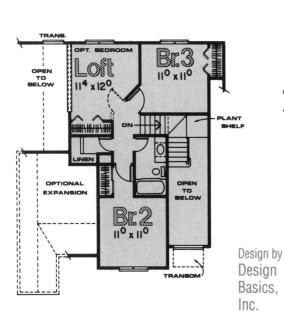

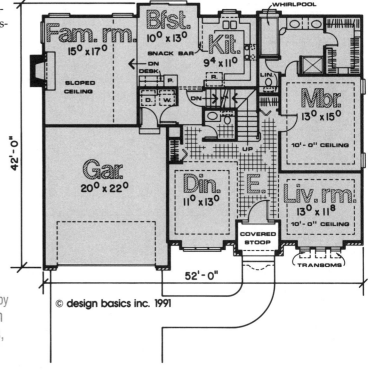

Design by
Design
Basics,
Inc.

© design basics inc. 1991

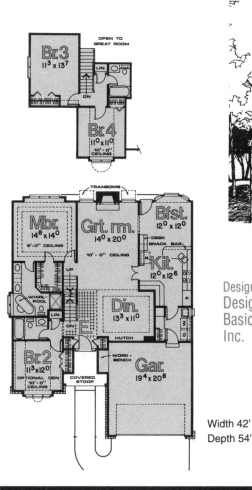

Open to Great Room

Br. 3
11³ x 13⁷

Br. 4
11⁰ x 11⁰
10'-0" ceiling

Mbr.
14⁸ x 14⁰
9'-0" ceiling

Grt. rm.
14⁰ x 20⁰
10'-0" ceiling

Bfst.
12⁰ x 12⁰

Kit.
12⁰ x 12⁶

Din.
13³ x 11⁰

Br. 2
11³ x 12⁰
optional den
10'-0" ceiling

Gar.
19⁴ x 20⁸

Covered Stoop

Design by
Design
Basics,
Inc.

Width 42'
Depth 54'

Design VH9381

First Floor: 1,517 square feet
Second Floor: 431 square feet
Total: 1,948 square feet

● Combined hip and gable roofs offer distinction to this impressive traditional home. To the right of the foyer is a formal dining room with a tray ceiling and built-in hutch space. The kitchen is conveniently located next to the dining area and the great room. The master suite, with a large walk-in closet, is located at the rear of the house, enjoying privacy and offering a restful retreat. The tiered ceiling adds interest and the master bath provides a pampering refuge. The second bedroom on the first floor may also be used as a den. The second floor contains Bedrooms 3 and 4 with a shared bath.

Photo by Jon Riley

Design by
Donald A.
Gardner,
Architects, Inc.

BED RM.
10-4 × 11-9

BED RM.
12-4 × 13-6

BONUS RM.
11-0 × 20-0

DECK

spa

GREAT RM.
15-4 × 18-0
(cathedral ceiling)
fireplace

KIT./BRKFST.
16-8 × 16-0

master bath

walk-in closet

walk-in closet

MASTER BED RM.
13-0 × 13-6

FOYER
7-8 × 9-0

DINING
12-4 × 12-4

UTILITY
10-0 × 6-4

PORCH

storage

GARAGE
20-0 × 20-0

Design VH9661

First Floor: 1,416 square feet
Second Floor: 445 square feet
Total: 1,861 square feet
Bonus Room: 284 square feet

● An arched entrance and windows provide a touch of class to the exterior of this plan. The foyer leads to all areas of the house, minimizing corridor space. The dining room displays round columns at the entrance while the great room boasts a cathedral ceiling, a fireplace and an arched window over the exterior doors to the deck. In the master suite is a walk-in closet and a lavish bath. On the second level are two bedrooms and a full bath. Please specify basement or crawlspace foundation when ordering.

Width 58'-3"
Depth 68'-9"

Design by
Design
Basics,
Inc.

Design VH9293

First Floor: 1,593 square feet
Second Floor: 633 square feet
Total: 2,226 square feet

● Entering through the foyer, a view of the great room with windows out the back and a fireplace centered beneath a cathedral ceiling is sure to please. The formal dining room features a boxed window and hutch space. A snack bar, a desk and a walk-in pantry are found in the kitchen. The formal master suite lies behind double doors and includes a spectacular master bath with an angled whirlpool tub, His and Hers vanities and three closets. Three second-floor bedrooms share a compartmented bath.

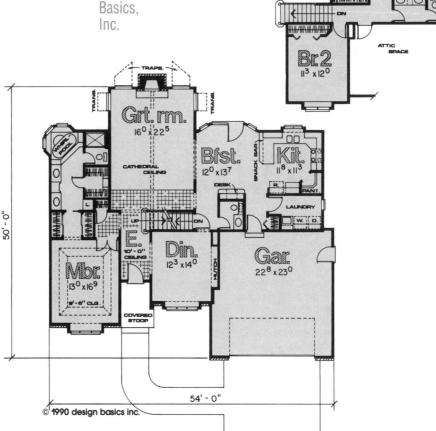

© 1990 design basics inc.

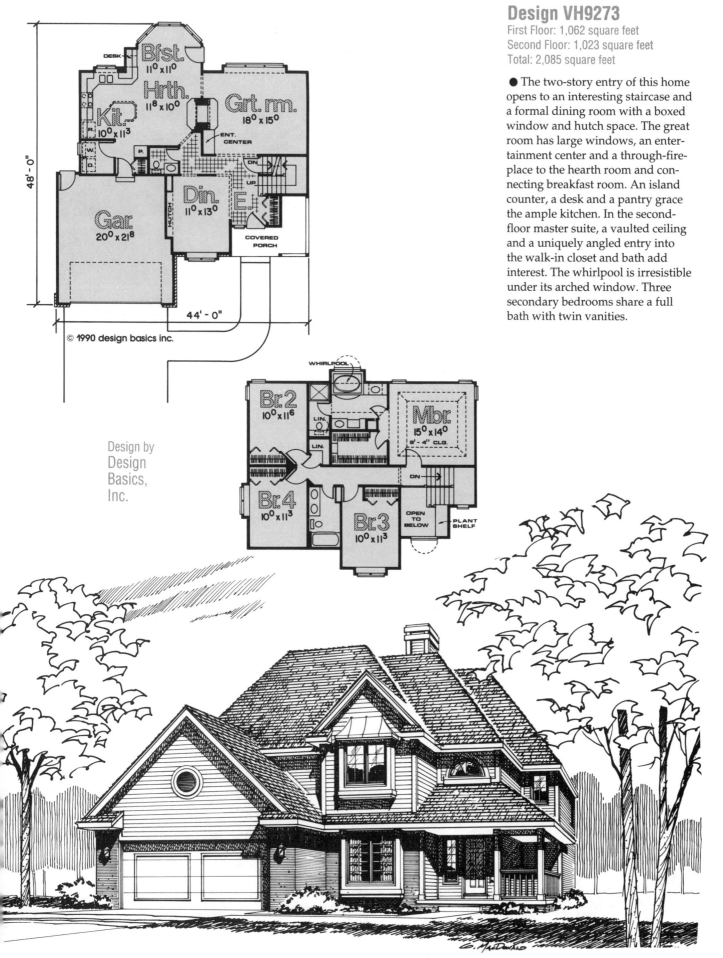

Design VH9273

First Floor: 1,062 square feet
Second Floor: 1,023 square feet
Total: 2,085 square feet

● The two-story entry of this home opens to an interesting staircase and a formal dining room with a boxed window and hutch space. The great room has large windows, an entertainment center and a through-fireplace to the hearth room and connecting breakfast room. An island counter, a desk and a pantry grace the ample kitchen. In the second-floor master suite, a vaulted ceiling and a uniquely angled entry into the walk-in closet and bath add interest. The whirlpool is irresistible under its arched window. Three secondary bedrooms share a full bath with twin vanities.

Bfst.
11⁰ x 11⁰

Hrth.
11⁸ x 10⁰

Grt. rm.
18⁰ x 15⁰

Kit.
10⁰ x 11³

ENT. CENTER

DESK

Din.
11⁰ x 13⁰

E.

Gar.
20⁰ x 21⁸

HUTCH

COVERED PORCH

48' - 0"

44' - 0"

© 1990 design basics inc.

Design by
Design Basics, Inc.

WHIRLPOOL

Br. 2
10⁰ x 11⁶

LIN.

LIN.

Mbr.
15⁰ x 14⁰
9' - 4" CLG.

DN

Br. 4
10⁰ x 11³

Br. 3
10⁰ x 11³

OPEN TO BELOW

PLANT SHELF

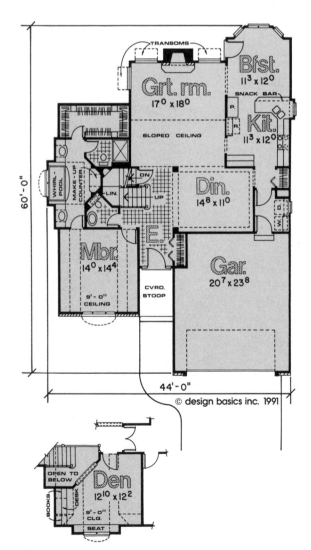

© design basics inc. 1991

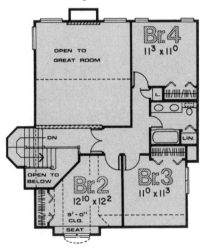

Design VH9338

First Floor: 1,509 square feet
Second Floor: 661 square feet
Total: 2,170 square feet

● Alluring! The exterior of this compact four bedroom, 1½-story home gracefully combines brick details and siding. Elegant columns enhance the open feeling of the formal dining room. Bright windows and the raised-hearth fireplace combine with a ceiling that soars to 16 feet, heightening the drama of the spacious great room. A generous kitchen with pantry and snack bar serves a sunny, bayed breakfast area. In the main floor master suite, be sure to savor the elegance of its tiered ceiling. Homeowners will enjoy the pampering master bath/dressing area with a whirlpool, His and Hers vanities, make-up counter and a large walk-in closet. Upstairs, three secondary bedrooms were designed to accommodate young adults and house guests. Bedroom 2 may be converted to an optional den/loft with a built-in desk and bookshelves. At 2,170 square feet, this home suits a variety of lifestyles!

Design by
Design
Basics,
Inc.

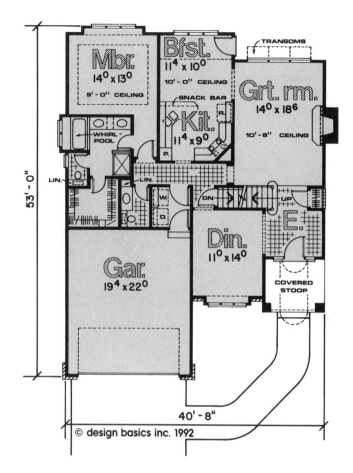

Mbr.
14⁰ x 13⁰

9' - 0" CEILING

Bfst.
11⁴ x 10⁰

10' - 0" CEILING

TRANSOMS

Grt. rm.
14⁰ x 18⁶

10' - 8" CEILING

SNACK BAR

Kit.
11⁴ x 9⁰

WHIRL-POOL

LIN.

LIN.

DN

UP

W.

D.

Din.
11⁰ x 14⁰

Gar.
19⁴ x 22⁰

COVERED STOOP

53' - 0"

40' - 8"

© design basics inc. 1992

OPEN TO BELOW

DN

Br. 2
10⁰ x 10⁰

Br. 3
10⁰ x 10⁰

Design by
Design
Basics,
Inc.

Design VH7216

First Floor: 1,327 square feet
Second Floor: 348 square feet
Total: 1,675 square feet

● Suited for a narrow lot, this home demonstrates design efficiency. A Palladian arch supported by stylish columns shelters the entry stoop. Off the entry, a wide-cased opening leads to the bright formal dining room. The entry also enjoys glass-block accents spotlighting the decorator plant shelf above the guest coat closet. The great room, with its 10'-8" ceiling, full wall of windows and brick fireplace, creates an inviting atmosphere. The breakfast area achieves a light, open sensation with a ten-foot ceiling and large windows. The master bedroom, with a nine-foot boxed ceiling and an expansive window area, affords maximum privacy. Two secondary bedrooms are upstairs.

Design by
Alan Mascord
Design Associates, Inc.

SPA

DEN/
BR. 4
10/0 X 13/4

VAULTED
MASTER
12/0 X 15/8

FOYER
BELOW

DN.

PLANT
SHELF

LIN.

VAULTED
BR. 2
10/4 X 11/0

VAULTED
BR. 3
10/4 X 11/0

◀ 40' ▶

▲
56'-6"
▼

NOOK
10/0 X 12/0

VAULTED
DINING
10/6 X 13/0

12/0 X 13/6

FAMILY
16/0 X 15/6

PAN. REF. O.

VAULTED
LIVING
12/0 X 14/0

UP

W. D.

GARAGE
21/4 X 20/8

Design VH9535

First Floor: 1,110 square feet
Second Floor: 1,080 square feet
Total: 2,190 square feet

● The vaulted living room, with
its fireplace and porch access, opens
this design. An attached dining room
makes formal meals a pleasure. In
the kitchen, an island cooktop and
an ample nook will satisfy the house
gourmet. The family room—also
with a fireplace—is open to this area.
Upstairs, the vaulted master suite
enjoys a private luxury bath with a
spa tub. A den or fourth bedroom is
accessible through double doors. Two
secondary bedrooms each feature a
vaulted ceiling and plenty of closet
space. A full hall bath with a cheery
window serves these areas well.

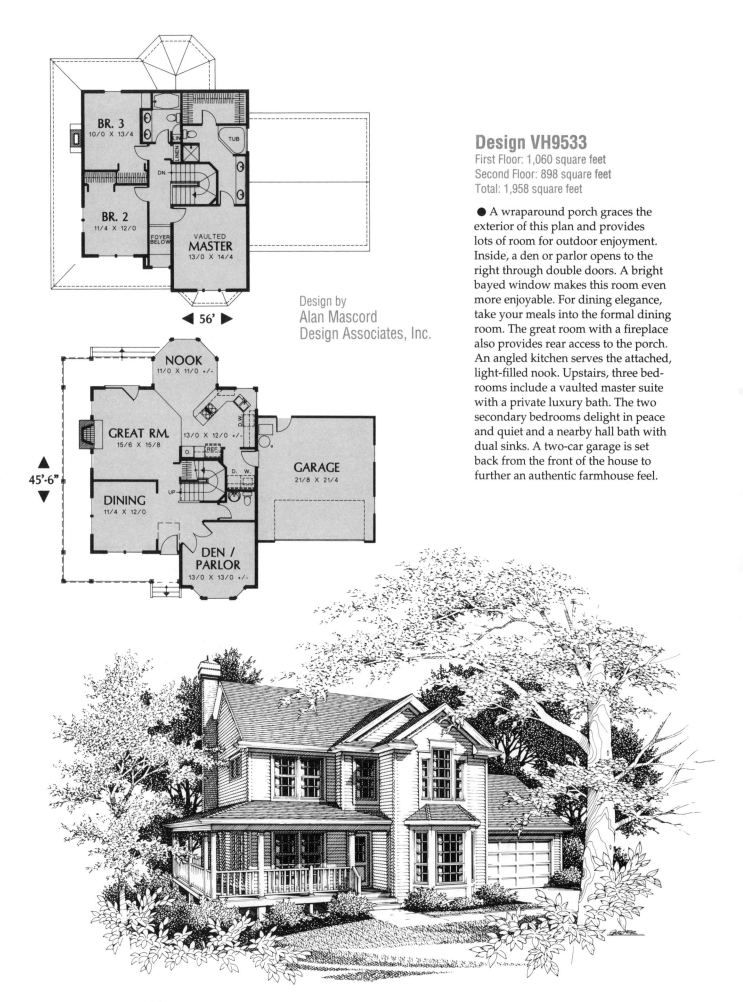

BR. 3
10/0 X 13/4

BR. 2
11/4 X 12/0

DN.

LINEN

TUB

VAULTED
MASTER
13/0 X 14/4

FOYER
BELOW

◄ 56' ►

Design by
Alan Mascord
Design Associates, Inc.

NOOK
11/0 X 11/0 +/-

GREAT RM.
15/6 X 15/8

13/0 X 12/0 +/-

D. W.

O.

REF.

D. W.

UP

GARAGE
21/8 X 21/4

DINING
11/4 X 12/0

DEN /
PARLOR
13/0 X 13/0 +/-

▲
45'-6"
▼

Design VH9533

First Floor: 1,060 square feet
Second Floor: 898 square feet
Total: 1,958 square feet

● A wraparound porch graces the exterior of this plan and provides lots of room for outdoor enjoyment. Inside, a den or parlor opens to the right through double doors. A bright bayed window makes this room even more enjoyable. For dining elegance, take your meals into the formal dining room. The great room with a fireplace also provides rear access to the porch. An angled kitchen serves the attached, light-filled nook. Upstairs, three bedrooms include a vaulted master suite with a private luxury bath. The two secondary bedrooms delight in peace and quiet and a nearby hall bath with dual sinks. A two-car garage is set back from the front of the house to further an authentic farmhouse feel.

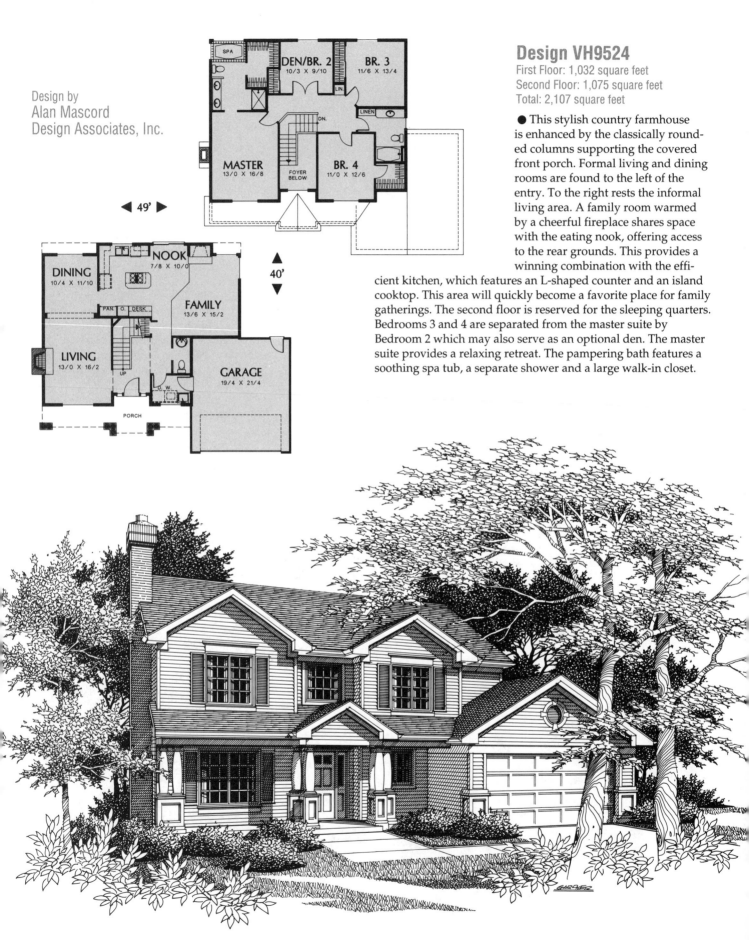

Design by
Alan Mascord
Design Associates, Inc.

◀ 49' ▶

SPA

DEN/BR. 2
10/3 X 9/10

BR. 3
11/6 X 13/4

LIN.

LINEN

MASTER
13/0 X 16/8

FOYER
BELOW

DN.

BR. 4
11/0 X 12/6

40'
▲
▼

DINING
10/4 X 11/10

NOOK
7/8 X 10/0

PAN. O. DESK

FAMILY
13/6 X 15/2

LIVING
13/0 X 16/2

UP

D. W.

GARAGE
19/4 X 21/4

PORCH

Design VH9524

First Floor: 1,032 square feet
Second Floor: 1,075 square feet
Total: 2,107 square feet

● This stylish country farmhouse is enhanced by the classically rounded columns supporting the covered front porch. Formal living and dining rooms are found to the left of the entry. To the right rests the informal living area. A family room warmed by a cheerful fireplace shares space with the eating nook, offering access to the rear grounds. This provides a winning combination with the efficient kitchen, which features an L-shaped counter and an island cooktop. This area will quickly become a favorite place for family gatherings. The second floor is reserved for the sleeping quarters. Bedrooms 3 and 4 are separated from the master suite by Bedroom 2 which may also serve as an optional den. The master suite provides a relaxing retreat. The pampering bath features a soothing spa tub, a separate shower and a large walk-in closet.

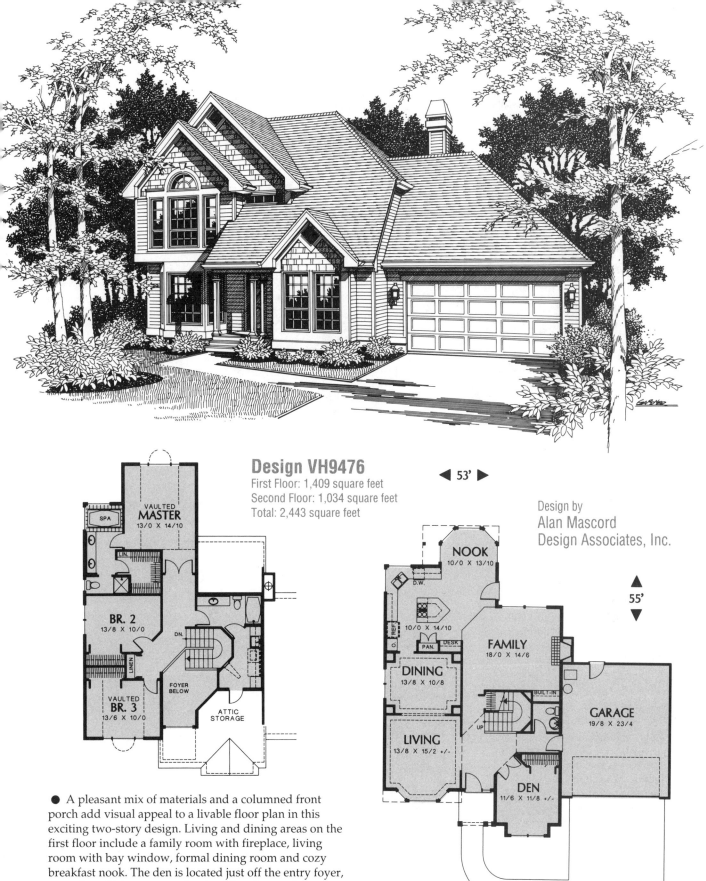

Design VH9476

First Floor: 1,409 square feet
Second Floor: 1,034 square feet
Total: 2,443 square feet

◄ 53' ►

Design by
**Alan Mascord
Design Associates, Inc.**

▲
55'
▼

VAULTED MASTER
13/0 X 14/10

SPA

LIN.

BR. 2
13/8 X 10/0

DN.

LINEN

VAULTED BR. 3
13/6 X 10/0

FOYER BELOW

ATTIC STORAGE

NOOK
10/0 X 13/10

D.W.

10/0 X 14/10

REF.

PAN.   DESK

FAMILY
18/0 X 14/6

DINING
13/8 X 10/8

BUILT-IN

GARAGE
19/8 X 23/4

LIVING
13/8 X 15/2 +/-

UP

DEN
11/6 X 11/8 +/-

● A pleasant mix of materials and a columned front porch add visual appeal to a livable floor plan in this exciting two-story design. Living and dining areas on the first floor include a family room with fireplace, living room with bay window, formal dining room and cozy breakfast nook. The den is located just off the entry foyer, away from living areas and noise. Upstairs are three bedrooms including a master suite with full bath. Attic storage over the garage is reached through the second bathroom.

Design VH8051

First Floor: 1,078 square feet
Second Floor: 921 square feet
Total: 1,999 square feet

Design by
Larry E. Belk
Designs

● This charming clapboard home is loaded with character and perfect for a narrow lot. High ceilings throughout give the home an open, spacious feeling. The great room and the dining room are separated by columns with connecting arches. The efficient, U-shaped kitchen features a corner sink with a window view and a bayed breakfast area with access to the rear porch. A bedroom and a bath (with a shower tucked under the stair) are conveniently located for guests on the first floor. Upstairs, the master bedroom features a vaulted ceiling and a luxurious master bath with dual vanities, a whirlpool tub and a separate shower. Access to a covered patio from the master bedroom provides a relaxing outdoor retreat. A secondary bedroom and full bath are also located on the second floor with a large rear balcony completing this compact, highly livable plan. This plan is available with either a crawlspace or slab foundation. Please specify when ordering.

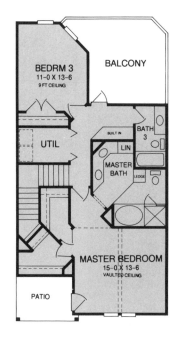

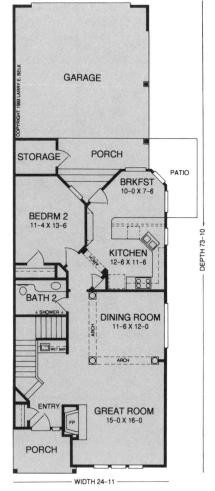

Design VH8052

First Floor: 904 square feet
Second Floor: 1,058 square feet
Total: 1,962 square feet

● This fine clapboard home is reminiscent of the popular "shotgun" homes of the past. Designed for a narrow lot and perfect for urban infill or riverfront living, this home features two balconies on the upper level. A two-way fireplace located between the formal living room and dining room provides visual impact. Built-in bookcases flanking an arched opening between these rooms add drama. The sunny breakfast area and the efficient kitchen, with its convenient features, will be treasures valued by the busy cook. A pass-through from the kitchen to the dining room simplifies serving and a walk-in pantry provides lots of storage. On the second floor, the master bedroom provides access to a large balcony and the relaxing master bath is designed with a large separate shower and an angled whirlpool tub. Two secondary bedrooms and a full bath are located at the rear of the plan. This plan is available with either a crawlspace or slab foundation. Please specify when ordering.

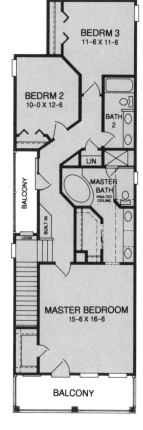

BEDRM 3
11-6 X 11-6

BEDRM 2
10-0 X 12-6

BATH 2

LIN

BALCONY

MASTER BATH
VAULTED CEILING

BUILT IN

LEDGE

MASTER BEDROOM
15-6 X 16-6

BALCONY

Design by
Larry E. Belk
Designs

GARAGE

COPYRIGHT 1993 LARRY E. BELK

BRKFST
10-6 X 11-4
10 FT CEILING

PAN

KITCHEN
11-6 X 10-6
10 FT CEILING

PATIO

PASS THRU

DINING ROOM
15-6 X 13-0
TRAYED CEILING

PWDR

TWO WAY FP

ARCH   ARCH

LIVING ROOM
15-6 X 15-0
10 FT CEILING

ENTRY

PORCH

DEPTH 74-0

WIDTH 22-0

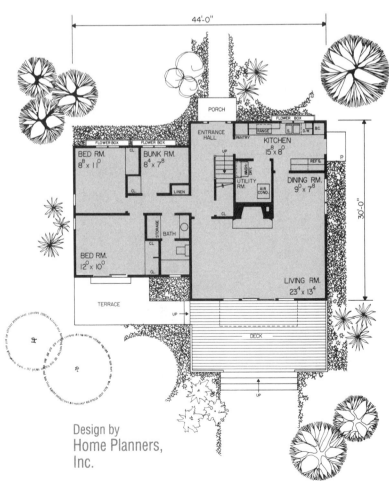

44'-0"

PORCH

FLOWER BOX

ENTRANCE HALL

PANTRY

RANGE

S.

D.W.

B.C.

KITCHEN
15⁸ x 8⁰

FLOWER BOX

FLOWER BOX

BED RM.
8⁸ x 11⁰

BUNK RM.
8⁴ x 7⁸

CL.

LINEN

UP

UTILITY RM.

WASH. DRY.

AIR COND.

REF'G.

DINING RM.
9⁰ x 7⁸

P

STORAGE

BATH

CL.

CL.

CL.

BED RM.
12⁰ x 10⁰

30'-0"

LIVING RM.
23⁴ x 13⁴

TERRACE

UP

DECK

UP

Design by
Home Planners,
Inc.

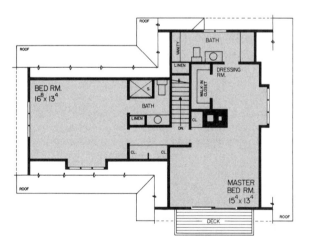

ROOF

ROOF

ROOF

BATH

LINEN

VANITY

DRESSING RM.

WALK IN CLOSET

BED RM.
16⁸ x 13⁴

S.

LINEN

BATH

DN

CL.

CL.

CL.

CL.

MASTER BED RM.
15⁴ x 13⁴

DECK

ROOF

Design VH2481

First Floor: 1,160 square feet
Second Floor: 828 square feet
Total: 1,988 square feet

● Five rooms for sleeping! A complete master suite plus three bedrooms and a bunk room. Three full baths, one on the first floor and two upstairs. The living room will enjoy easy access to a large deck plus a fireplace. The dining room is conveniently located between the living area and the efficient kitchen which has a pantry and nearby laundry/utility room. Surely a great planned work center for a vacation home.

Farmhouse Favor

Design VH9123
Square Footage: 829

● Build small, then add on as the family grows or as needs increase. The economical Phase 1 project of this home allows for all the livability of much larger plans: an ample living area, hexagonal dining area, U-shaped kitchen and large bedroom with full bath and huge closet. When you outgrow the Basic

Plan, you can add the two additional bedrooms with walk-in closets. The utility room provides adequate space for a washer and dryer. The covered front porch is not only charming, but adds a welcome indoor/outdoor relationship.

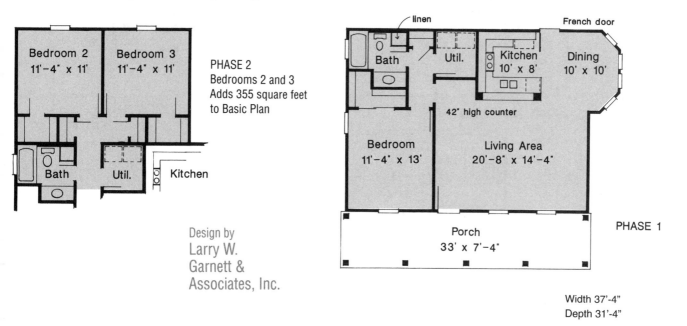

Bedroom 2
11'-4" x 11'

Bedroom 3
11'-4" x 11'

PHASE 2
Bedrooms 2 and 3
Adds 355 square feet
to Basic Plan

Bath

Util.

Kitchen

Design by
Larry W.
Garnett &
Associates, Inc.

linen

French door

Bath

Util.

Kitchen
10' x 8'

Dining
10' x 10'

42" high counter

Bedroom
11'-4" x 13'

Living Area
20'-8" x 14'-4"

Porch
33' x 7'-4"

PHASE 1

Width 37'-4"
Depth 31'-4"

● This economical plan offers an impressive visual statement with its comfortable and well-proportioned appearance. The entrance foyer leads to all areas of the house. The great room, dining area and kitchen are all open to one another allowing visual interaction. The great room and dining area both have a cathedral ceiling. The fireplace is flanked by book shelves and cabinets. The master suite has a cathedral ceiling, walk-in closet and master bath with double-bowl vanity, whirlpool tub and shower. The plan is available with a crawl-space foundation.

Design by
Donald A.
Gardner,
Architects, Inc.

Design VH9664
Square Footage: 1,287

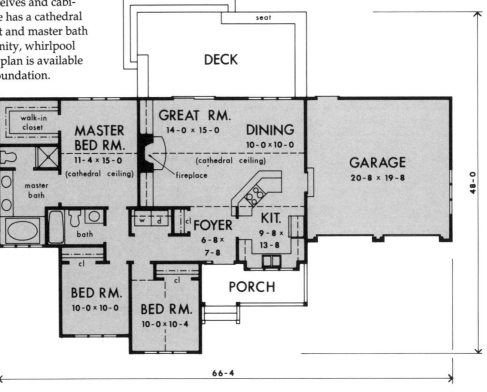

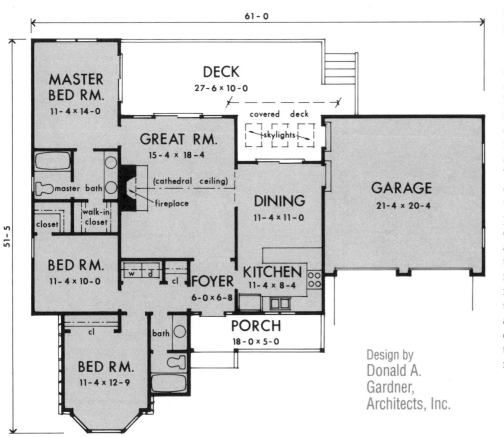

MASTER
BED RM.
11-4 × 14-0

DECK
27-6 × 10-0

covered deck
skylights

GREAT RM.
15-4 × 18-4

61-0

51-5

(cathedral ceiling)
fireplace

master bath

walk-in
closet

closet

GARAGE
21-4 × 20-4

DINING
11-4 × 11-0

BED RM.
11-4 × 10-0

w d   cl

FOYER
6-0 × 6-8

KITCHEN
11-4 × 8-4

cl

bath

PORCH
18-0 × 5-0

BED RM.
11-4 × 12-9

Design by
Donald A.
Gardner,
Architects, Inc.

Design VH9620
Square Footage: 1,310

● A multi-paned bay window, dormers, a cupola, a covered porch and a variety of building materials dress up this one-story cottage. The entrance foyer leads to an impressive great room with cathedral ceiling and fireplace. The U-shaped kitchen, adjacent to the dining room, provides an ideal layout for food preparation. An expansive deck offers shelter while admitting cheery sunlight through skylights. A luxurious master bedroom located to the rear of the house takes advantage of the deck area and is assured privacy from two other bedrooms at the front of the house. These family bedrooms share a full bath.

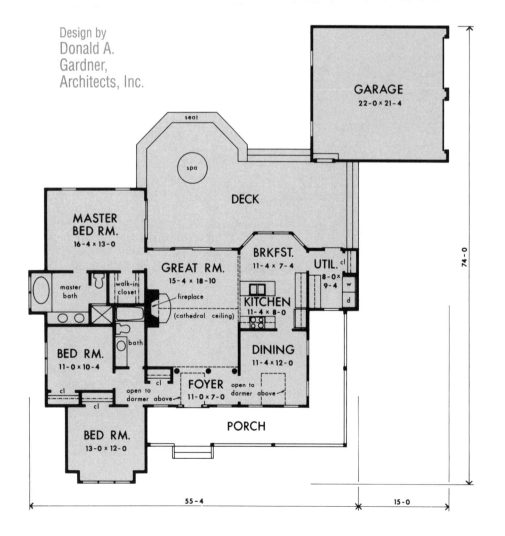

Design by
Donald A.
Gardner,
Architects, Inc.

GARAGE
22-0 × 21-4

**MASTER
BED RM.**
16-4 × 13-0

seat

spa

DECK

master
bath

walk-in
closet

GREAT RM.
15-4 × 18-10

fireplace

(cathedral ceiling)

BRKFST.
11-4 × 7-4

UTIL.
8-0 ×
9-4

KITCHEN
11-4 × 8-0

BED RM.
11-0 × 10-4

bath

cl

DINING
11-4 × 12-0

cl

FOYER
11-0 × 7-0

open to
dormer above

open to
dormer above

cl

cl

BED RM.
13-0 × 12-0

PORCH

55-4

15-0

74-0

Design VH9713
Square Footage: 1,590

● The open floor plan of
this country farmhouse packs
in all of today's amenities in
only 1,590 square feet.
Columns separate the foyer
from the great room with its
cathedral ceiling and fireplace. Serving meals has
never been easier—the
kitchen makes use of direct
access to the dining room as
well as a breakfast nook
overlooking the deck and
spa. A handy utility room
even has room for a counter
and cabinets. Three bed-
rooms make this an especially desirable design. The master bedroom, off of the great
room, provides private
access to the deck. This
design is flexible enough to
be accommodated by a nar-
row lot if the garage is relocated. This plan includes a
crawl-space foundation.

Design VH9679
Square Footage: 1,512

● A multi-pane bay window, dormers, a cupola, a covered porch and a variety of building materials all combine to dress up this intriguing country cottage. The generous entry foyer leads to a formal dining room and an impressive great room with a cathedral ceiling and a fireplace. The kitchen includes a breakfast area with a bay window overlooking the deck. The great room and master bedroom also access the deck. The master bath has a double-bowl vanity, a shower and a garden tub. Two additional bedrooms are located at the front of the house for privacy and share a full bath.

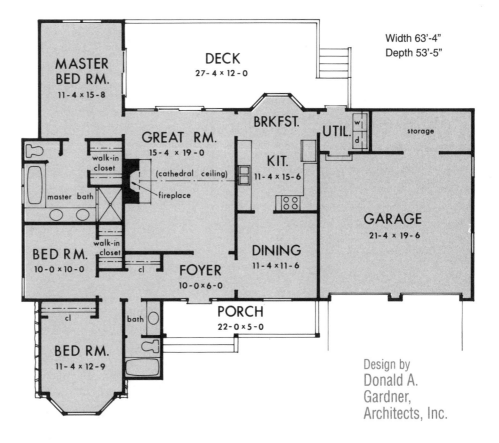

Width 63'-4"
Depth 53'-5"

MASTER BED RM.
11-4 x 15-8

DECK
27-4 x 12-0

BRKFST.

UTIL.

storage

GREAT RM.
15-4 x 19-0

walk-in closet

(cathedral ceiling)

fireplace

KIT.
11-4 x 15-6

master bath

walk-in closet

cl

FOYER
10-0 x 6-0

DINING
11-4 x 11-6

GARAGE
21-4 x 19-6

BED RM.
10-0 x 10-0

bath

PORCH
22-0 x 5-0

cl

BED RM.
11-4 x 12-9

Design by
Donald A.
Gardner,
Architects, Inc.

83

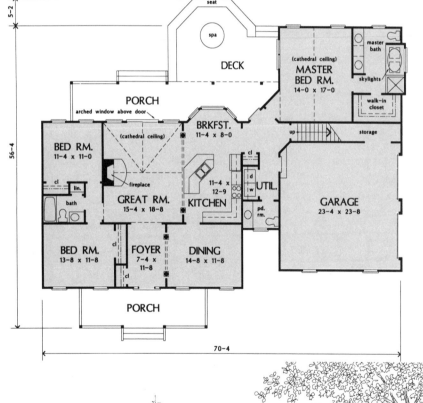

Floor plan labels:

seat
spa
DECK
PORCH
arched window above door
(cathedral ceiling)
MASTER BED RM.
14-0 x 17-0
(cathedral ceiling)
master bath
skylights
walk-in closet
BED RM.
11-4 x 11-0
cl
lin.
bath
BRKFST.
11-4 x 8-0
up
storage
fireplace
GREAT RM.
15-4 x 18-8
KITCHEN
11-4 x 12-9
d
w
UTIL.
cl
pd. rm.
GARAGE
23-4 x 23-8
BED RM.
13-8 x 11-8
FOYER
7-4 x 11-8
DINING
14-8 x 11-8
PORCH
5-2
56-4
70-4

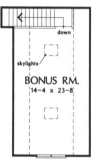

down
skylights
BONUS RM.
14-4 x 23-8

Design by
Donald A.
Gardner,
Architects, Inc.

Design VH9749

Square Footage: 1,864
Bonus Room: 420 square feet

● Quaint and cozy on the outside with porches front and back, this three-bedroom country home surprises with an open floor plan featuring a large great room with a cathedral ceiling. Nine-foot ceilings add volume throughout the home. A central kitchen with an angled counter opens to the breakfast and great rooms for easy entertaining. The privately located master bedroom has a cathedral ceiling and adjacent access to the deck. Operable skylights over the tub accent the luxurious master bath. Two secondary bedrooms share a full hall bath. A bonus room makes expanding easy. Please specify basement or crawlspace foundation when ordering.

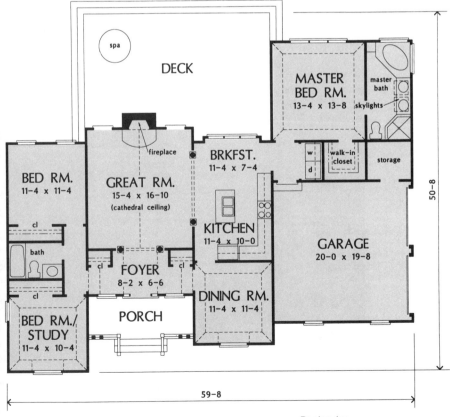

spa

DECK

MASTER
BED RM.
13-4 x 13-8

master
bath

skylights

fireplace

BRKFST.
11-4 x 7-4

w
d

walk-in
closet

storage

BED RM.
11-4 x 11-4

GREAT RM.
15-4 x 16-10
(cathedral ceiling)

KITCHEN
11-4 x 10-0

GARAGE
20-0 x 19-8

cl

bath

FOYER
8-2 x 6-6

cl

cl

50-8

BED RM./
STUDY
11-4 x 10-4

PORCH

DINING RM.
11-4 x 11-4

59-8

Design by
Donald A.
Gardner,
Architects, Inc.

Design VH9726
Square Footage: 1,498

● This charming one-story home utilizes multi-pane windows, columns, dormers and a covered porch to offer a welcoming front exterior. Inside, the great room with a dramatic cathedral ceiling commands attention; the kitchen and breakfast room are just beyond a set of columns. The tiered ceilinged dining room presents a delightfully formal atmosphere for dinner parties or family gatherings. A tray ceiling in the master bedroom will please, as will a large walk-in closet and a gracious master bath with dual lavatories, a garden tub, and a separate shower. The secondary bedrooms are located at the opposite end of the house for privacy. This plan is available with a crawlspace foundation.

Design VH3465
Square Footage: 1,410

L

● An L-shaped veranda employs tapered columns to support a standing-seam metal roof. Horizontal siding with brick accents and multi-pane windows enhance the exterior of this home. Most notable, however, is the metal roof with its various planes. Complementing this is a massive stucco chimney that captures the ambience of the West. A hardworking interior will delight those building within a modest budget. A 36' front room provides plenty of space for both living and family dining activities. A fireplace makes a delightful focal point. The kitchen, set aside, will be free of annoying cross-room traffic. Adjacent to the kitchen is the passageway to the garage. To one side is the laundry area, to the other, the stairs to the basement. The centrally located main bath has twin lavatories and a nearby linen closet. One of the two secondary bedrooms has direct access to the veranda. The master bedroom is flanked by the master bath and its own private covered porch.

Quote One™
Cost to build? See page 300 to order complete cost estimate to build this house in your area!

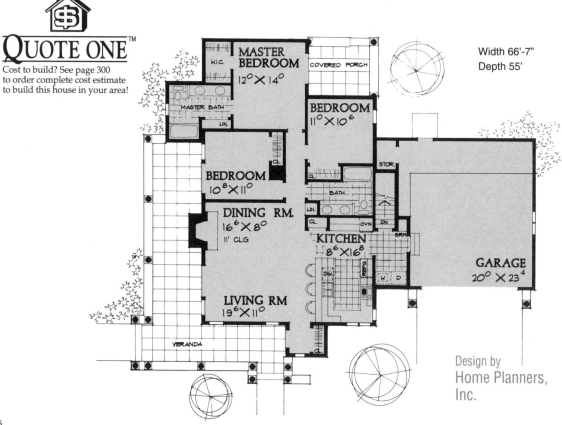

Width 66'-7"
Depth 55'

Design by
Home Planners, Inc.

Design VH3460
Square Footage: 1,389

L

● A double dose of charm, this special farmhouse plan offers two elevations in its blueprint package—one showcases a delightful wraparound porch. The formal living room has a warming fireplace and a sunny bay window. The kitchen separates this area from the more casual family room. In the kitchen, you'll find an efficient snack bar as well as a pantry for additional storage space. Three bedrooms include two family bedrooms served by a full bath and a lovely master suite with its own private bath. Notice the location of the washer and dryer—convenient to all of the bedrooms.

California Engineered Plans and California Stock Plans are available for this home. Call 1-800-521-6797 for more information.

Design by
Home Planners,
Inc.

QUOTE ONE™
Cost to build? See page 300
to order complete cost estimate
to build this house in your area!

Design VH3469

First Floor: 1,066 square feet
Second Floor: 1,006 square feet
Total: 2,072 square feet

L

● Our neo-classic farmhouse offers plenty of room for delightful diversions; a sheet-metal roof adds old-fashioned flair; front and rear porches accommodate out-of-doors lounging. Inside, a large living area with a fireplace affords grand lounging; a dining room, cozy interludes. A fully functional kitchen, powder room and utility room round out the first floor. The second floor provides well-arranged sleeping quarters—with large master bedroom—and two full baths. Don't forget the interesting mud yard separating the garage from the house.

Design by
Home Planners,
Inc.

WIDTH 70'-4"
DEPTH 50'-4"

Quote One™
Cost to build? See page 300
to order complete cost estimate
to build this house in your area!

Design VH3467

First Floor: 1,276 square feet
Second Floor: 658 square feet
Total: 1,934 square feet

L

● A projecting front gable supported by columns effectively frames the paneled front door of this house while creating an impressive and inviting entrance. Inside, both formal living and dining rooms flank the foyer and deliver an extra measure of livability through thoughtful traffic patterns. A fireplace in the living room is bordered by glass doors leading to a side porch. For more casual living, the kitchen opens over a snack bar to the family living area. Note the central fireplace and sliding glass doors to the raised deck outside. Three bedrooms include a master suite with a large walk-in closet, a private bath and glass doors to the rear deck.

Design by
Home Planners,
Inc.

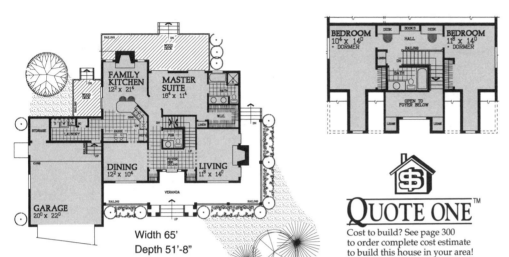

Width 65'
Depth 51'-8"

QUOTE ONE™

Cost to build? See page 300
to order complete cost estimate
to build this house in your area!

Design by
Home Planners,
Inc.

Design VH3468

First Floor: 1,618 square feet
Second Floor: 510 square feet
Total: 2,128 square feet

L

QUOTE ONE™

Cost to build? See page 300
to order complete cost estimate
to build this house in your area!

● Amenities abound in this contemporary farmhouse. A wraparound porch ensures a favorite spot for enjoying good weather. The great room sports a fireplace and lots of natural light. Grab a snack at the kitchen island/snack bar or in the breakfast room. The vaulted foyer grandly introduces the dining room and parlor—the master bedroom is just off this room. Inside it: a tray ceiling, a fireplace, a luxury bath and a walk-in closet. Stairs lead up to a quaint loft/bedroom, a full bath and an additional bedroom.

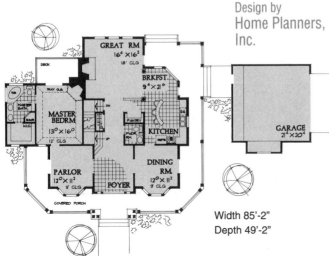

Width 85'-2"
Depth 49'-2"

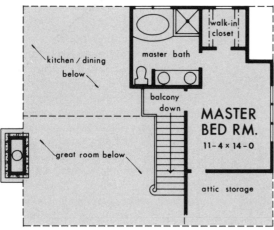

kitchen / dining below

master bath

walk-in closet

balcony down

great room below

MASTER BED RM.
11-4 × 14-0

attic storage

Design VH9663 First Floor: 1,002 square feet
Second Floor: 336 square feet; Total: 1,338 square feet

● A mountain retreat, this rustic version features covered porches front and rear. Open living is enjoyed in a great room and kitchen/dining room combination. The cathedral ceiling gives an open, inviting sense of space. Two bedrooms and a full bath on the first level are complemented by a master suite on the second level which includes a walk-in closet and a deluxe bath. There is also attic storage on the second level. This plan is available with either a basement or crawlspace foundation. Please specify when ordering.

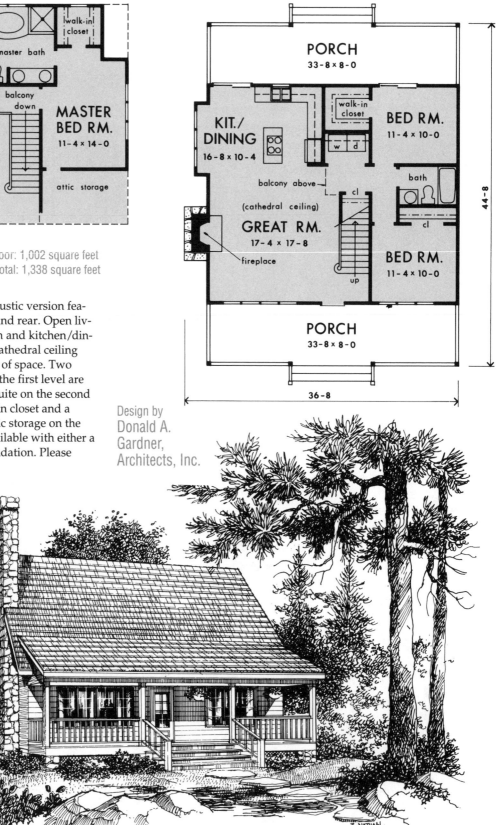

PORCH
33-8 × 8-0

KIT./ DINING
16-8 × 10-4

walk-in closet

w d

BED RM.
11-4 × 10-0

bath

balcony above

cl

(cathedral ceiling)

GREAT RM.
17-4 × 17-8

cl

fireplace

up

BED RM.
11-4 × 10-0

PORCH
33-8 × 8-0

44-8

36-8

Design by
Donald A.
Gardner,
Architects, Inc.

Design VH4061 First Floor: 1,008 square feet
Second Floor: 323 square feet; Total: 1,331 square feet

D

LOFT
15'-4" x 15'-4"

CLOSET

RAILING

DOWN

RAILING

ROUGH SAWN BEAM WITH BRACKETS

STONE

UPPER PART OF LIVING ROOM

LINE OF PORCH BELOW

36'-0"

WASH   TUB   DRY

LAUNDRY
ROOM

D.W.   RANGE

KITCHEN & DINING
20'-0" x 8'-0"

SINK

CLOSET

SHOWER
BATH

REFRIG.

CLOSET   CLOSET

STORAGE

WH

RAILING

FIREPLACE

STONE

BEDROOM
11'-8" x 13'-0"

LIVING ROOM
20'-0" x 19'-0"

UP

38'-0"

COATS

DN.

PORCH
36'-0" x 10'-0"

WOOD POSTS & RAILING

Quote One™

Cost to build? See page 300
to order complete cost estimate
to build this house in your area!

Design by
**Home Planners,
Inc.**

● This charming farmhouse design will be economical to build and a pleasure to occupy. Like most vacation homes, this design features an open plan. The large living area includes a living room, a dining room and a mas-sive stone fireplace. A partition separates the kitchen from the living room. Also downstairs are a bedroom, a full bath and a laundry room. Upstairs is a spacious sleeping loft overlooking the living room. Don't miss the large front porch—this will be a favorite spot for relaxing.

California Engineered Plans and California Stock Plans are available for this home. Call 1-800-521-6797 for more information.

Design VH9625

First Floor: 1,581 square feet
Second Floor: 549 square feet
Total: 2,130 square feet
Bonus Room: 334 square feet

● Great flexibility is available in this plan—the great room/dining room can be reworked into one large great room with the dining room relocated to the family room. A sun room with a cathedral ceiling and sliding glass doors to the deck is accessible from both the breakfast and dining rooms. A large kitchen boasts a convenient cooking island. The master bedroom has a fireplace, a walk-in closet and a spacious master bath. Two second-level bedrooms are equal in size and share a full bath with a double-bowl vanity. Both have a dormer window and a walk-in closet. A large bonus room over the garage is accessible from the utility room below. Please specify basement or crawlspace foundation when ordering.

Design by
Donald A. Gardner, Architect, Inc.

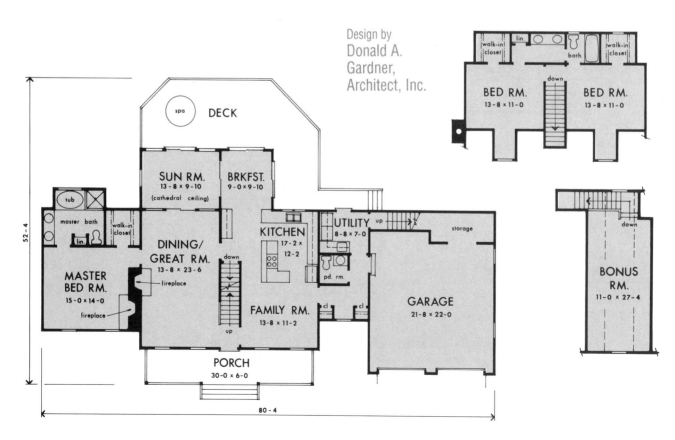

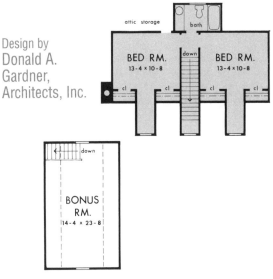

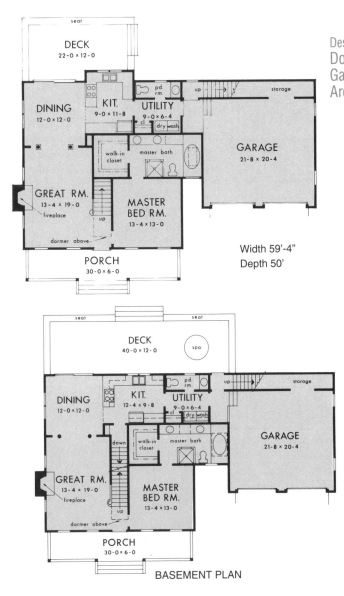

DECK
22-0 × 12-0

DINING
12-0 × 12-0

KIT.
9-0 × 11-8

UTILITY
9-0 × 6-4

dry | wash

pd. rm.

storage

GARAGE
21-8 × 20-4

walk-in closet

master bath

GREAT RM.
13-4 × 19-0
fireplace

MASTER BED RM.
13-4 × 13-0

dormer above

PORCH
30-0 × 6-0

Width 59'-4"
Depth 50'

attic storage

bath

BED RM.
13-4 × 10-8

down

BED RM.
13-4 × 10-8

cl | cl | cl | cl

down

BONUS RM.
14-4 × 23-8

DECK
40-0 × 12-0

spa

DINING
12-0 × 12-0

KIT.
12-4 × 9-8

UTILITY
9-0 × 6-4

dry | wash

pd. rm.

up

storage

walk-in closet

master bath

GARAGE
21-8 × 20-4

down

GREAT RM.
13-4 × 19-0
fireplace

MASTER BED RM.
13-4 × 13-0

dormer above

PORCH
30-0 × 6-0

BASEMENT PLAN

Design by
Donald A.
Gardner,
Architects, Inc.

Design VH9626

First Floor (crawlspace foundation): 1,057 square feet
First Floor (basement foundation): 1,110 square feet
Second Floor (crawlspace or basement): 500 square feet
Total (crawlspace foundation): 1,557 square feet
Total (basement foundation): 1,610 square feet
Bonus Room: 342 square feet

● This compact, two-story, cozy country cottage is perfect for the economically conscious family. Its entrance foyer is highlighted by a clerestory dormer above for natural light. The master suite is conveniently located on the first level for privacy and accessibility. Its attached master bath boasts a whirlpool tub with a skylight above, a separate shower and a double-bowl vanity. Second-level bed-rooms share a full bath and there's a wealth of storage on this level. An added advantage to this house is the bonus room above the garage. Please specify basement or crawlspace foundation when ordering.

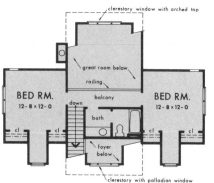

clerestory window with arched top

great room below

railing

balcony

BED RM.
12-8 x 12-0

BED RM.
12-8 x 12-0

down

cl

cl

bath

cl

cl

foyer below

clerestory with palladian window

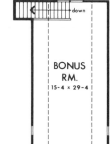

down

BONUS
RM.
15-4 x 29-4

Design VH9702

First Floor: 1,618 square feet
Second Floor: 570 square feet
Total: 2,188 square feet
Bonus Room: 495 square feet

● A wraparound covered porch, an open deck with a spa and seating, arched windows and dormers enhance the already impressive character of this three-bedroom farmhouse. The spacious great room boasts a fireplace, cabinets and bookshelves. The kitchen, with a cooking island, is conveniently located between a dining room and a breakfast room with an open view of the great room. A generous master bedroom has plenty of closet space as well as an expansive master bath. Bonus space over the garage allows for room to grow. The plan includes a crawlspace foundation.

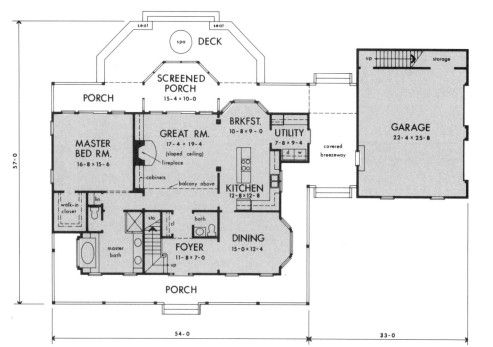

seat   spa   DECK   seat

SCREENED
PORCH
15-4 x 10-0

PORCH

up   storage

MASTER
BED RM.
16-8 x 15-6

GREAT RM.
17-4 x 19-4
(sloped ceiling)
fireplace

BRKFST.
10-8 x 9-0

UTILITY
7-8 x 9-4

covered breezeway

GARAGE
22-4 x 25-8

cabinets   balcony above

KITCHEN
12-8 x 12-8

d w

walk-in closet

lin.

57-0

master bath

sto.

cl

bath

FOYER
11-8 x 7-0

DINING
15-0 x 12-4

up

PORCH

54-0   33-0

Design by
Donald A.
Gardner,
Architects, Inc.

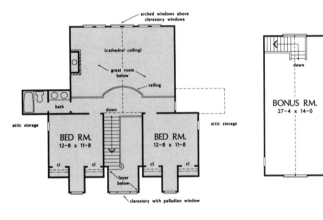

Design VH9723

First Floor: 2,064 square feet
Second Floor: 594 square feet
Total: 2,658 square feet
Bonus Room: 464 square feet

● You'll find country living at its best when meandering through this spacious four-bedroom farmhouse with wraparound porch. A front Palladian window dormer and rear clerestory windows at the great room add exciting visual elements to the exterior while providing natural light to the interior. The large great room boasts a fireplace, bookshelves and a raised cathedral ceiling, allowing a curved balcony overlook above. The great room, master bedroom and breakfast room are accessible to the rear porch for greater circulation and flexibility. Special features such as the large cooktop island in the kitchen, the wet bar, the bedroom/study and the generous bonus room over the garage and ample storage set this plan apart.

Design by
Donald A.
Gardner,
Architects, Inc.

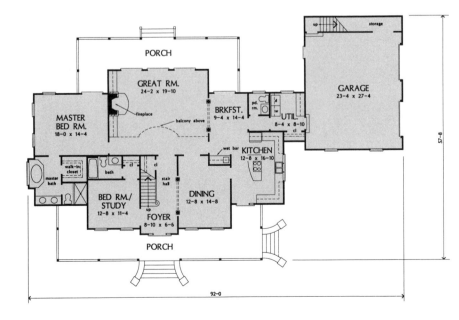

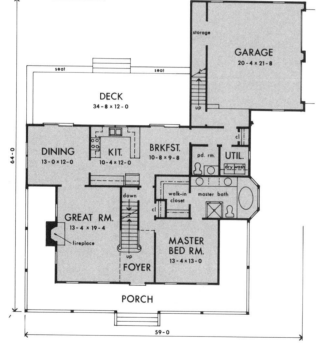

DECK
34-8 x 12-0

GARAGE
20-4 x 21-8

storage

seat   seat

DINING
13-0 x 12-0

KIT.
10-4 x 12-0

BRKFST.
10-8 x 9-8

pd. rm.

UTIL.

dry | wash

cl

64-0

walk-in
closet

master bath

GREAT RM.
13-4 x 19-4

fireplace

down

cl

MASTER
BED RM.
13-4 x 13-0

up

FOYER

PORCH

59-0

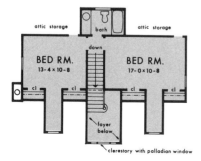

attic storage   attic storage

bath

down

BED RM.
13-4 x 10-8

BED RM.
17-0 x 10-8

cl   cl   cl   cl

foyer
below

clerestory with palladian window

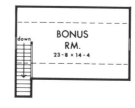

down

BONUS
RM.
23-8 x 14-4

Design VH9645

First Floor: 1,356 square feet
Second Floor: 542 square feet
Total: 1,898 square feet

● The welcoming charm of this country farmhouse is expressed by its many windows and its covered, wraparound porch. A two-story entrance foyer is enhanced by a Palladian window in a clerestory dormer above to allow natural lighting. A first-floor master suite allows privacy and accessibility. The master bath includes a whirlpool tub, a shower and a double-bowl vanity along with a walk-in closet. The first floor features nine-foot ceilings throughout with the exception of the kitchen area which features an eight-foot ceiling. The second floor provides two additional bedrooms, a full bath and plenty of storage space. Please specify basement or crawlspace foundation when ordering.

Design by
Donald A.
Gardner,
Architects, Inc.

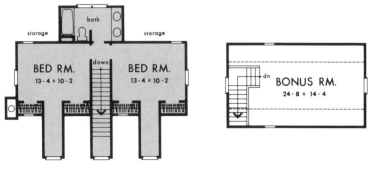

BED RM.
13-4 × 10-2

BED RM.
13-4 × 10-2

storage

storage

bath

down

BONUS RM.
24-8 × 14-4

dn

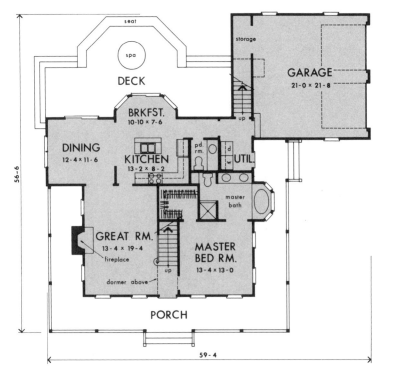

seat

spa

DECK

storage

GARAGE
21-0 × 21-8

BRKFST.
10-10 × 7-6

DINING
12-4 × 11-6

KITCHEN
13-2 × 8-2

pd. rm.

d w

UTIL.

master bath

up

GREAT RM.
13-4 × 19-4

fireplace

MASTER BED RM.
13-4 × 13-0

dormer above

up

56-6

PORCH

59-4

Design VH9690

First Floor: 1,145 square feet
Second Floor: 518 square feet
Total: 1,663 square feet

● Look this plan over and you'll be amazed at how much livability can be found in less than 2,000 square feet. A wraparound porch welcomes visitors to the home. Inside lies an enormous great room with fireplace. To the rear of the home, the breakfast and dining rooms have sliding glass doors to a large deck with room for a spa. The master bedroom contains a walk-in closet and airy bath with a whirlpool tub. Two bedrooms are found on the second floor, as well as a bonus room over the garage.

Design by
Donald A.
Gardner,
Architects, Inc.

Design by
Donald A.
Gardner,
Architects, Inc.

Design VH9644

First Floor: 943 square feet
Second Floor: 840 square feet
Total: 1,783 square feet

● Roundtop windows and an inviting covered porch offer an irresistible appeal for this three-bedroom plan. A two-story foyer provides a spacious feeling to this well-organized open layout. Round columns between the great room and kitchen add to the impressive quality of the plan. An expansive deck promotes casual outdoor living to its fullest. The master suite with walk-in closet and complete master bath is on the second floor along with two additional bedrooms and a full bath. The bonus room over the garage offers room for expansion.

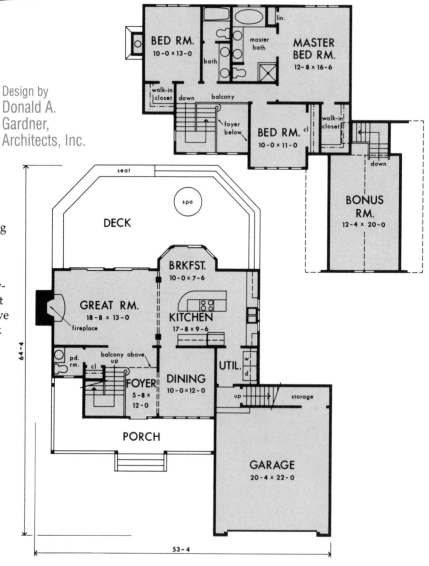

Design VH9667

First Floor: 1,357 square feet
Second Floor: 1,204 square feet
Total: 2,561 square feet

● This grand four-bedroom farmhouse with a wraparound porch has eye-catching features. The living room opens to the foyer and provides a formal entertaining area. The exceptionally large family room allows for more casual living. The lavish kitchen boasts a cooking island and serves the dining room and breakfast and deck areas. The master suite on the second level has a large walk-in closet and a master bath with a whirlpool tub, a shower and a double-bowl vanity. Three additional bedrooms share a full bath.

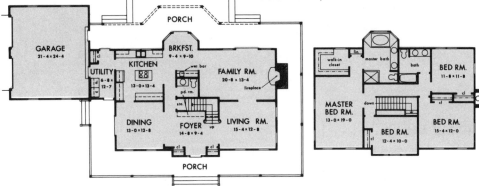

Design by
Donald A.
Gardner,
Architects, Inc.

Width 80'
Depth 57'

Design VH9673

First Floor: 1,526 square feet
Second Floor: 635 square feet
Total: 2,161 square feet

● This beautiful farmhouse boasts all the extras a three-bedroom design could offer. Clerestory windows with arched tops enhance the exterior and allow natural light to penetrate into the foyer and great room. A kitchen with island counter and breakfast area is open to the spacious great room through a cased opening with colonnade. The exquisite master suite has a generous bedroom, large walk-in closet and dramatically designed master bath providing emphasis on the whirlpool tub flanked by double columns. Access to the rear deck is possible from the screened porch, master bath and breakfast area. The second level has two bedrooms sharing a full bath and a loft/study area overlooking the great room.

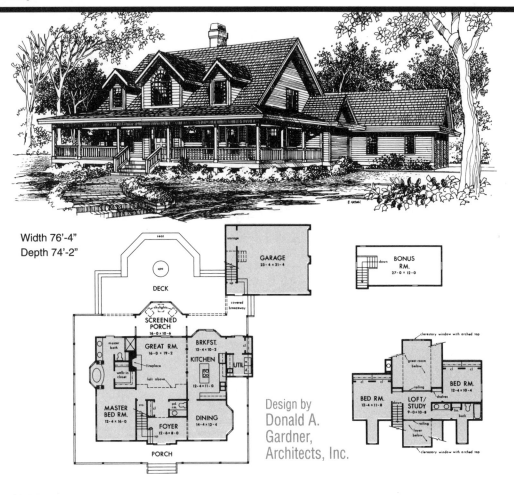

Width 76'-4"
Depth 74'-2"

Design by
Donald A.
Gardner,
Architects, Inc.

99

Design by
Donald A.
Gardner,
Architects, Inc.

Design VH9662

First Floor: 1,025 square feet
Second Floor: 911 square feet
Total: 1,936 square feet

● The exterior of this three-bedroom home is enhanced by its many gables, arched windows and wraparound porch. A large great room with impressive fireplace leads to both the dining room and screened porch with access to the deck. An open kitchen offers a country-kitchen atmosphere. The second-level master suite has two walk-in closets and an impressive bath. There is also bonus space over the garage. The plan is available with a crawl-space foundation.

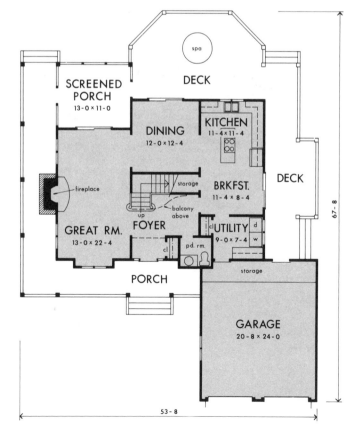

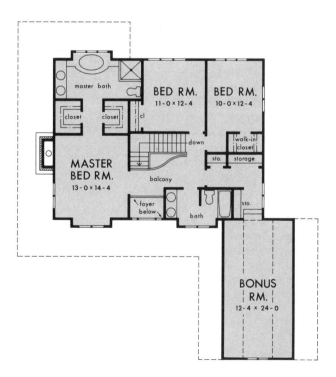

Design VH9621

First Floor: 1,325 square feet
Second Floor: 453 square feet
Total: 1,778 square feet

● This compact design has all the amenities available in larger plans with little wasted space. In addition, a front Palladian window, dormers and rear arched windows provide exciting visual elements to the exterior. The spacious great room has a fireplace, a cathedral ceiling and clerestory windows. A second-level balcony overlooks this gathering area. The kitchen is centrally located for maximum flexibility in layout and features a pass-through to the great room. Besides the generous master suite with its well-appointed full bath, there are two family bedrooms located on the second level sharing a full bath with a double vanity. Please specify basement or crawlspace foundation when ordering.

FRONT

REAR

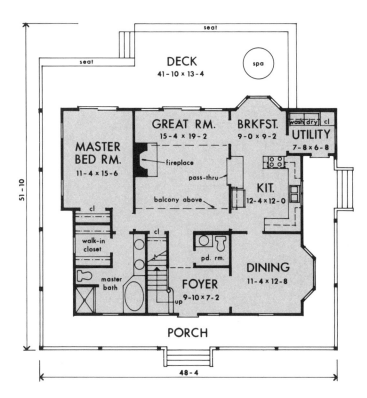

Design by
Donald A.
Gardner,
Architects, Inc.

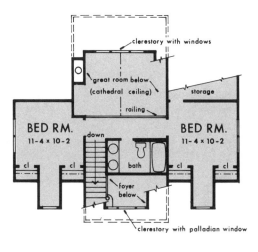

101

Design VH3461

First Floor: 1,391 square feet
Second Floor: 611 square feet
Total: 2,002 square feet

L

● A Palladian window set in a dormer provides a nice introduction to this 1½-story country home. The two-story foyer draws on natural light and a pair of columns to set a comfortable, yet elegant mood. The living room, to the left, presents a grand space for entertaining. From full-course dinners to family suppers, the dining room will serve its purpose well. The kitchen delights with an island work station and openness to the family room. Here, a raised-hearth fireplace provides added comfort. Sleeping accommodations are comprised of four bedrooms, one a first-floor master suite. With a luxurious private bath, including dual lavatories, this room will surely be a favorite retreat. Upstairs, three secondary bedrooms meet the needs of the growing family.

QUOTE ONE™

Cost to build? See page 300 to order complete cost estimate to build this house in your area!

Design by
Home Planners, Inc.

Design VH9632

First Floor: 1,756 square feet
Second Floor: 565 square feet
Total: 2,321 square feet

Design by
Donald A. Gardner, Architects, Inc.

● A wraparound covered porch at the front and sides of this house and an open deck at the back provide plenty of outside living area. The spacious great room features a fireplace, a cathedral ceiling and a clerestory with an arched window. The first-floor master bedroom contains a generous closet and a master bath with a garden tub, a double-bowl vanity and a shower. The second floor sports two bedrooms and a full bath. Please specify basement or crawlspace foundation when ordering.

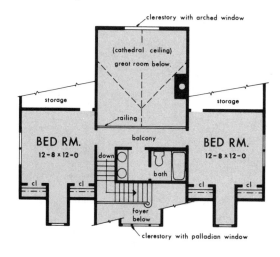

Copyright 1992 Stephen S. Fuller

Design VH9861

First Floor: 1,960 square feet
Second Floor: 965 square feet
Total: 2,925 square feet

● The facade of this charming home is Americana at its best, with a rocking-chair porch, a bay window and dormers above, finished in stone and wood siding and faithfully detailed.

The main level features an easy flow, beginning with the dining room to the right of the foyer. The great room features a large hearth and French doors to the patio, and leads directly to the breakfast area and kitchen. Storage closets and a counter-top desk area highlight the kitchen which, along with the laundry room, is conveniently located to the rear of the home. Left of the foyer is an attractive study with

a large bay window. The master suite, featuring a bay-windowed sitting area, large master bath with double vanities, a shower and ample closet space, completes the main level. On the upper level, Bedroom 2 features a full bath and has three dormer windows overlooking the front lawn. The third and fourth bedrooms share another full bath. This home is designed with a basement foundation.

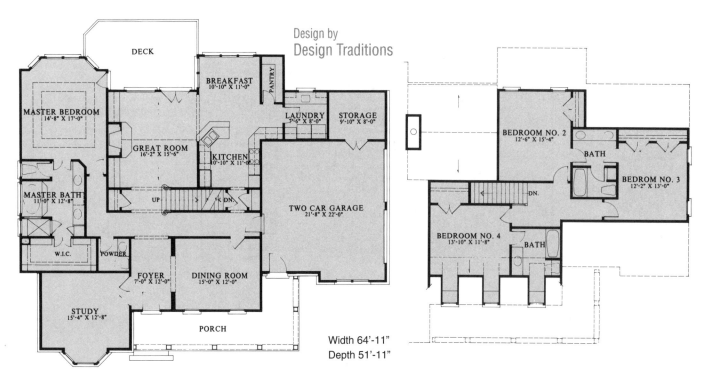

Design by
Design Traditions

Width 64'-11"
Depth 51'-11"

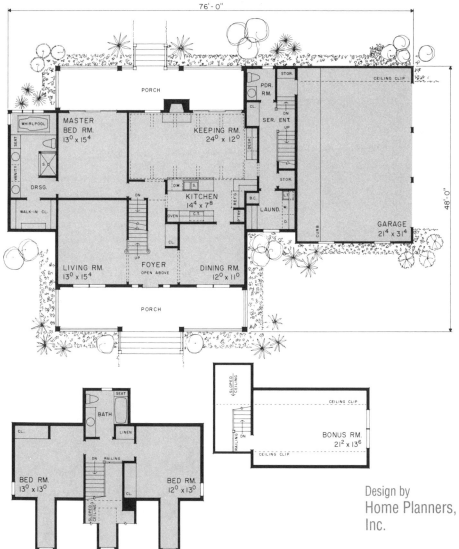

Design VH3566

First Floor: 1,635 square feet
Second Floor: 586 square feet
Total: 2,221 square feet
Bonus Room: 321 square feet

L **D**

● Don't be fooled by the humble appearance of this farmhouse. All the amenities abound. Covered porches are located to both the front and rear of the home. A grand front entrance opens into living and dining rooms. The family will surely enjoy the ambience of the keeping room with its fireplace and beamed ceiling. A service entry, with laundry nearby, separates the garage from the main house. An over-the-garage bonus room allows for room to grow or a nice study. Two quaint bedrooms and full bath make up the second floor. Each bedroom features a lovely dormer window.

Design by
Home Planners,
Inc.

Cost to build? See page 300
to order complete cost estimate
to build this house in your area!

Design VH3507

First Floor: 1,360 square feet
Second Floor: 1,172 square feet
Total: 2,532 square feet

L

Design by
**Home Planners,
Inc.**

QUOTE ONE™

Cost to build? See page 300
to order complete cost estimate
to build this house in your area!

● After a brisk walk to the creek for some fly fishing or an invigorating day of raking leaves, enjoy some spiced hot apple cider by one of the four fireplaces highlighted in this delightful farmhouse. Leading inside is an elevated front entrance with a dual set of steps, an appealing patterned railing and a muntined door flanked by carriage lamps, all of which projects an engaging image of the raised cottage so popular in the South. To the left of the foyer is the formal living room with a corner fireplace. To the right is a formal dining room which also enjoys a fireplace. Open planning is the byword of the spacious family living area. An efficient kitchen possesses a cooking island, a snack bar, a planning desk and a breakfast area with access to the veranda. Twin pillars support an archway opening to the large family room which is enhanced by yet another fireplace. The expansive master bedroom is complemented by a sitting area and a warming fireplace. A luxurious master bath offers a vanity flanked by twin lavatories, a whirlpool bath, a shower and a large walk-in closet.

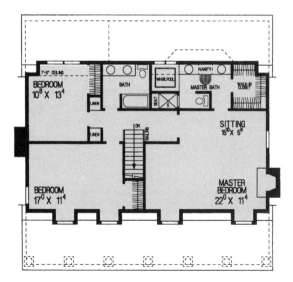

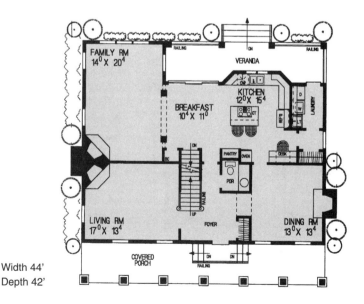

Width 44'
Depth 42'

Capes, Cottages & Cabins

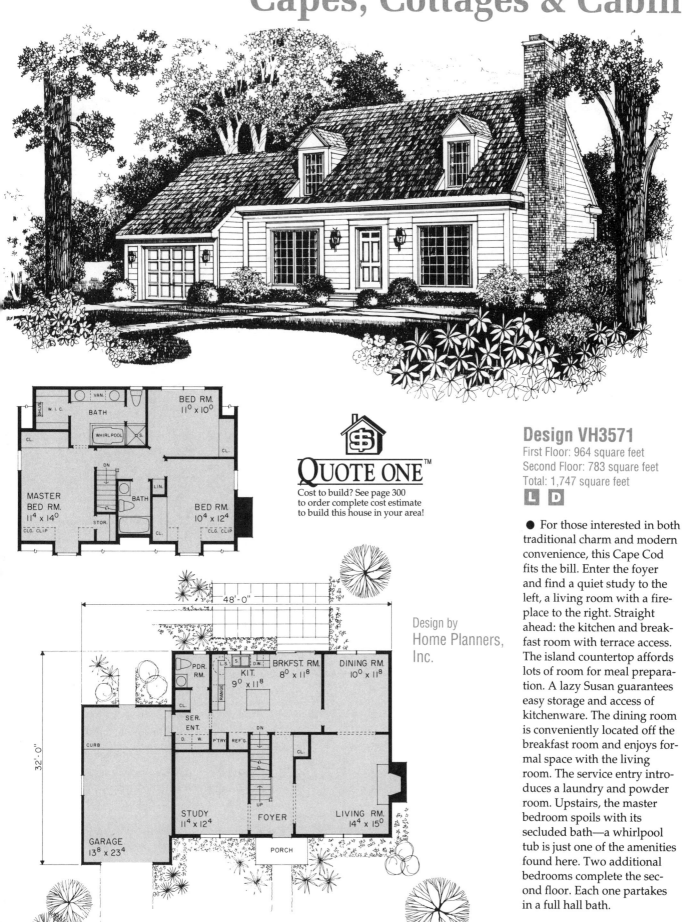

Quote One™

Cost to build? See page 300 to order complete cost estimate to build this house in your area!

Design by Home Planners, Inc.

Design VH3571

First Floor: 964 square feet
Second Floor: 783 square feet
Total: 1,747 square feet

L **D**

● For those interested in both traditional charm and modern convenience, this Cape Cod fits the bill. Enter the foyer and find a quiet study to the left, a living room with a fireplace to the right. Straight ahead: the kitchen and breakfast room with terrace access. The island countertop affords lots of room for meal preparation. A lazy Susan guarantees easy storage and access of kitchenware. The dining room is conveniently located off the breakfast room and enjoys formal space with the living room. The service entry introduces a laundry and powder room. Upstairs, the master bedroom spoils with its secluded bath—a whirlpool tub is just one of the amenities found here. Two additional bedrooms complete the second floor. Each one partakes in a full hall bath.

Design VH8894

First Floor: 846 square feet
Second Floor: 400 square feet
Total: 1,246 square feet

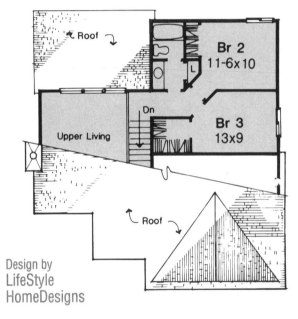

Design by
LifeStyle
HomeDesigns

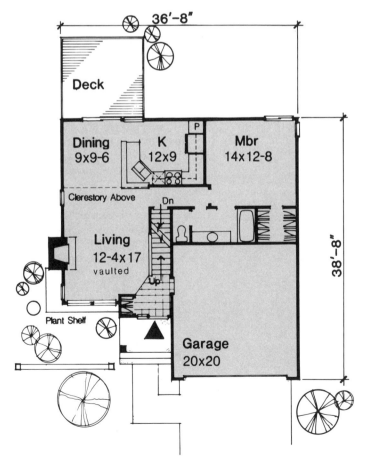

● A sloping roofline and wood siding lend a fresh look to this stunning starter home. Inside options include a second floor that can be built unfinished and completed as budgets allow. On the first floor, a tiled entryway reveals a vaulted living room with a fireplace. A rear kitchen serves a dining room that accesses a rear deck for outside enjoyments. Master-suite enhancements include corner windows, a walk-in closet and private passage to a full bath. Two bedrooms on the second floor include one with a walk-in closet and share a full hall bath.

Design VH1394

First Floor: 832 square feet
Second Floor: 512 square feet
Total: 1,344 square feet

● The growing family with a restricted building budget will find this a great investment - a convenient living floor plan inside an attractive facade.

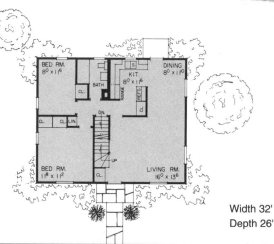

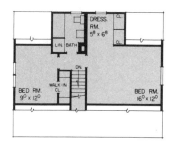

Design by
Home Planners, Inc.

Width 32'
Depth 26'

Design VH2162

First Floor: 741 square feet
Second Floor: 504 square feet
Total: 1,245 square feet

● This economical design delivers great exterior appeal and fine livability. In addition to kitchen eating space there is a separate dining room.

Width 42'-8"
Depth 37'

Design by
Home Planners, Inc.

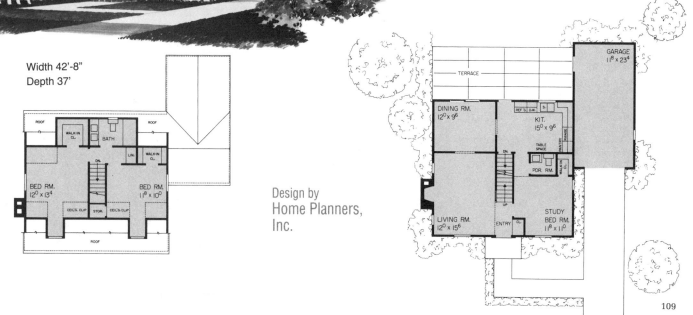

Expanding the Half-House

Design VH2682 First Floor(Basic Plan): 976 square feet
First Floor(Expanded Plan): 1,230 square feet; Second Floor(Both Plans): 744 square feet
Total(Basic Plan): 1,720 square feet; Total(Expanded Plan): 1,974 square feet

L D

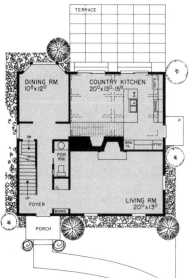

Width 32'
Depth 32'

● Here is an expandable
Colonial with a full measure
of Cape Cod Charm. For
those who wish to build the
basic house, there is an
abundance of low-budget
livability. Twin fireplaces
serve the formal living room
and the informal country
kitchen. Note the spaciousness of both areas. A dining
room and powder room are
also on the first floor of this
basic plan. Upstairs three
bedrooms and two full baths.

Build Small and Add On Later

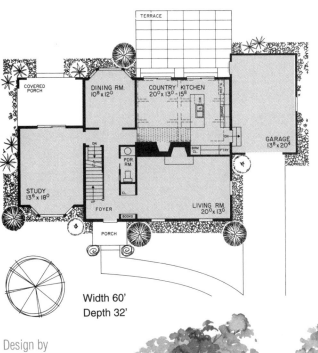

Width 60'
Depth 32'

Design by
Home Planners,
Inc.

● This expanded version of the basic house on the opposite page is equally as reminiscent of Cape Cod. Common in the 17th-Century was the addition of appendages to the main structure. This occurred as family size increased or finances improved. This version provides for the addition of wings to accommodate a large study and a garage. Utilizing the alcove behind the study results in a big, covered porch. Certainly a charming design whichever version you decide to build for your family.

Design VH3609

First Floor: 1,623 square feet
Second Floor: 596 square feet
Total: 2,219 square feet

L **D**

● This home's front-projecting garage allows utilization of a narrow, less expensive building site. Open planning, sloping ceilings and an abundance of windows highlight the formal dining room/great room area. Notice the second bay window in the dining room. The great room has a central fireplace as its focal point. The master bedroom has a big walk-in closet and twin lavatories, a garden tub, a stall shower and a compartmented toilet with a linen closet in the master bath. Upstairs are two bedrooms, a bath with twin lavatories, plus an outstanding computer/study area.

Design by
Home Planners,
Inc.

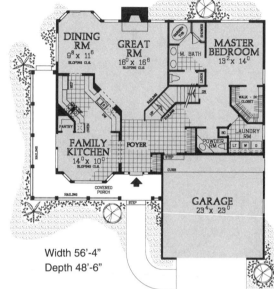

Width 56'-4"
Depth 48'-6"

Design VH3620

First Floor: 1,295 square feet
Second Floor: 600 square feet
Total: 1,895 square feet

● This country home extends a warm welcome. Inside, Colonial columns and pilasters provide a charming entrance to the two-story family/great room enhanced by a fireplace and three sets of French doors opening onto the rear wraparound porch. An arched opening leads the way to the L-shaped country kitchen highlighted by a bay-windowed eating area with a window seat. The spacious first-floor master suite is complemented by French doors opening onto the porch. A bay window in the master bath effectively surrounds an old-fashioned claw-foot tub. The second floor holds two secondary bedrooms and a full bath. Plans for a detached garage are included.

Width 50'
Depth 55'-3"

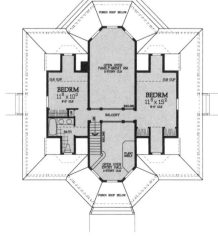

Design by
Home Planners,
Inc.

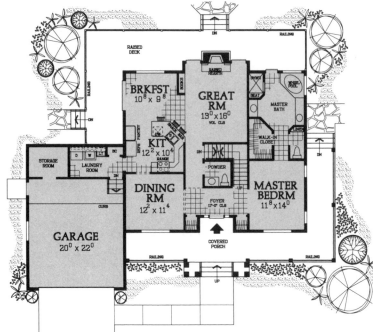

Design VH3615

First Floor: 1,355 square feet
Second Floor: 582 square feet
Total: 1,937 square feet

L

● A portico makes a strong architectural statement and provides shelter for this home's front entrance. The central foyer, with its two-story ceiling and dramatic glass area, routes traffic directly to all zones. To the left of the foyer is the formal dining room, which is but a step away from the angular kitchen. The great room has a high volume ceiling and a raised-hearth fireplace flanked by doors to the deck. To the right of the foyer is the master suite. The master bath is compartmented and includes double lavatories, a walk-in closet, a whirlpool, a stall shower with a seat, linen storage and access to the rear deck. This modest 1½-story home has a two-bedroom upstairs which features a balcony overlooking the great room below.

Width 65'
Depth 55'-8"

QUOTE ONE™
Cost to build? See page 300
to order complete cost estimate
to build this house in your area!

Design by
Home Planners,
Inc.

113

Design VH9094

First Floor: 627 square feet
Second Floor: 90 square feet
Total: 717 square feet

● Whether you're thinking about a vacation home or a "granny flat" addition to your existing home, this little cottage might be the answer for you. The main-level living area provides a full kitchen with a bay window over the sink and an attached dining area. The bedroom provides access to a side yard. There is also an abundance of closets. An incline ladder in the living room leads to a loft area overlooking the living room below.

Loft
8' x 9'

Living Below
vaulted ceiling

clerestory window

Br
12' x 12'

incline ladder

Kit

Living
13' x 15'

Dining

WIDTH 24'
DEPTH 36'-4"

Design by
Larry W.
Garnett &
Associates, Inc.

114

Design VH9045

Square Footage: 902 (Plus Optional Loft:
127 additional square feet)

● This adorable European-
style doll-house embodies the
very essence of charm. For the
single home owner, empty-
nesters, or as a cozy country
retreat, it could not be any
more perfect. Simple floor
planning includes an open living area with cathedral ceiling
and exposed wood trusses, a
kitchen/dining area, two bedrooms and a full bath with
compartmented stool and tub.
For added space —possibly for
use as a studio or additional
sleeping — there's an optional
loft available with sloped ceiling. The two-car garage offers
an ample storage area.

Design by
Larry W.
Garnett &
Associates, Inc.

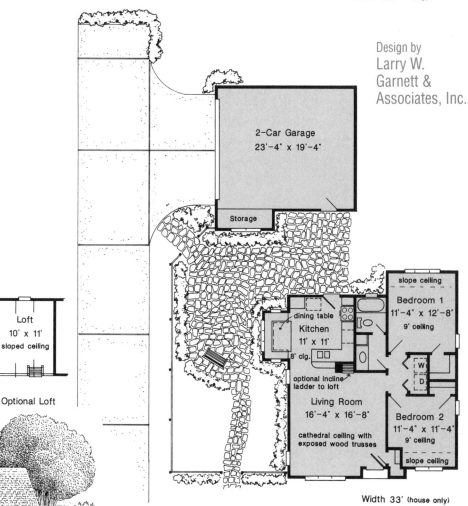

4' wall →

Loft
10' x 11'
sloped ceiling

Optional Loft

2-Car Garage
23'-4" x 19'-4"

Storage

dining table

Kitchen
11' x 11'
8' clg.

slope ceiling

Bedroom 1
11'-4" x 12'-8"
9' ceiling

optional incline
ladder to loft

W
D

Living Room
16'-4" x 16'-8"

Bedroom 2
11'-4" x 11'-4"
9' ceiling

cathedral ceiling with
exposed wood trusses

slope ceiling

Width 33' (house only)
Depth 33'-4" (house only)

115

Design VH9150

First Floor: 588 square feet
Second Floor: 397 square feet
Total: 985 square feet

Design by
Larry W.
Garnett &
Associates, Inc.

● This quaint little Victorian cottage serves perfectly as a starter or second home; or maybe you have it in mind for a lakefront location. Beyond the front porch, the living room defines the front of the house. A full kitchen, a dining room and a powder room account for the back of the house. Each of these areas appreciates an abundance of natural lighting and excellent space utilization. Upstairs, two family bedrooms share a full bath. Bedroom 1 enjoys twin closets. Economical construction makes this house even more attractive. You'll find a detached garage with storage space just beyond the back door and arbor making a delightful outdoor living space.

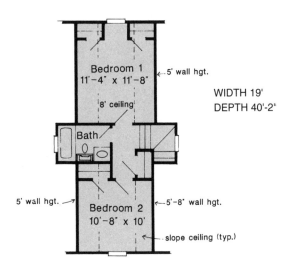

WIDTH 19'
DEPTH 40'-2"

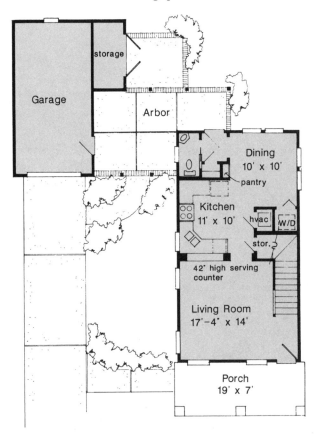

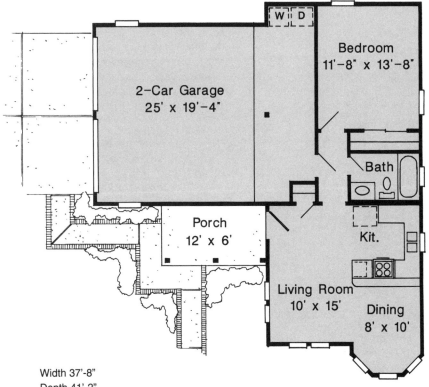

2-Car Garage
25' x 19'-4"

Bedroom
11'-8" x 13'-8"

Bath

Porch
12' x 6'

Kit.

Living Room
10' x 15'

Dining
8' x 10'

Width 37'-8"
Depth 41'-2"

Design by
Larry W.
Garnett &
Associates, Inc.

Design VH8901
Square Footage: 582

● Perfect for narrow lots, lakeside or otherwise, this darling little Victorian-style cottage will serve as a wonderful retreat. The covered front porch leads to a bright living room and dining room area. A handy closet stores coats and outer wear. The U-shaped kitchen includes a windowed sink area. It directly accesses the bay-windowed dining area. A full bath with natural light is conveniently located. The bedroom, with lots of closet space and views out two sides, sits quietly at the rear of the plan. In the two-car garage, space exists for the placement of a washer and a dryer.

Design VH3302

First Floor: 1,326 square feet
Second Floor: 542 square feet
Total: 1,868 square feet

L

● A cottage fit for a king! Appreciate the highlights: a two-story foyer, a rear living zone (gathering room, terrace, and dining room), pass-through snack bar in kitchen, a two-story master bedroom. Two upstairs bedrooms share a full bath.

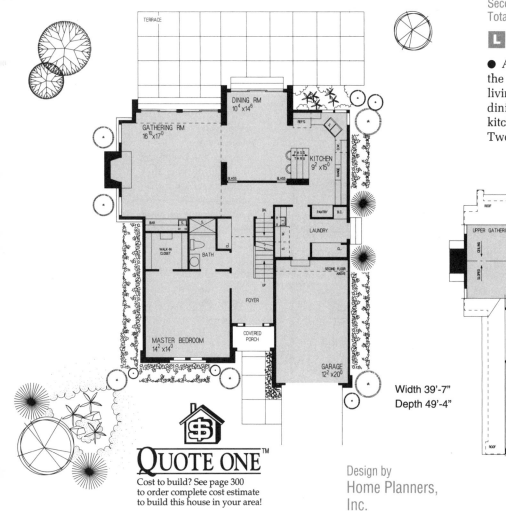

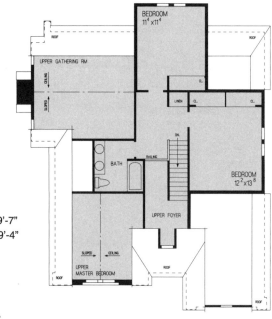

Width 39'-7"
Depth 49'-4"

QUOTE ONE™

Cost to build? See page 300 to order complete cost estimate to build this house in your area!

Design by
Home Planners, Inc.

Design VH3619

First Floor: 1,171 square feet
Second Floor: 600 square feet
Total: 1,771 square feet

L D

● In this gracious home, the entry hall soars two stories, opening through an archway on the right to a banquet-sized formal dining room. Nearby, the efficient country kitchen shares space with a bay-windowed eating area. The first-floor master suite offers room to kick off your shoes and curl up with a good book by the bay window or access the porch through French doors. An abundance of closet space precedes the amenity-filled master bath. The second floor holds two family bedrooms that share a full bath. Plans for a detached garage are included.

QUOTE ONE™
Cost to build? See page 300 to order complete cost estimate to build this house in your area!

Design by
Home Planners, Inc.

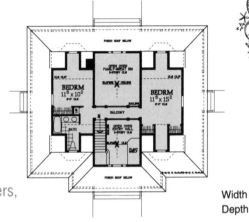

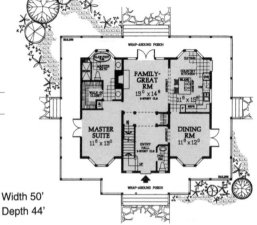

Width 50'
Depth 44'

Design VH9133

First Floor: 440 square feet
Loft: 126 square feet
Total: 566 square feet

● Charming exterior details make the most of this quaint cottage: dormer windows, a covered entry and wood siding. The interior floor plan is perfect for use as a guest house, a vacation residence or for comfortably accommodating an extended-stay family. The bay-windowed dinette is complemented by a small kitchen and an ample living area. The upstairs loft serves as an additional bedroom or as studio space.

Design by
Larry W. Garnett & Associates, Inc.

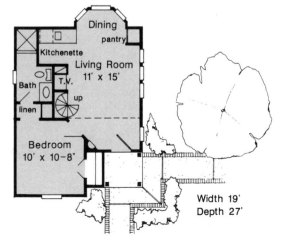

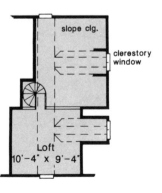

Width 19'
Depth 27'

Design VH9666

First Floor: 1,027 square feet
Second Floor: 580 square feet
Total: 1,607 square feet

● This economical, rustic three-bedroom plan sports a relaxing country image with both front and back covered porches. The openness of the expansive great room to kitchen/dining areas and loft/study areas is reinforced with a shared cathedral ceiling for impressive space. The first level allows for two bedrooms, a full bath and a utility area. The master suite on the second level has a walk-in closet and a master bath with whirlpool tub, shower and double-bowl vanity. The plan is available with a crawl-space foundation.

Design by
Donald A.
Gardner,
Architects, Inc.

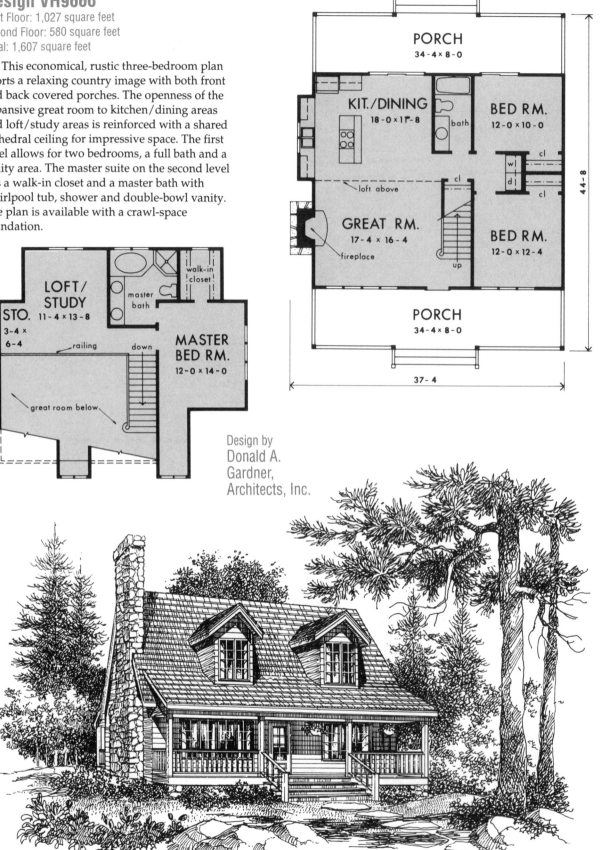

Design VH9697

First Floor: 1,039 square feet
Second Floor: 583 square feet
Total: 1,622 square feet

 Charming and compact, this delightful two-story plan fits the needs of either a small family or empty nesters. Or, for the vacation home builder, it functions as a cozy retreat with a fireplace and lots of outdoor living space. The master suite is on the first floor, away from two secondary bedrooms. The kitchen features an island and an attached dining area with a box window. A two-story great-room allows plenty of room for entertaining and relaxing.

Design by
Donald A.
Gardner,
Architects, Inc.

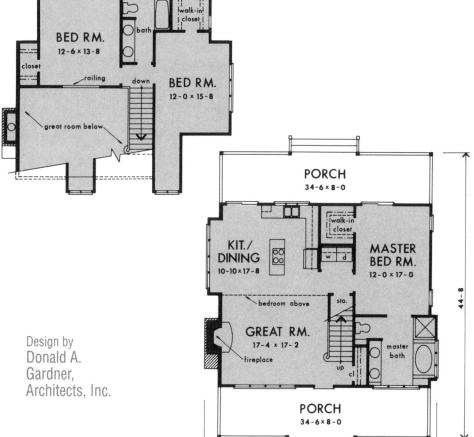

Build This Vacation Home In Three Stages

Design VH1425 Basic Unit: 576 square feet; Expanded Unit: 1,152 square feet

● Here is a vacation home that can be easily built in three stages. This procedure will stretch your building budget and enable you to continue as your finances permit. Blueprints show details for the construction of the basic unit first. This features the kitchen, bath, bedroom and living room. The second stage can be either the addition of the two extra bedrooms, or the screened porch. Each addition is a modular 12 x 24 foot unit. The ceilings are sloping thus contributing to the feeling of spaciousness. The finished house has excellent storage facilities. If desired, the screened porch could be modified to be built as a family room addition. Such a move would permit year 'round use. Note the perfectly rectangular shape of this home which will result in economical construction costs.

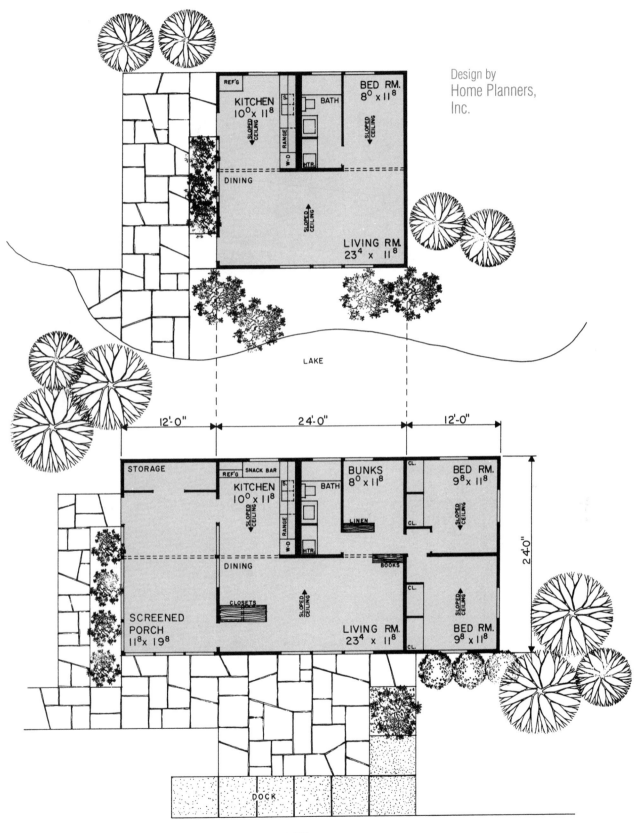

Design by
Home Planners,
Inc.

REF'G
KITCHEN
10⁰ x 11⁸
SLOPED CEILING
RANGE
W-D
HTR.
BATH
BED RM.
8⁰ x 11⁸
SLOPED CEILING
DINING
SLOPED CEILING
LIVING RM.
23⁴ x 11⁸

LAKE

12'-0" 24'-0" 12'-0"

STORAGE
REF'G
SNACK BAR
KITCHEN
10⁰ x 11⁸
SLOPED CEILING
RANGE
W-D
HTR.
BATH
LINEN
BUNKS
8⁰ x 11⁸
CL.
CL.
BED RM.
9⁸ x 11⁸
SLOPED CEILING
DINING
BOOKS
CL.
SLOPED CEILING
SCREENED
PORCH
11⁸ x 19⁸
CLOSETS
SLOPED CEILING
LIVING RM.
23⁴ x 11⁸
CL.
BED RM.
9⁸ x 11⁸
SLOPED CEILING

24'-0"

DOCK

LAKE

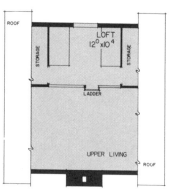

Design VH1492
First Floor: 608 square feet
Second Floor: 120 square feet
Total: 728 square feet

● It will not matter one bit where this log cabin is built, for there will be many paths beaten to its doors. The massive stone chimney seems to foretell of the warm hospitality awaiting inside. The big living area is dominated, as well it should be, by the centered fireplace.

Design by
Home Planners,
Inc.

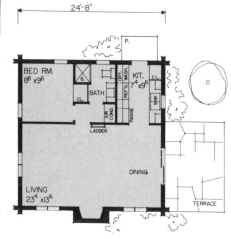

● The rustic charm of this 40' x 20' rectangle will be hard to beat. Its appeal is all the more enticing when all that livability is the result of such economy of construction. In addition to the two bedrooms, there are two bunk rooms. Then, there is the big living/dining area with fireplace.

Design VH1489
Square Footage: 800

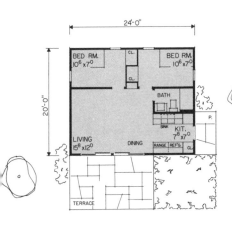

Design VH1486
Square Footage: 480

● You'll be anxious to start building this delightful little vacation home. Whether you do it yourself, or engage professional help, you will not have to wait long for its completion.

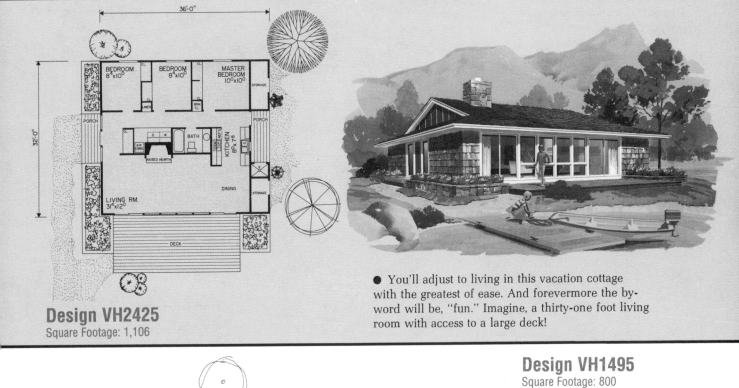

Design VH2425
Square Footage: 1,106

● You'll adjust to living in this vacation cottage with the greatest of ease. And forevermore the by-word will be, "fun." Imagine, a thirty-one foot living room with access to a large deck!

Design VH1495
Square Footage: 800

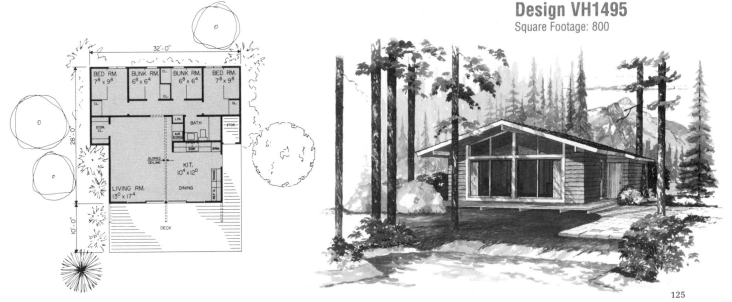

Design VH9813

First Floor: 1,724 square feet
Second Floor: 700 square feet
Total: 2,424 square feet

● This cozy English cottage might be found hidden away in a European garden. All the charm of gables, stonework and multi-level rooflines combines to create this home. To the left of the foyer you will see the sun-lit dining room, highlighted by a dramatic tray ceiling and expansive windows with transoms. This room and the living room flow together to form one large entertainment area. In the gourmet kitchen are a work island, an oversized pantry and a bright adjoining octagonal breakfast room with a gazebo ceiling. The great room features a pass-through wet bar, a fireplace and bookcases or an entertainment center. The master suite enjoys privacy at the rear of the home. An open-rail loft above the foyer leads to additional bedrooms with walk-in closets, private vanities and a shared bath. This home is designed with a basement foundation.

Design by
Design Traditions

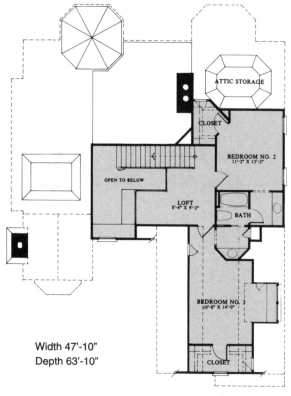

Width 47'-10"
Depth 63'-10"

126

Shingled-Sided Style

Width 39'-8"
Depth 32'

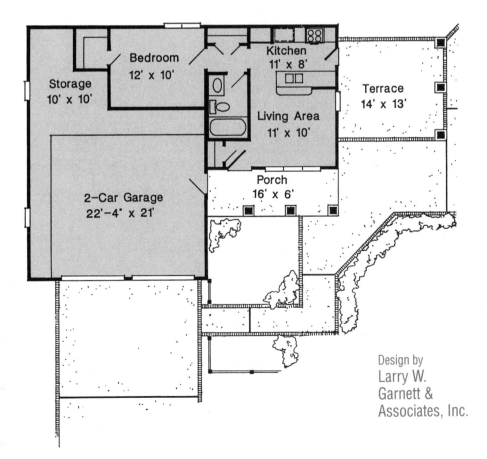

Design by
Larry W.
Garnett &
Associates, Inc.

Design VH8978
Square Footage: 468

● This delightful cottage features a columned porch and a side terrace—perfect for outdoor relaxation. Inside, the front-facing living room shares space with the efficiently patterned kitchen and has a window overlooking the terrace. A coat closet sits right next to the front door. A large storage closet, between the kitchen and bath, will serve nicely as a pantry or a linen closet. The bedroom, with a large, walk-in closet, enjoys peace and quiet at the rear of the plan. A step away, the full hall bath is also convenient to living areas. In the two-car garage, a large storage area accommodates all your recreational equipment.

Design VH3314

Square Footage: 1,951

● Scaled down but definitely upscale, this plan leaves nothing out. Two verandas, front and back, provide outdoor enjoyment along with a screened porch that extends the formal and casual eating areas. A galley kitchen serves all areas. The glow from the fireplace in the gathering room will warm any gathering. Two family bedrooms share a full bath while the master suite enjoys its own luxury bath.

California Engineered Plans and California Stock Plans are available for this home. Call 1-800-521-6797 for more information.

Quote One™

Cost to build? See page 300 to order complete cost estimate to build this house in your area!

Design by
Home Planners, Inc.

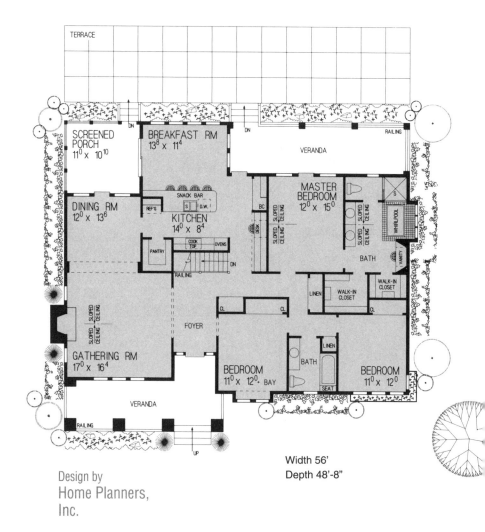

Width 56'
Depth 48'-8"

Design VH3496
Square Footage: 2,033

L

● Get more out of your home-building dollars with this unique one-story bungalow. A covered front porch provides sheltered entry into a spacious living room. A bookshelf and a column are special touches. The dining room enjoys a sloped ceiling, a wet bar and direct access to the rear covered patio. In the nearby kitchen, a breakfast bar accommodates quick meals. The adjacent family room rounds out this casual living area. The large master suite pampers with a sitting area, patio access and a luxurious bath which features a corner tub, a separate shower and dual lavatories. Two secondary bedrooms share a full hall bath.

Design by
Home Planners,
Inc.

QUOTE ONE™

Cost to build? See page 300
to order complete cost estimate
to build this house in your area!

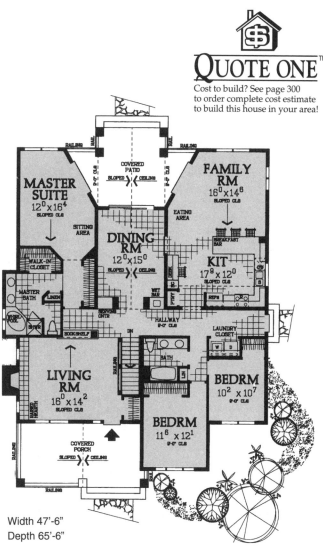

Width 47'-6"

Depth 65'-6"

Copyright 1992 Stephen S. Fuller, Inc.

Design VH9854
Square Footage: 2,770

● This English cottage with its cedar shake exterior displays the best qualities of a traditional design. With the bay window and recessed entry, visitors will feel welcomed. The foyer opens to both the dining room and the great room with its fireplace and built-in cabinetry. Surrounded by windows, the breakfast room opens to a gourmet kitchen and a laundry room conveniently located near the garage entrance. To the right of the foyer is a hall powder room. Two bedrooms with large closets are joined by a full bath with individual vanities and a window seat. Through double doors at the end of a short hall, the master suite awaits with a tray ceiling and an adjoining sunlit sitting room. The master bath has His and Hers walk-in closets, separate vanities, an individual shower and a garden tub with a bay window. This home is designed with a basement foundation.

Design by
Design Traditions

DECK

SITTING
12'-0"x 12'-0"

W.I.C.

MASTER BATH

BREAKFAST
12'-0"x 13'-6"

DN.

GREAT ROOM
20'-6"x 18'-6"

MASTER SUITE
16'-6"x 15'-0"

W.I.C.

KITCHEN
14'-13"x 13'-6"

POWDER

BEDROOM NO.3
12'-0"x 12'-0"

FOYER

DINING ROOM
13'-6" X 14'-6"

BATH

LAUNDRY
9'-0" X 8'-6"

BEDROOM NO.2
12'-3"x 14'-0"

STORAGE

STOOP

TWO CAR GARAGE
21'-6"x 27'-6"

Width 73'-6"
Depth 78'

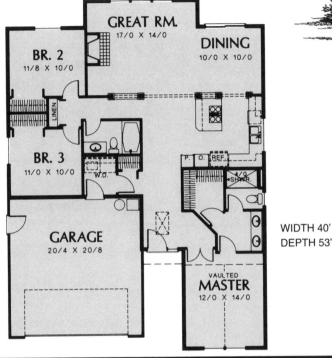

GREAT RM.
17/0 X 14/0

DINING
10/0 X 10/0

BR. 2
11/8 X 10/0

LINEN

BR. 3
11/0 X 10/0

W.O.

P. O. REF.

4/0
SHWR.

GARAGE
20/4 X 20/8

WIDTH 40'
DEPTH 53'

VAULTED
MASTER
12/0 X 14/0

Design VH9506

Square Footage: 1,463

● A combination of shingles and wood siding adds interest to this three-bedroom home. The skylit foyer offers a commanding view of the great room where a fireplace demands attention. Columns add definition to the living areas. The kitchen extends to an island cooktop and has convenient access to the dining room. Here, sliding glass doors open to the rear yard. For added convenience, a utility room opens off the garage while providing passage to the house. Closets separate Bedrooms 2 and 3, thus allowing for more quiet; the rooms share a full hall bath. The vaulted master suite takes advantage of its front location and features a private bath with dual lavatories and a walk-in closet.

Design VH8076

Square Footage: 2,733

● The heart of this beautiful home is its breakfast and keeping room which are complemented by the full kitchen. They are flanked by a large living room with double French doors and the master bedroom with French doors into the elegant master bath. Three other bedrooms, or two bedrooms and a study, are positioned at the opposite end of the house for privacy. Bedrooms 2 and 3 have their own walk-in closets. Please specify slab or crawlspace foundation when ordering.

NOTE: STAIRS LEAD TO EXPANDABLE AREA
ABOVE KEEPING ROOM/KITCHEN/GARAGE.

BEDROOM 2
14-6 X 11-0

BREAKFAST AND KEEPING RM.
22-6 X 13-0
EXPANDABLE AREA ABOVE KEEPING ROOM
10 FT CEILING

MASTER BEDROOM
16-0 X 19-2
10 FT CEILING

MASTER BATH

LIVING ROOM
18-0 X 16-0
10 FT CEILING

KITCHEN
15-0 X 13-10
EXPANDABLE AREA ABOVE
10 FT CEILING

LIN

PWDR

UTIL

BATH 2

PAN

BEDROOM 3
11-0 X 11-6

BEDRM 4/STUDY
12-6 X 13-0

FOYER
10 FT CEILING

DINING ROOM
11-8 X 13-4
10 FT CEILING

GARAGE
EXPANDABLE AREA ABOVE

Width 88'
Depth 54'-2"

PORCH
BARREL CEILING

Design VH9422
Square Footage: 1,417

● This compact ranch leaves nothing out in the way of great features. Most rooms of the home have ten-and-a-half-foot ceilings, allowing transom windows to be used extensively. The kitchen and breakfast nook look out on an outdoor living area. Note the uniquely shaped great room with a fireplace and a vaulted ceiling. The master suite has rear-yard access and is complemented by a second smaller bedroom. Because of the narrow width of this home, it can sit comfortably on many small-sized lots.

Design by
Alan Mascord
Design Associates, Inc.

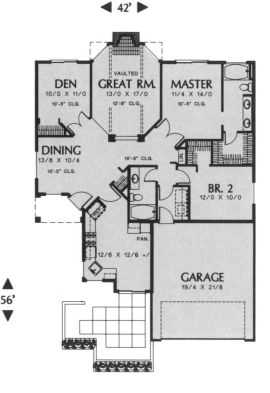

Design by
Alan Mascord
Design Associates, Inc.

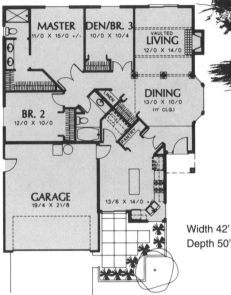

Design VH9429
Square Footage: 1,367

Width 42'
Depth 50'

● Featuring a combination of cedar shingles and vertical cedar siding, this ranch home has a compact, convenient floor plan. Both kitchen and nook face the front where a courtyard wall provides privacy for outdoor relaxation. The entry and dining room both have eleven-foot ceilings, allowing for attractive transom windows. This area is also enhanced by a series of columns separating the vaulted living room from the dining room. Opening off the hallway with a pair of French doors is a den which could be used as a third bedroom.

Design by
Alan Mascord
Design Associates, Inc.

Design VH9508
Square Footage: 1,523

● The repeated roof treatments and varying exterior materials add interest to this darling home. Inside, the great room commands attention with its fireplace, high ceiling and overall spaciousness. Double doors lead to a den where built-ins enhance an already attractive room—perfect for quiet getaways. A built-in desk adds to the inviting character of the kitchen and breakfast nook. The great room could easily support a formal dining area serviced by the angular kitchen passageway. The sleeping quarters consist of a master suite with a private bath and a walk-in closet, and a secondary bedroom for family or guests. A utility area ties the house and garage together well.

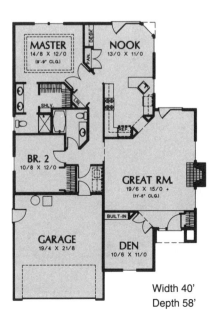

Width 40'
Depth 58'

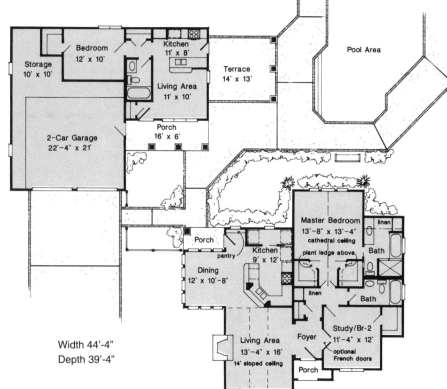

Bedroom
12' x 10'

Kitchen
11' x 8'

Storage
10' x 10'

Living Area
11' x 10'

Terrace
14' x 13'

Pool Area

2-Car Garage
22'-4" x 21'

Porch
16' x 6'

Design VH9096

Square Footage: 1,268
Guest Cottage: 468 square feet

● The perfect plan for those with a live-in relative, long-term guest or a family member who works at home, this plan allows a separate cottage with complete livability. The main house features a living room with fireplace and sloped ceiling, a glass-enclosed dining room with porch, kitchen with plenty of counter space and two bedrooms with two baths (or make one a study). The separate cottage is attached to the garage and has its own living area, galley kitchen and bedroom with walk-in closet and full bath. It also features a front porch and private side terrace. It can work as complete living quarters or a private studio or office. A bright solution to today's living patterns.

Porch

pantry

Kitchen
9' x 12'

Dining
12' x 10'-8"

Master Bedroom
13'-8" x 13'-4"
cathedral ceiling

plant ledge above

linen

Bath

linen

Bath

Living Area
13'-4" x 16'
14' sloped ceiling

Foyer

Study/Br-2
11'-4" x 12'

optional
French doors

Porch

Width 44'-4"
Depth 39'-4"

Design by
Larry W.
Garnett &
Associates, Inc.

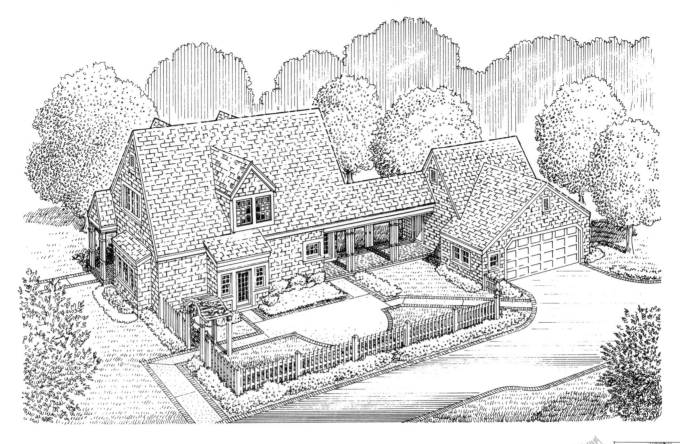

Design VH9044

First Floor: 814 square feet
Second Floor: 467 square feet
Total: 1,281 square feet

● Here's an adorable shingled cottage that offers more that just another charming face. Because the living room opens directly to the dining room, an appearance of space is created. Abundant windows further enhance the roomy feeling. The kitchen overlooks a garden side yard. The pampering master bedroom includes a huge walk-in closet and a bath with separate tub and shower. Upstairs are two more bedrooms and an alcove loft that can be used as a study area. Note the two-story foyer and linen storage in the upstairs bath. A guest half-bath is thoughtfully placed at entry.

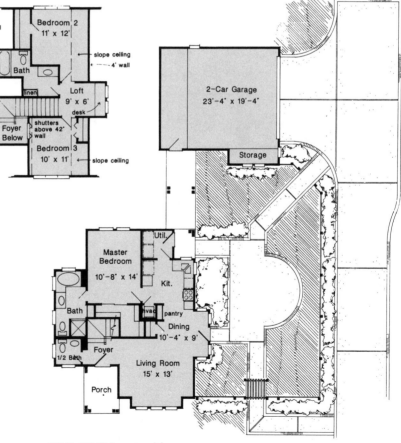

Width 31'-4" (house only)
Depth 35'-8" (house only)

Design by
Larry W.
Garnett &
Associates, Inc.

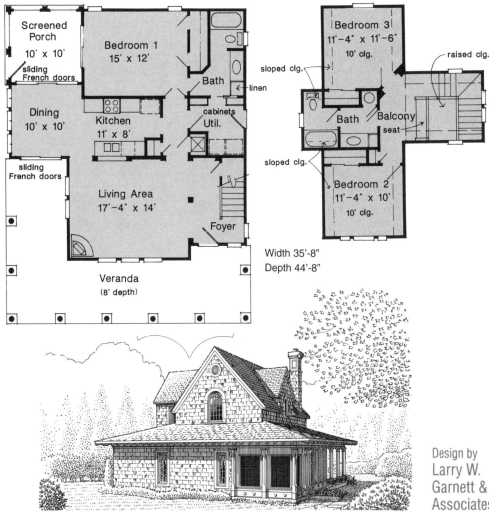

Floor Plan Labels

Screened Porch
10' x 10'

sliding French doors

Bedroom 1
15' x 12'

Bath

linen

Dining
10' x 10'

Kitchen
11' x 8'

cabinets

Util.

sliding French doors

Living Area
17'-4" x 14'

Foyer

Veranda
(8' depth)

Bedroom 3
11'-4" x 11'-6"
10' clg.

sloped clg.

raised clg.

Bath

Balcony

seat

sloped clg.

Bedroom 2
11'-4" x 10'
10' clg.

Width 35'-8"
Depth 44'-8"

Design VH9131

First Floor: 978 square feet
Second Floor: 464 square feet
Total: 1,442 square feet

● From the covered front veranda to the second-story Palladian window, this home exudes warmth and grace. Though smaller in square footage, the floor plan offers plenty of room. The living area is complemented by a cozy corner fireplace and is attached to a dining area with French doors to a screened porch and the front veranda. The galley-style kitchen is the central hub of the first floor. A large bedroom on this floor has an attached full bath and serves equally well as guest bedroom or master bedroom. The second floor holds two bedrooms and another full bath. An open balcony area here overlooks the foyer below.

Design by
Larry W. Garnett & Associates, Inc.

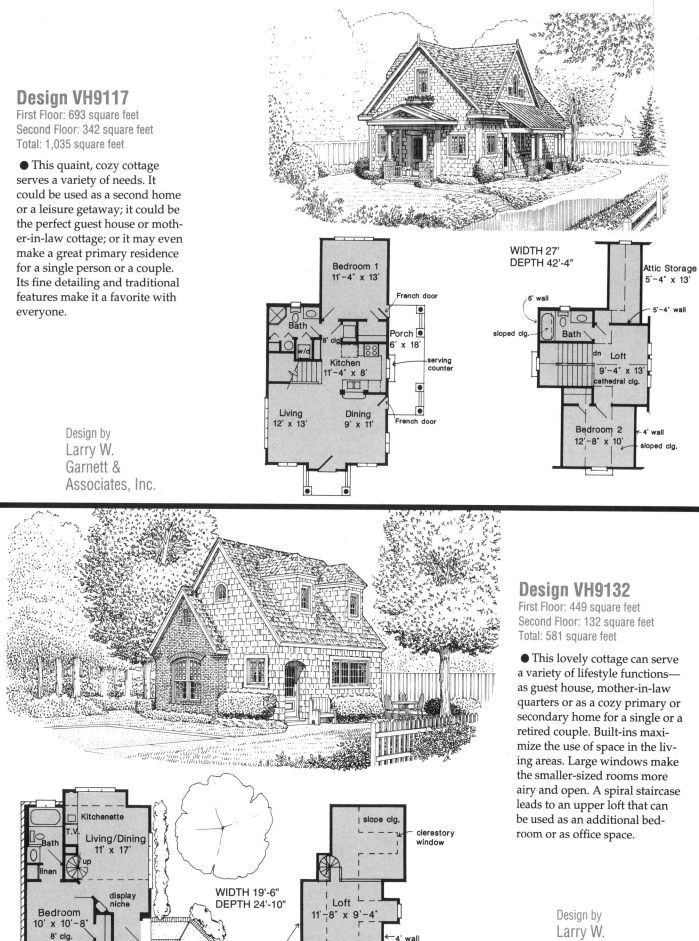

Design VH9117

First Floor: 693 square feet
Second Floor: 342 square feet
Total: 1,035 square feet

● This quaint, cozy cottage
serves a variety of needs. It
could be used as a second home
or a leisure getaway; it could be
the perfect guest house or mother-in-law cottage; or it may even
make a great primary residence
for a single person or a couple.
Its fine detailing and traditional
features make it a favorite with
everyone.

Design by
Larry W.
Garnett &
Associates, Inc.

Bedroom 1
11'-4" x 13'

French door

Bath

8' clg.

w/d

Porch
6' x 18'

Kitchen
11'-4" x 8'

serving
counter

Living
12' x 13'

Dining
9' x 11'

French door

WIDTH 27'
DEPTH 42'-4"

Attic Storage
5'-4" x 13'

6' wall

5'-4" wall

sloped clg.

Bath

dn

Loft
9'-4" x 13'
cathedral clg.

Bedroom 2
12'-8" x 10'

4' wall

sloped clg.

Design VH9132

First Floor: 449 square feet
Second Floor: 132 square feet
Total: 581 square feet

● This lovely cottage can serve
a variety of lifestyle functions—
as guest house, mother-in-law
quarters or as a cozy primary or
secondary home for a single or a
retired couple. Built-ins maxi-
mize the use of space in the living areas. Large windows make
the smaller-sized rooms more
airy and open. A spiral staircase
leads to an upper loft that can
be used as an additional bedroom or as office space.

Kitchenette

T.V.

Bath

Living/Dining
11' x 17'

linen

up

display
niche

Bedroom
10' x 10'-8"
8' clg.

WIDTH 19'-6"
DEPTH 24'-10"

slope clg.

clerestory
window

Loft
11'-8" x 9'-4"

4' wall

4' wall

Design by
Larry W.
Garnett &
Associates, Inc.

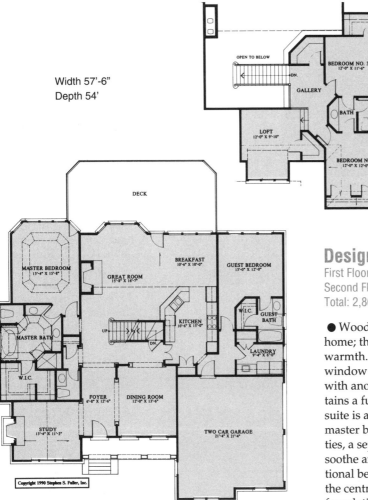

Width 57'-6"
Depth 54'

OPEN TO BELOW

BEDROOM NO. 3
12'-0" X 11'-6"

GALLERY

DN.

BATH

LOFT
12'-0" X 9'-10"

BEDROOM NO. 2
12'-0" X 12'-0"

DECK

MASTER BEDROOM
13'-4" X 15'-8"

BREAKFAST
10'-6" X 10'-0"

GREAT ROOM
15'-8" X 16'-7"

GUEST BEDROOM
13'-0" X 12'-0"

W.I.C.

GUEST BATH

MASTER BATH

KITCHEN
10'-6" X 15'-0"

UP

DN.

LAUNDRY
9'-4" X 6'-0"

W.I.C.

FOYER
6'-4" X 12'-6"

DINING ROOM
12'-0" X 13'-6"

TWO CAR GARAGE
21'-4" X 21'-4"

STUDY
13'-4" X 11'-2"

Design by
Design Traditions

Design VH9898
First Floor: 2,070 square feet
Second Floor: 790 square feet
Total: 2,860 square feet

● Wood shingles add a cozy touch to the exterior of this home; the arched covered front porch adds its own bit of warmth. Interior rooms include a great room with a bay window and a fireplace, a formal dining room and a study with another fireplace. A guest room on the first floor contains a full bath and a walk-in closet. The relaxing master suite is also on the first floor and features a pampering master bath with His and Hers walk-in closets, dual vanities, a separate shower and a whirlpool tub just waiting to soothe and rejuvenate. The second floor holds two additional bedrooms, a loft area and a gallery which overlooks the central hall. This home is designed with a basement foundation.

Design VH9908 First Floor: 1,944 square feet
Second Floor: 1,055 square feet; Total: 2,999 square feet

● Interesting rooflines, multi-level eaves and a two-story double-bay window create a unique cottage farmhouse appearance for this charming home. A combination of columns and stone create a cozy and inviting porch. The grand foyer leads to the formal dining room and large great room, both graced with columns. The great room features a cozy fireplace and opens to the deck through French door. The breakfast room, divided from the great room by an open stair-case, shares space with an efficient L-shaped kitchen and nearby laundry room, making domestic endeavors easy to accomplish. The right wing is devoted to a sumptuous, amenity-filled master suite with convenient access to the study for after-hours research or quiet reading. The second floor contains three secondary bedrooms and two baths for family and guests. This home is designed with a basement foundation.

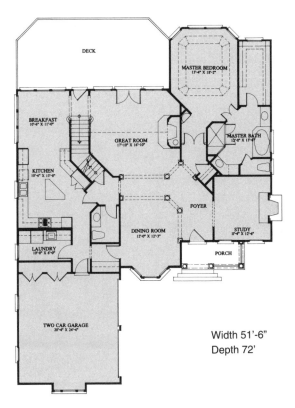

Width 51'-6"
Depth 72'

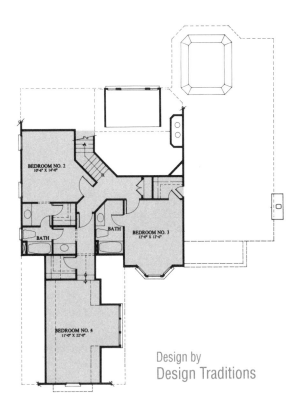

Design by
Design Traditions

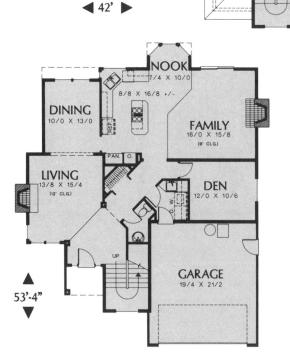

Design VH9495

First Floor: 1,321 square feet
Second Floor: 1,155 square feet
Total: 2,476 square feet

● If you love the look of cedar
shingles and cedar siding, you'll
find much to appreciate in this
home. From the tall entryway to
the formal and informal living
areas, it is both attractive and
practical. Fireplaces are found in
the family room and the living
room; the dining room boasts outdoor access. A den is tucked away
between the family room and the
garage, insuring privacy. The
kitchen includes an island cooktop
and an attached bayed nook eating
area. The bedrooms are upstairs
and include a master suite with
cove ceiling and spa tub. Family
bedrooms feature excellent closet
space. The shared bath contains a
double-bowl vanity.

Design by
Alan Mascord
Design Associates, Inc.

◄ 42' ►

53'-4"

MASTER
16/8 X 14/8
(9'-3" CLG.)

SPA

BR. 2
11/10 X 11/0

BR. 3
11/10 X 10/0

BR. 4
11/4 X 11/0

LINEN

DN.

NOOK
7/4 X 10/0

8/8 X 16/8 +/-

DINING
10/0 X 13/0

FAMILY
16/0 X 15/8
(9' CLG.)

PAN. O.

LIVING
13/8 X 15/4
(12' CLG.)

DEN
12/0 X 10/6

W.

UP

GARAGE
19/4 X 21/2

Design VH9534

First Floor: 762 square feet
Second Floor: 738 square feet
Total: 1,500 square feet

● As a starter or fine family home, this two-story design functions well. An attractive traditional exterior introduces the interior by way of a covered front porch. The living room opens directly off the foyer and features a fireplace and an expansive window seat. Sharing space with this area is the gourmet kitchen. It delights with an island cooktop, a sunny sink and a pantry. Room for a dinette set is right near a side door. Accommodations for a washer and dryer, a rear deck and a powder room complete the first floor. Upstairs, three bedrooms all include vaulted ceilings. The master bedroom enjoys its own private bath and a deck.

Design by
Alan Mascord
Design Associates, Inc.

Width 34'
Depth 36'

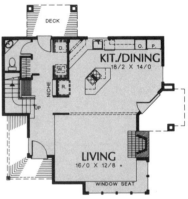

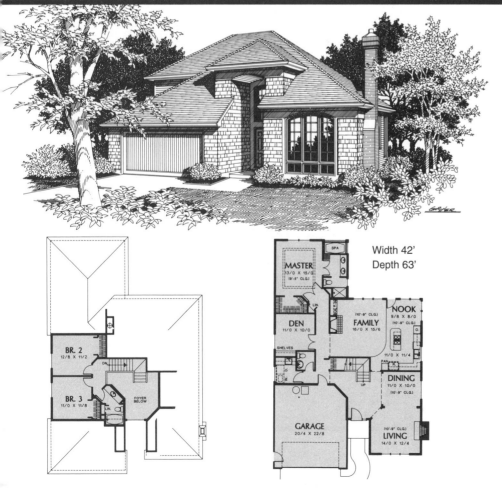

Design VH9483

First Floor: 1,697 square feet
Second Floor: 433 square feet
Total: 2,130 square feet

● High, sloping rooflines allow for a volume look with expansive windows in this two-story plan. The living areas are clustered on the first floor along with a private master suite tucked privately to the rear. The living room and family room both have fireplaces. Two family bedrooms are found on the second floor along with a full bath.

Width 42'
Depth 63'

Design by
Alan Mascord
Design Associates, Inc.

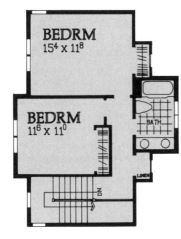

BEDRM
15⁴ x 11⁸

BEDRM
11⁶ x 11⁰

BATH

LINEN

DN

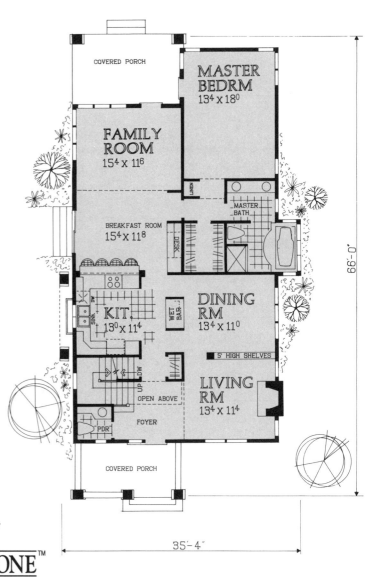

COVERED PORCH

MASTER
BEDRM
13⁴ x 18⁰

FAMILY
ROOM
15⁴ x 11⁶

LINEN

MASTER
BATH

BREAKFAST ROOM
15⁴ x 11⁸

DESK

DINING
RM
13⁴ x 11⁰

KIT
13⁰ x 11⁴

SINK

WET
BAR

DW

DW

UP

5' HIGH SHELVES

LIVING
RM
13⁴ x 11⁴

OPEN ABOVE

PDR

FOYER

COVERED PORCH

66'-0"

35'-4"

Design VH3497

First Floor: 1,581 square feet
Second Floor: 592 square feet
Total: 2,173 square feet

● For the best in traditional styling, this 1 ½-story bungalow design takes the cake. A shingled exterior complements raised roof lines and a front porch. Inside, the entry gives way to a living room with a fireplace and a dining room serviced by a U-shaped kitchen and a wet bar. An airy breakfast room is situated nearby. In the family room, a back porch acts as a pleasant enhancement. The first-floor master bedroom suite leaves room for a sitting area. Upstairs, two secondary bedrooms share a full bath with dual lavatories. No matter what your family's style, this home will provide all the desired livability.

Design by
Home Planners,
Inc.

QUOTE ONE™

Cost to build? See page 300
to order complete cost estimate
to build this house in your area!

Design VH3495

First Floor: 1,457 square feet
Second Floor: 1,288 square feet
Total: 2,745 square feet

L D

● The very best in modern design comes into play with this extraordinary two-story home. Columns and half walls define the formal living and dining rooms—a curved niche adds appeal to the latter. Beyond the centrally located stair-

case, the family room extends to its occupants a sloped ceiling, and an angled corner fireplace. At the other side of the house, the bright breakfast area—adjacent to the kitchen—enjoys the use of a patio. In the kitchen, an abundance of counter and storage space sets the stage for convenient food preparation. Notice, too, the powder room nestled between the kitchen and the laundry room. Two full bathrooms grace the upstairs: one in the master suite includes a soaking tub and separate shower; one in the hallway serves the three secondary bedrooms.

Width 42'
Depth 63'-4"

Design by
Home Planners,
Inc.

QUOTE ONE™

Cost to build? See page 300
to order complete cost estimate
to build this house in your area!

Design VH9536

First Floor: 1,200 square feet
Second Floor: 1,339 square feet
Total: 2,539 square feet

● A covered front porch introduces this home's comfortable living pattern. The two-story foyer opens to a living room with a fireplace and lots of natural light. The formal dining room looks out over the living room. In the kitchen, an island cooktop, a pantry, a built-in planning desk and a nook with double doors to outside livability aims to please. A spacious family room with another fireplace will accommodate casual living. Upstairs, five bedrooms—or four and a den— make room for all family members and guests. The master bedroom suite exudes elegance with an elegant ceiling and a pampering spa bath. A full hall bath with a skylight and dual lavatories serves the secondary bedrooms.

Design by
Alan Mascord
Design Associates, Inc.

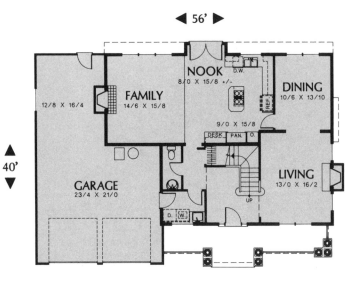

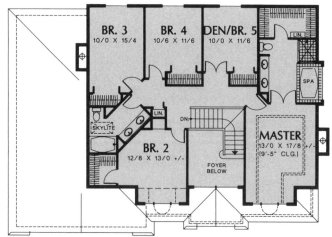

Multi-Level Vacation Homes

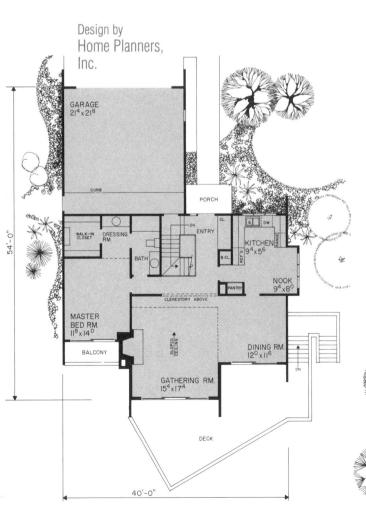

Design by
Home Planners,
Inc.

GARAGE
21⁴ x 21⁸

CURB

PORCH

WALK-IN CLOSET
DRESSING RM.
BATH
ENTRY
KITCHEN
9⁴ x 5⁶

NOOK
9⁴ x 8⁰

PANTRY

CLERESTORY ABOVE

MASTER BED RM.
11⁸ x 14⁰

BALCONY

SLOPED CEILING

GATHERING RM.
15⁴ x 17⁴

DINING RM.
12⁰ x 11⁶

DECK

54'-0"

40'-0"

Design VH2485 Main Level: 1,108 square feet
Lower Level: 983 square feet; Total: 2,091 square feet

● This hillside vacation home gives the appearance of being a one-story from the road. However, since it is built off the edge of a slope, the rear exterior is a full two-story structure. Notice the projecting deck and how it shelters the terrace. Each of the generous glass areas is protected from the summer sun by the overhangs and the extended walls. The clerestory windows of the front exterior provide natural light to the center of the plan.

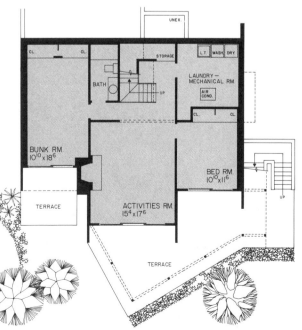

UNEX.

STORAGE

LT WASH. DRY.

LAUNDRY — MECHANICAL RM.

AIR COND.

BATH

BUNK RM.
10¹⁰ x 18⁶

BED RM.
10¹⁰ x 11⁶

TERRACE

ACTIVITIES RM.
15⁴ x 17⁶

TERRACE

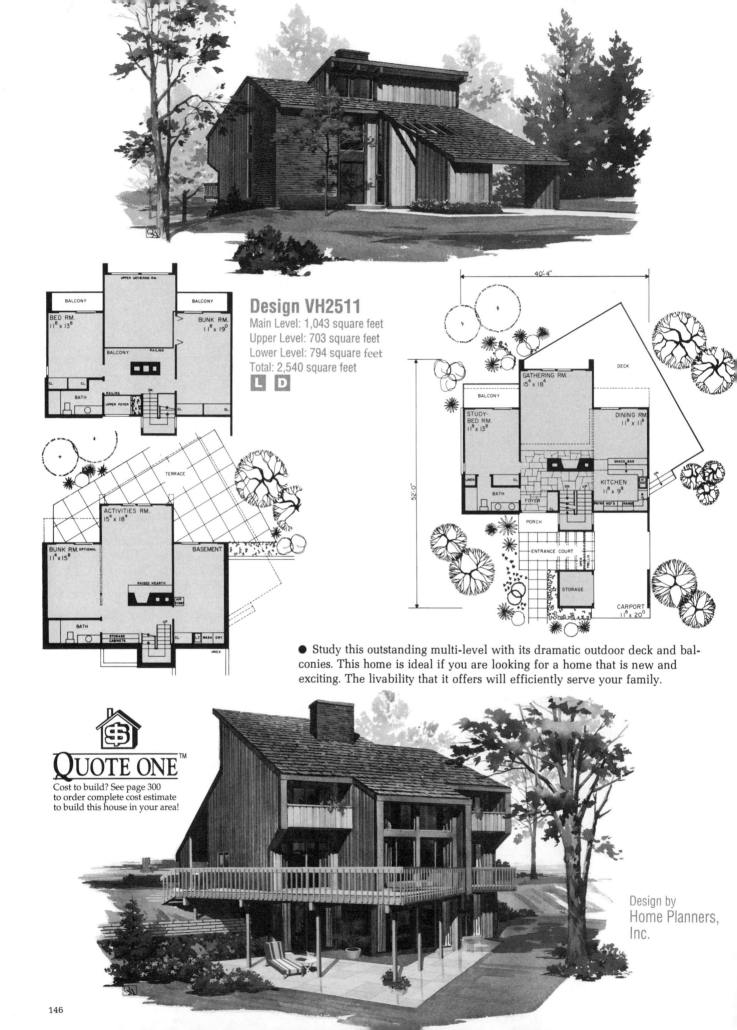

Design VH2511

Main Level: 1,043 square feet
Upper Level: 703 square feet
Lower Level: 794 square feet
Total: 2,540 square feet

L **D**

● Study this outstanding multi-level with its dramatic outdoor deck and balconies. This home is ideal if you are looking for a home that is new and exciting. The livability that it offers will efficiently serve your family.

QUOTE ONE™

Cost to build? See page 300
to order complete cost estimate
to build this house in your area!

Design by
Home Planners,
Inc.

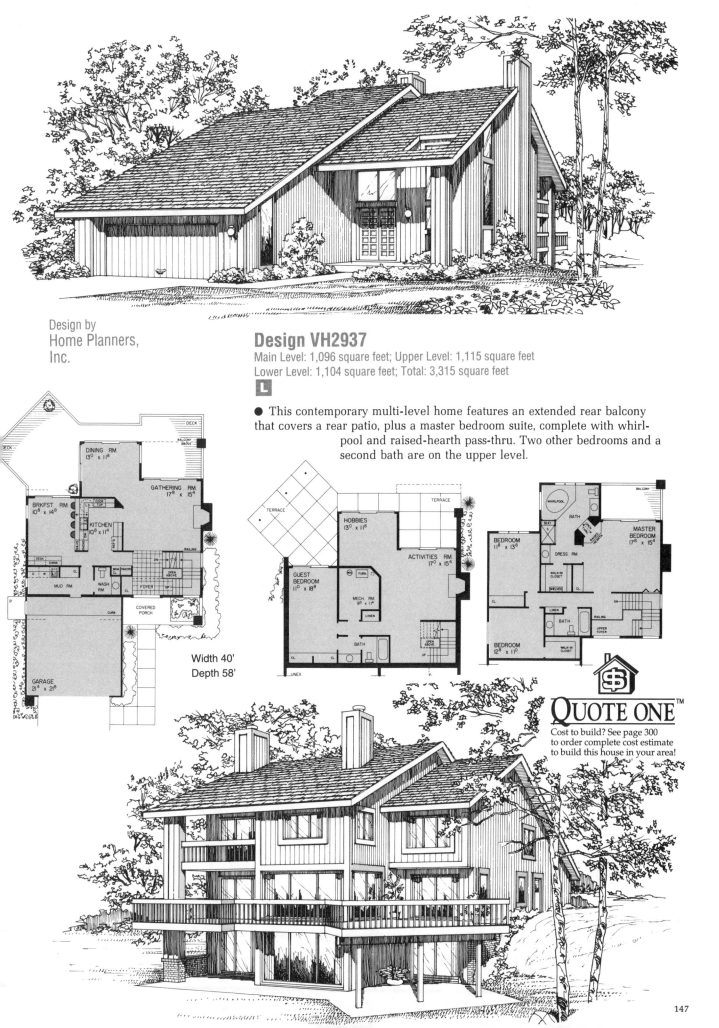

Design by
**Home Planners,
Inc.**

Design VH2937

Main Level: 1,096 square feet; Upper Level: 1,115 square feet
Lower Level: 1,104 square feet; Total: 3,315 square feet

L

● This contemporary multi-level home features an extended rear balcony that covers a rear patio, plus a master bedroom suite, complete with whirlpool and raised-hearth pass-thru. Two other bedrooms and a second bath are on the upper level.

Width 40'
Depth 58'

Quote One™
Cost to build? See page 300
to order complete cost estimate
to build this house in your area!

Design VH2716 Main Level: 1,013 square feet
Upper Level: 885 square feet; Lower Level: 1,074 square feet; Total: 2,972 square feet

L

● A genuine master suite! It overlooks the gathering room through shuttered windows and includes a private balcony, a 9' by 9' sitting/dressing room and a full bath. There's more, a two-story gathering room with a raised hearth fireplace, sloped ceiling and sliding glass doors onto the main balcony. Plus, a family room and a study both having a fireplace. A kitchen with lots of built-ins and a separate dining nook.

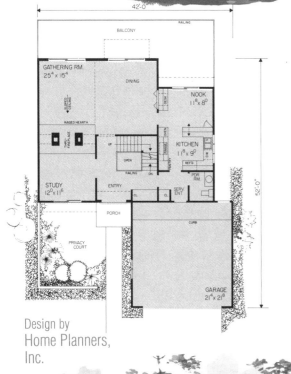

Design by
Home Planners,
Inc.

Design VH9484

Main Level: 1,573 square feet
Lower Level: 1,404 square feet
Total: 2,977 square feet

● There's something for every member of the family in this captivating hillside plan. The first floor holds a huge great room for family and formal gatherings, a dining room distinguished by columns, an island kitchen with an attached nook and outdoor deck area, and a master suite with a giant-sized bath. The game room downstairs is joined by three bedrooms or two bedrooms and a den. Look for another deck at this level.

Design by
Alan Mascord
Design Associates, Inc.

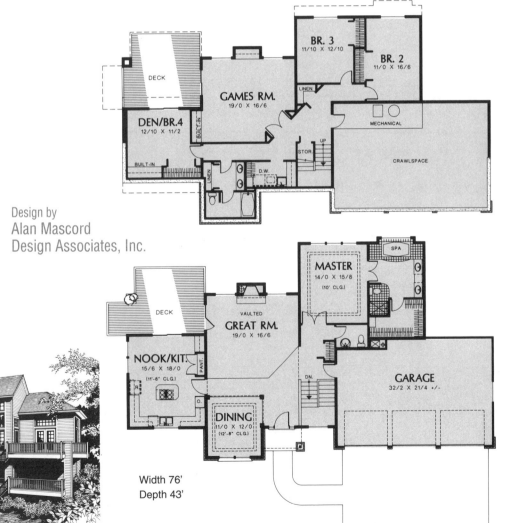

Width 76'
Depth 43'

Design by
Home Planners,
Inc.

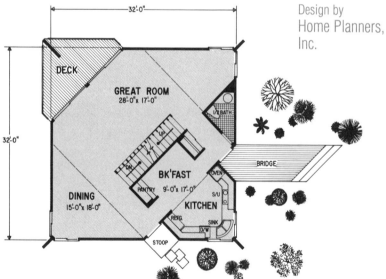

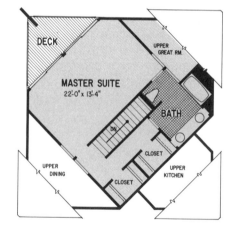

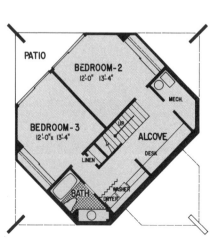

Design VH4134

Entry Level: 1,015 square feet
Upper Level: 574 square feet
Lower Level: 708 square feet
Total: 2,297 square feet

● This unusual contemporary features three levels of livability. A wooden bridge leads to the middle entry level containing the great room, dining area, and kitchen. Interesting shapes and angles make this a dramatic space. Downstairs is the children's suite with two bedrooms, shared bath, and alcove with built-in desk. The large master suite, found on the upper level, is truly a private retreat with a generous bath and its own deck. The split-sleeping-area design ensures maximum peace and quiet.

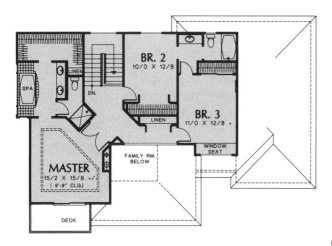

Design VH9488

Main Level: 1,713 square feet
Upper Level: 998 square feet
Lower Level: 102 square feet
Total: 2,813 square feet

Design by
**Alan Mascord
Design Associates, Inc.**

Width 54'-6"
Depth 37'

● Designed for sloping lots, this home has much to offer in addition to its visual appeal. It is especially suited to homes that orient with a view to the front (note the decks in the master bedroom and den). The two-story family room, with through fireplace to the den, is complemented by the more formal parlor with 10'-1" ceiling. The parlor is separated from the dining room by a step with columned accents. The kitchen/nook area has an island range and is enhanced by a 9' ceiling. Three bedrooms upstairs include a master with lavish bath and 9'-9" tray ceiling. Two family bedrooms share a full bath.

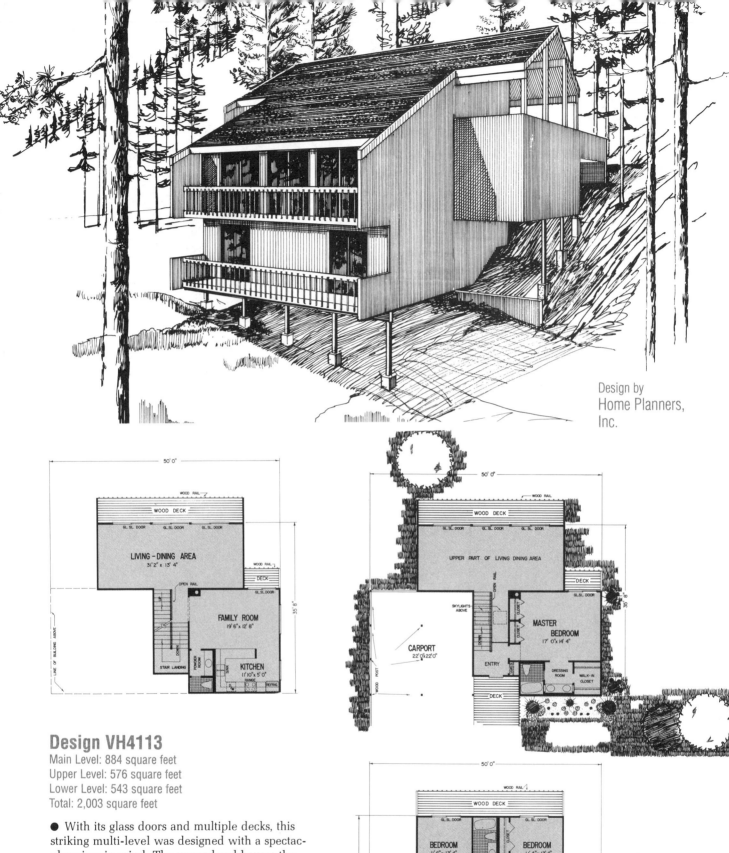

Design by
Home Planners,
Inc.

Design VH4113

Main Level: 884 square feet
Upper Level: 576 square feet
Lower Level: 543 square feet
Total: 2,003 square feet

● With its glass doors and multiple decks, this striking multi-level was designed with a spectacular view in mind. The upper level houses the large master bedroom. Down the open stair is the spacious living and dining area. Just steps away is the open kitchen and family room, a communal spot for cooking and relaxing together. The lower level contains two more bedrooms, a full bath, and a shared deck. Both parents and children will appreciate the privacy of the split sleeping area.

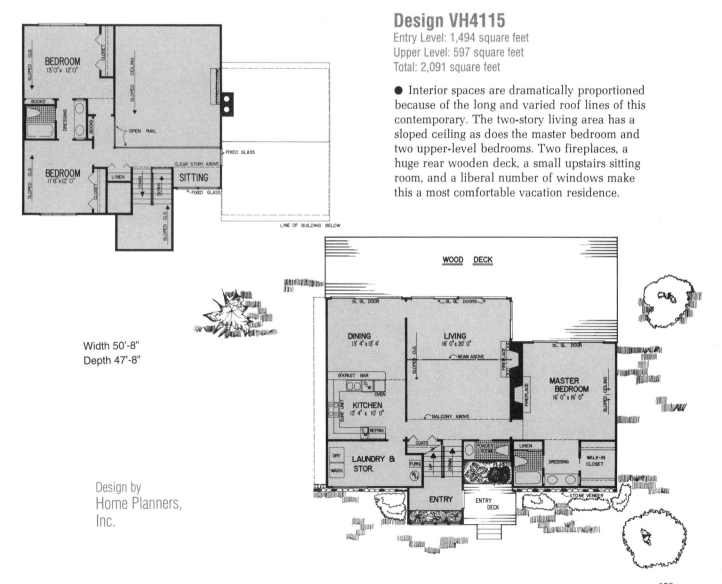

Design VH4115

Entry Level: 1,494 square feet
Upper Level: 597 square feet
Total: 2,091 square feet

● Interior spaces are dramatically proportioned because of the long and varied roof lines of this contemporary. The two-story living area has a sloped ceiling as does the master bedroom and two upper-level bedrooms. Two fireplaces, a huge rear wooden deck, a small upstairs sitting room, and a liberal number of windows make this a most comfortable vacation residence.

Width 50'-8"
Depth 47'-8"

Design by
Home Planners, Inc.

◀ 43' ▶

Design VH9538

First Floor: 1,538 square feet
Second Floor: 1,089 square feet
Total: 2,627 square feet

● Accentuate your sloping lot
with this attractive two-story
home. The foyer opens to
columned views. A volume great
room with a deck, a fireplace and
built-ins commands attention. The
gourmet kitchen features an island
cooktop, a sunny corner sink and a
nook with a pass-through to the
great room. A dining room, a dou-
ble-doored den and a spacious
laundry room with a nearby powder room complete the first floor.
Upstairs, the master bedroom suite
utilizes a scissor vault ceiling
design. An attached, private luxury
bath and a walk-in closet will surely satisfy. Two secondary bedrooms share a compartmented
hall bath.

50'

Design by
Alan Mascord
Design Associates, Inc.

Design VH9509

Main Level: 1,022 square feet
Upper Level: 813 square feet
Total: 1,835 square feet

● This house not only accommodates a narrow lot, but it also fits a sloping site. Notice how the two-car garage is tucked away under the first level of the house. The angled corner entry gives way to a two-story living room with a tiled hearth. The dining room shares an interesting angled space with this area and enjoys easy service from the efficient kitchen. A large pantry and an angled corner sink add character to this area. The family room offers double doors to a refreshing balcony. A powder room and a laundry room complete the main level. Upstairs, three bedrooms include a vaulted master suite with a private bath. Bedrooms 2 and 3 each take advantage of direct access to a full bath.

Design by
Alan Mascord
Design Associates, Inc.

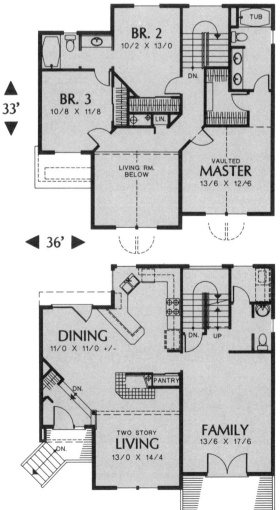

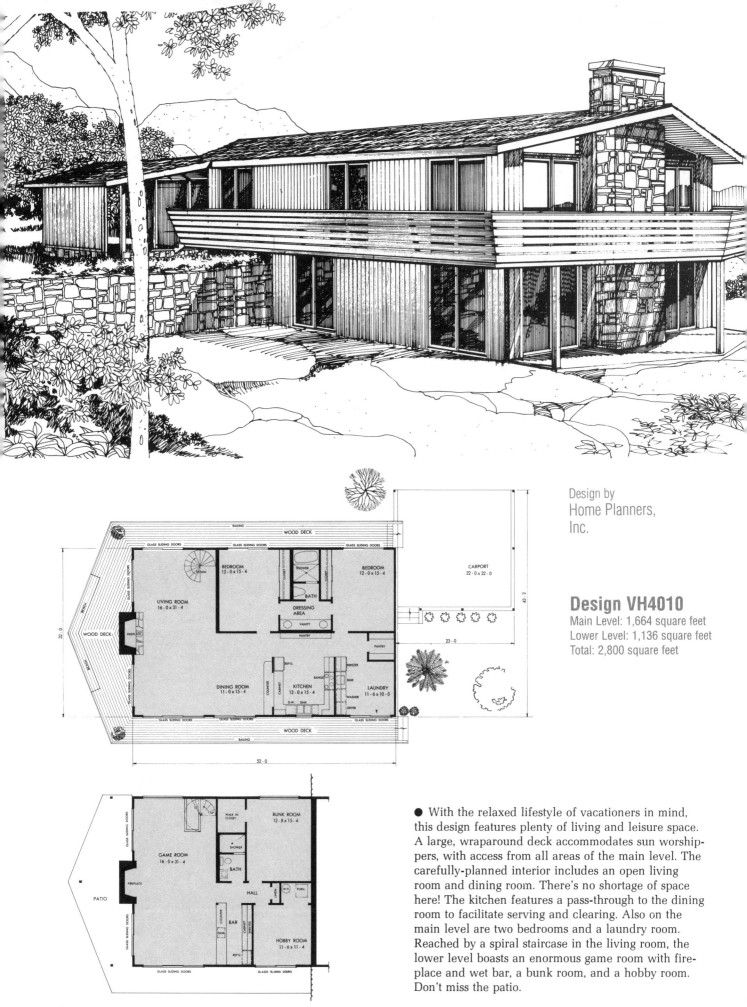

Design by
Home Planners,
Inc.

Design VH4010
Main Level: 1,664 square feet
Lower Level: 1,136 square feet
Total: 2,800 square feet

● With the relaxed lifestyle of vacationers in mind, this design features plenty of living and leisure space. A large, wraparound deck accommodates sun worshippers, with access from all areas of the main level. The carefully-planned interior includes an open living room and dining room. There's no shortage of space here! The kitchen features a pass-through to the dining room to facilitate serving and clearing. Also on the main level are two bedrooms and a laundry room. Reached by a spiral staircase in the living room, the lower level boasts an enormous game room with fireplace and wet bar, a bunk room, and a hobby room. Don't miss the patio.

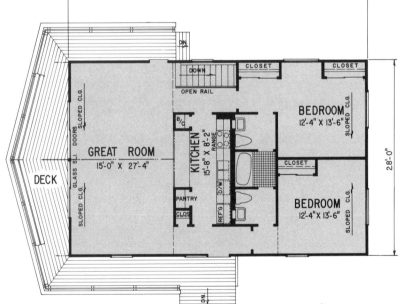

GREAT ROOM
15'-0" X 27'-4"

DECK

KITCHEN
15'-8" X 8'-2"

PANTRY

CLOS

BEDROOM
12'-4" X 13'-6"

CLOSET

BEDROOM
12'-4" X 13'-6"

CLOSET

CLOSET

OPEN RAIL

DOWN

SLOPED CLG.

GLASS SLI. DOORS

44'-0"

28'-0"

Design by
**Home Planners,
Inc.**

Design VH4027
Square Footage: 1,232

● Good things come in small packages, too! The size and shape of this design will help hold down construction costs without sacrificing livability. The enormous great room is a multi-purpose living space with room for a dining area and several seating areas. Also notice the sloped ceilings. Sliding glass doors provide access to the wraparound deck and sweeping views of the outdoors. The well-equipped kitchen includes a pass-through and pantry. Two bedrooms, each with sloped ceilings, and compartmented bath round out the plan.

PLAY ROOM
14'-8" X 26'-4"

LAUNDRY

FURN

WASH

DRY

BEDROOM
12'-8" X 13'-2"

CLOSET

CLOSET

BEDROOM
12'-8" X 10'-10"

GLASS SLI. DOORS

UP

44'-0"

28'-0"

Optional Basement

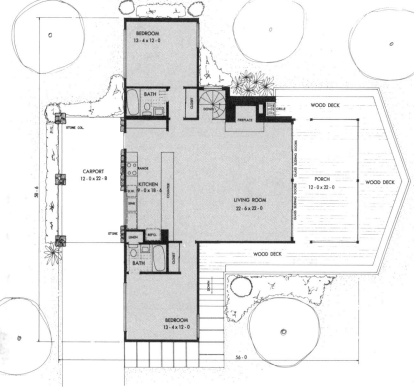

● This plan features the kind of indoor-outdoor relationship found in vacation homes. Sliding glass doors in the living room open onto a screened porch which, in turn, leads to a large deck. Note the built-in grille. The large living room with welcoming fireplace has enough space to accommodate an eating area. The sleeping quarters are split with two private bedrooms and baths on the entry level and a spacious dormitory with fireplace on the lower level. Just steps away is a covered patio.

Design by
Home Planners,
Inc.

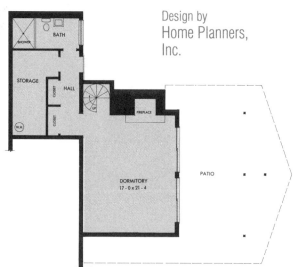

Design VH4012

Main Level: 1,216 square feet
Lower Level: 786 square feet
Total: 2,002 square feet

Design by
Home Planners,
Inc.

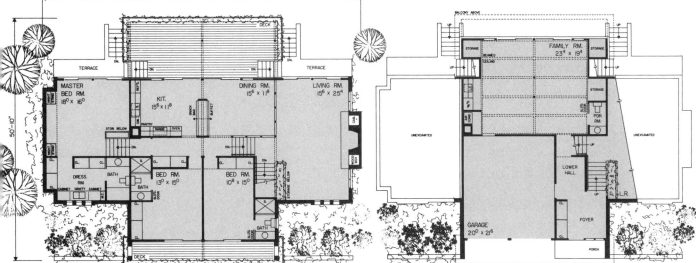

69'-3"

50'-10"

MASTER
BED RM.
18⁰ x 16⁰

KIT.
15⁶ x 11⁸

DINING RM.
15⁶ x 11⁸

LIVING RM.
15⁶ x 25⁴

TERRACE

TERRACE

DECK

STOR. BELOW   PANTRY   RANGE   OVEN   SNACK BAR   BUFFET

DRESS.
RM.

BATH

BED RM.
13⁰ x 15⁰

BED RM.
10⁸ x 15⁰

CABINET   VANITY   CABINET

BATH

BATH

DECK

BALCONY ABOVE

FAMILY RM.
23⁴ x 19⁴

STORAGE   BEAMED CEILING   STORAGE

STORAGE

UNEXCAVATED

AIR COND.

LOWER
HALL

UNEXCAVATED

GARAGE
20⁰ x 21⁶

PDR.

L.R.

FOYER

PORCH

BALCONY ABOVE

Design VH2247

Main Level: 979 square feet
Upper Level: 1,049 square feet
Lower Level: 915 square feet
Total: 2,943 square feet

159

Design VH2761

Main Level: 1,242 square feet

Lower Level: 1,242 square feet

Total: 2,484 square feet

L

● Here is another one-story that doubles its livability by exposing the lowest level at the rear. Formal living on the main level and informal living, the activity room and study, on the lower level. Observe the wonderful outdoor living facilities. The deck acts as a cover for the terrace.

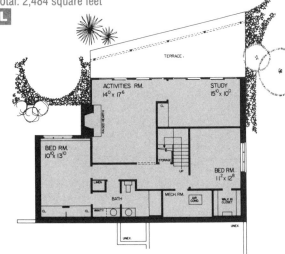

Design by
Home Planners,
Inc.

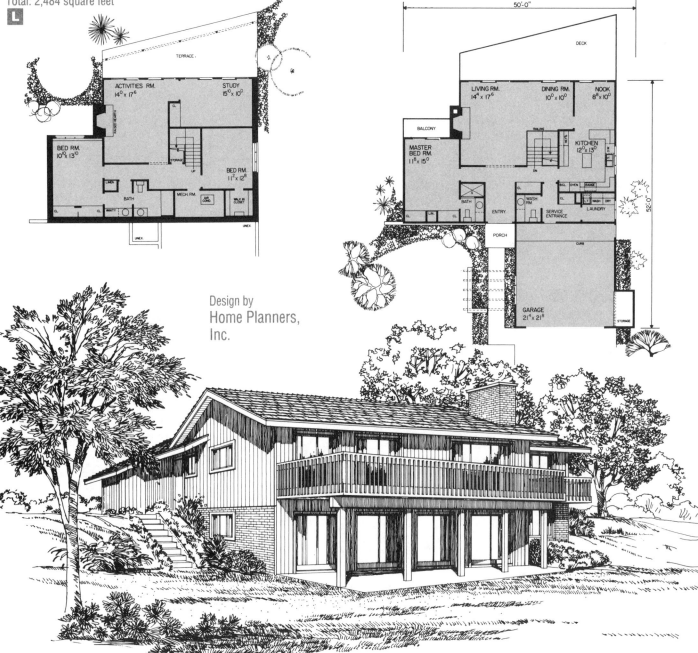

● Four bedrooms! Or three plus a study, it's your choice. A fireplace in the study/bedroom guarantees a cozy atmosphere. The warmth of a fireplace also will be enjoyed in the gathering room and activities room. Lots of living space, too. An exceptionally large gathering room with sliding glass doors that open onto the main terrace to enjoy the scenic outdoors. A formal dining room, too. And a kitchen that promises to turn a novice cook into a pro. Check out the counter space, the pantry and the island range. This house is designed to make living pleasant.

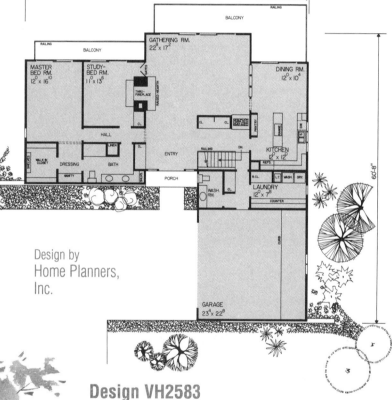

Design by
Home Planners,
Inc.

Design VH2583

Main Level: 1,838 square feet
Lower Level: 1,558 square feet
Total: 3,396 square feet

Design VH2896

Upper Level: 1,856 square feet; Lower Level: 1,454 square feet
Total: 3,310 square feet

● This design is very inviting with its contemporary appeal. A large kitchen with an adjacent snack bar makes light meals a breeze. The adjoining breakfast room offers a scenic view through sliding glass doors. Notice the sloped ceiling in the dining and gathering rooms. A fireplace in the gathering room adds a cozy air. An interesting feature is the master bedroom's easy access to the study. Also, take note of the sliding doors in the master bedroom which lead to a private balcony. On the lower level, a large activities room will be a frequently used spot by family members. The fireplace and wet bar add a nice touch for entertaining friends. Also, notice the sliding glass doors which lead to the terrace. Take note of the two or optional three bedrooms - the choice is yours.

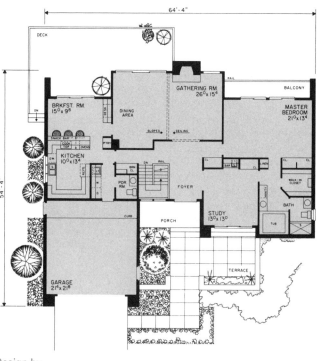

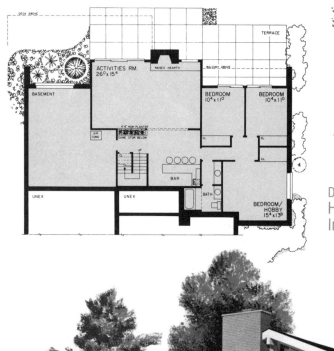

Design by
Home Planners, Inc.

162

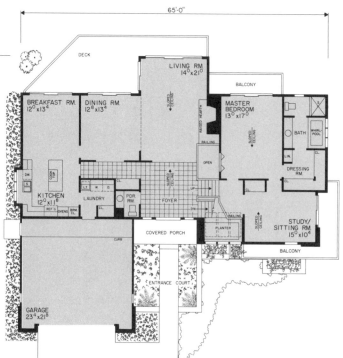

65'-0"

DECK

LIVING RM.
14⁰x21⁰

BALCONY

BREAKFAST RM.
12⁰x13⁴

DINING RM.
12⁸x13⁴

MASTER BEDROOM
13⁰x17⁰

BATH

WHIRL-POOL

KITCHEN
12⁰x11⁸

LAUNDRY

PDR RM.

FOYER

OPEN

RAILING

DRESSING RM.

STUDY/SITTING RM.
15⁰x10⁴

COVERED PORCH

PLANTER

BALCONY

ENTRANCE COURT

GARAGE
23⁴x21⁸

Design by
Home Planners,
Inc.

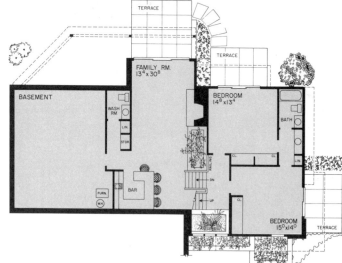

TERRACE

TERRACE

FAMILY RM.
13⁴x30⁸

BASEMENT

WASH RM.

BEDROOM
14⁸x13⁴

BATH

FURN.

BAR

BEDROOM
15⁰x14⁰

TERRACE

Design VH2679 Main Level: 1,179 square feet
Upper Level: 681 square feet; Lower Level: 680 square feet
Family Room Level: 643 square feet; Total: 3,183 square feet

● This spacious modern Contemporary home offers plenty of livability on many levels. Main level includes a breakfast room in addition to a dining room. Adjacent is a sloped-ceiling living room with raised hearth. The upper level features isolated master bedroom suite with adjoining study or sitting room and balcony. Family room level includes a long rectangular family room with adjoining terrace on one end and adjoining bar with washroom at the other end. A spacious basement is included. Two other bedrooms are positioned in the lower level with their own view of the terrace and quiet privacy. Note the rear deck.

Design VH2841

Main Level: 1,044 square feet; Upper Level: 851 square feet
Lower Level: 753 square feet; Total: 2,648 square feet

L

● This spacious tri-level with traditional stone exterior offers excellent comfort and zoning for the modern family. The rear opens to balconies and a deck that creates a covered patio below. A main floor gathering room is continued above with an upper gathering room. The lower level offers an activities room with raised hearth, in addition to an optional bunk room with bath. A modern kitchen on main level features a handy snack bar, in addition to a dining room. A study on main level could become an optional bedroom. The master bedroom is located on the upper level, along with a rectangular bunk room with its own balcony.

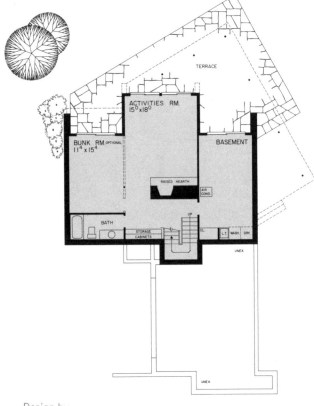

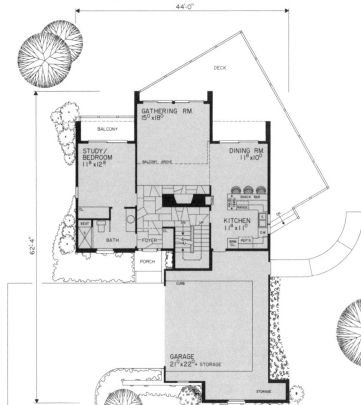

Design by
Home Planners,
Inc.

164

Design VH1974 Main Level: 1,680 square feet; Lower Level: 1,344 square feet; Total: 3,024 square feet

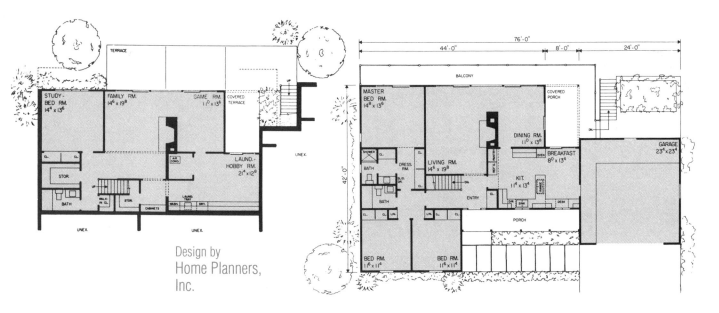

Design by
Home Planners,
Inc.

● You would never guess from looking at the front of this traditional design that it possessed such a strikingly different rear. From the front, you would guess that all of its livability is on one floor. Yet, just imagine the tremendous amount of livability that is added to the plan as a result of exposing the lower level - 1,344 square feet of it. Living in this hillside house will mean fun. Obviously, the most popular spot will be the balcony. Then again, maybe it could be the terrace adjacent to the family room. Both the terrace and the balcony have a covered area to provide protection against unfavorable weather. The interior of the plan also will serve the family with ease.

PLAN IS DESIGNED FOR
DAYLIGHT BASEMENT LOTS.

Design VH9537

Main Floor: 1,687 square feet
Lower Floor: 1,251 square feet
Total: 2,938 square feet

● This striking home is perfect for daylight basement lots. An elegant dining room fronts the plan. It is near an expansive kitchen that features plenty of cabinet and counter space. A nook surrounded by a deck adds character and the comfortable great room, with its raised ceiling and fireplace, enhances these areas. The master bedroom suite includes private deck access and a superb bath with a spa tub and dual lavatories. Downstairs, two bedrooms, a laundry room with lots of counter space and a rec room with a fireplace cap off this plan. A three-car garage furthers the custom feel of the home.

Design by
Alan Mascord
Design Associates, Inc.

Width 82'-7"
Depth 54'-9"

Design VH9539

Main Level: 2,219 square feet
Lower Level: 1,324 square feet
Total: 3,543 square feet

● Sleek lines define the contemporary feel of this home. Double entry doors lead to a columned gallery and an expressive great room. It showcases a fireplace, built-ins and a curving wall of windows. The nearby kitchen utilizes efficient zoning. A nook here opens to a wraparound deck. A dining room and a den finish the first-floor living areas. In the master bedroom suite, large proportions and an elegant bath with a see-through fireplace aim to please. The two bedrooms in the lower level have in-room vanities; one has direct access to the compartmented bath. A games room with a fireplace and built-ins leads to outdoor activities.

Design by
Alan Mascord
Design Associates, Inc.

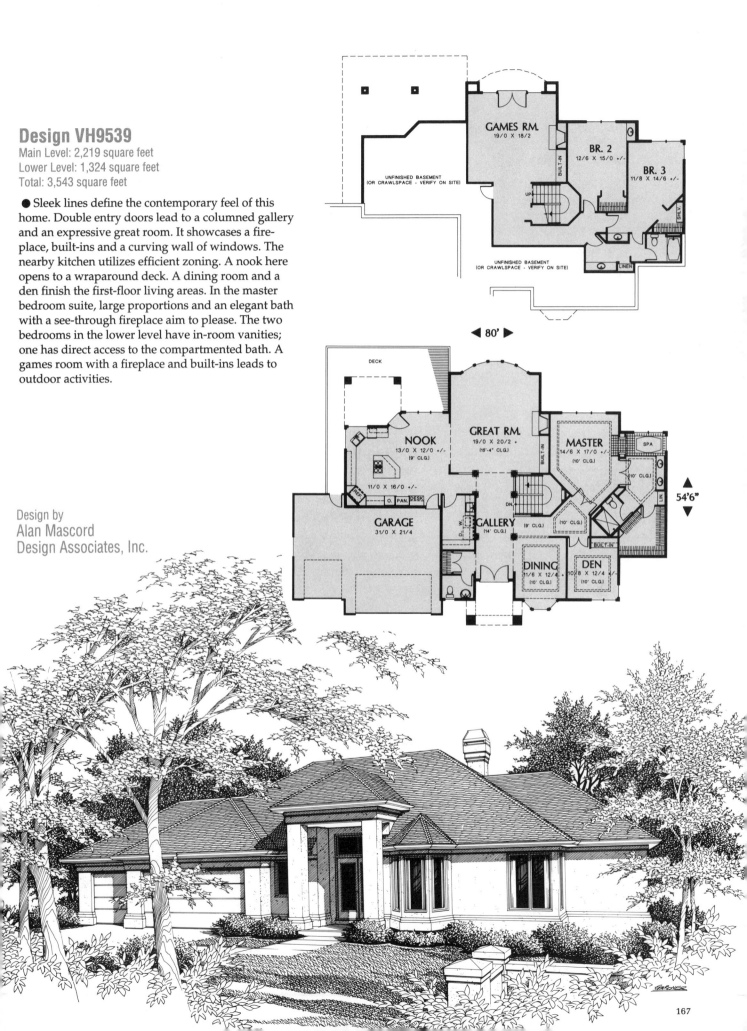

GAMES RM.
19/0 X 18/2

BR. 2
12/6 X 15/0 +/-

BR. 3
11/8 X 14/6 +/-

UNFINISHED BASEMENT
(OR CRAWLSPACE - VERIFY ON SITE)

UNFINISHED BASEMENT
(OR CRAWLSPACE - VERIFY ON SITE)

◀ 80' ▶

DECK

NOOK
13/0 X 12/0 +/-
(9' CLG.)

11/0 X 16/0 +/-

GREAT RM.
19/0 X 20/2 +
(15'-4" CLG.)

MASTER
14/6 X 17/0 +/-
(10' CLG.)

SPA

GARAGE
31/0 X 21/4

GALLERY
(14' CLG.)

DINING
11/6 X 12/4
(10' CLG.)

DEN
10/8 X 12/4
(10' CLG.)

54'6"

167

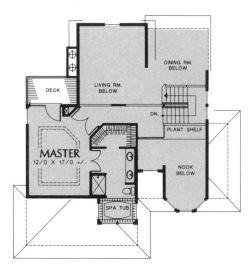

Design VH9510

Main Level: 800 square feet
Upper Level: 462 square feet
Lower Level: 732 square feet
Total: 1,994 square feet

● With undeniable style, this home would easily serve steep, daylight-basement lots. The lower level houses two bedrooms and the family room where sliding glass doors provide outdoor access. A utility area is tucked away near the full bath here. On the main level, the foyer opens to a two-story kitchen which affords room enough for a dinette set. A formal living room/dining room combination speaks for the rest of this level. Notice that the dining room is vaulted and enjoys a balcony overlooking the backyard. With true flair, the master bedroom impresses with its private upper-level location. A deck opens off the back of the room. The bath spoils with its dual lavatories and bumped-out spa tub.

Design by
Alan Mascord
Design Associates, Inc.

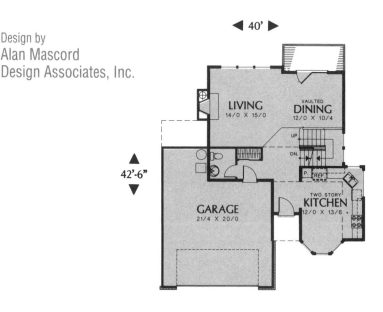

A-Frame Adaptations

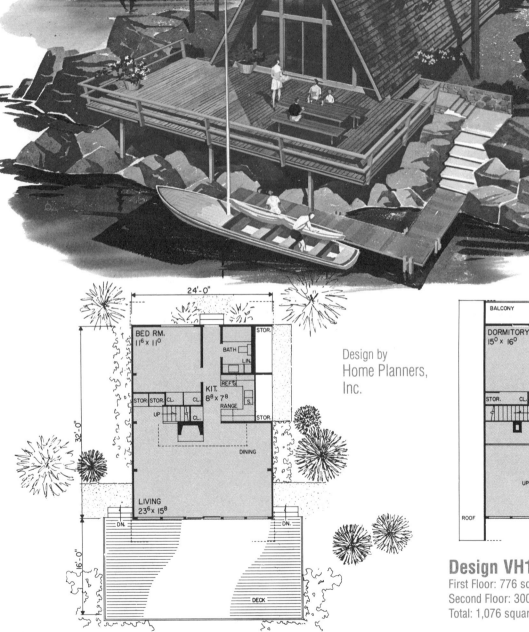

Design by
Home Planners,
Inc.

Design VH1406
First Floor: 776 square feet
Second Floor: 300 square feet
Total: 1,076 square feet

● A spacious 23-foot by 15-foot living room is really something to talk about. And when it has a high, vaulted ceiling and a complete wall of windows it is even more noteworthy. Because of the wonderful glass area, the livability of the living room seems to spill right out onto the huge wood deck. In addition to the bedroom downstairs, there is the sizable dormitory upstairs for sleeping quite a crew. Sliding glass doors open onto the outdoor balcony from the dormitory. Don't miss the fireplace, the efficient kitchen and the numerous storage facilities. The outside storage units are accessible from just below the roof line and are great for all the recreational equipment. Don't be without the exceptional wood deck. It will make a vital contribution to your outdoor vacation enjoyment.

Design by
Home Planners,
Inc.

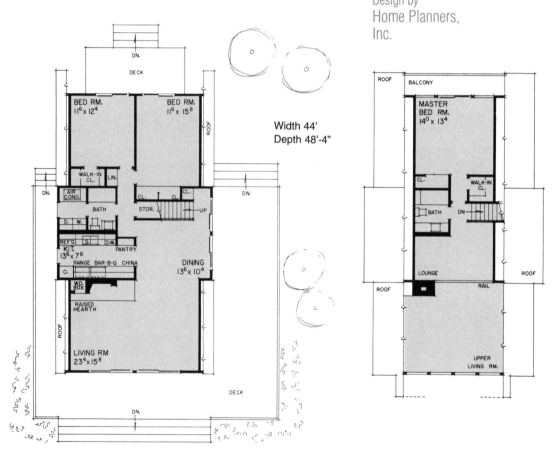

Width 44'
Depth 48'-4"

Design VH1451 First Floor: 1,224 square feet; Second Floor: 464 square feet; Total: 1,688 square feet

● This dramatic A-frame will surely command its share of attention wherever located. Its soaring roof and large glass areas put this design in a class all of its own. Raised wood decks on all sides provide delightful outdoor living areas. In addition, there is a balcony outside the second floor master bedroom. The living room will be the focal point of the interior. It will be wonderfully spacious with all that glass and the high roof. The attractive raised hearth fireplace will be a favorite feature. Another favored highlight will be the lounge area of the second floor where it is possible to look down into the living room. The work center has all the conveniences of home. Note the barbecue unit, pantry and china cabinet which are sure to help provide ease of living.

Design VH1448

First Floor: 776 square feet
Second Floor: 300 square feet
Total: 1,076 square feet

● This sun-filled A-frame will be a welcome addition to any setting. The 23-foot living room offers a comfortable fireplace and plenty of room for a dining area with the added luxury of a snack-bar pass-through to the U-shaped kitchen. While the master bedroom is located downstairs for privacy, additional sleeping arrangements are available in the upstairs dormitory with its own special balcony. Notice the abundant storage space available on both floors and the large deck for outdoor entertaining.

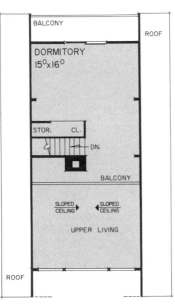

BALCONY

ROOF

DORMITORY
15⁰x16⁰

STOR.   CL.

DN.

BALCONY

SLOPED CEILING   SLOPED CEILING

UPPER LIVING

ROOF

Design by
Home Planners, Inc.

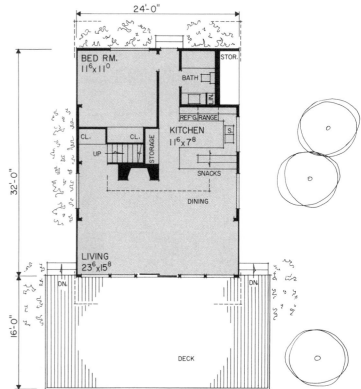

24'-0"

BED RM.
11⁶x11⁰

STOR.

BATH

REF'G. RANGE

CL.   CL.

KITCHEN
11⁶x7⁸

S.

UP   STORAGE

SNACKS

DINING

32'-0"

LIVING
23⁶x15⁸

DN.   DN.

16'-0"

DECK

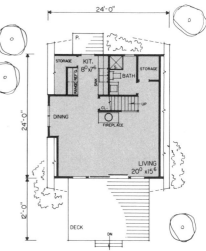

Design VH1490

First Floor: 576 square feet; Second Floor: 362 square feet; Total: 938 square feet

● Wherever situated—in the northern woods, or on the southern coast—these enchanting A-frames will function as perfect retreats. Whether called upon to serve as ski lodges or summer havens, they will perform admirably. The size of the first floor of each design is identical. However, the layouts are quite different. Design VH1490 has a two-bedroom second floor while Design VH1491, below, has a loft on the second floor.

Design by
Home Planners,
Inc.

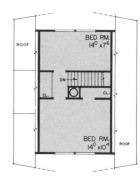

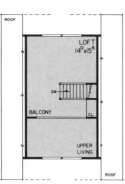

Design VH1491

First Floor: 576 square feet; Second Floor: 234 square feet; Total: 810 square feet

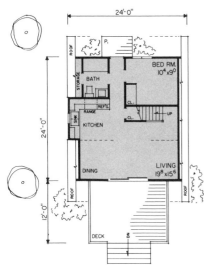

Design VH1470

First Floor: 1,000 square feet; Second Floor: 482 square feet
Loft: 243 square feet; Total: 1,725 square feet

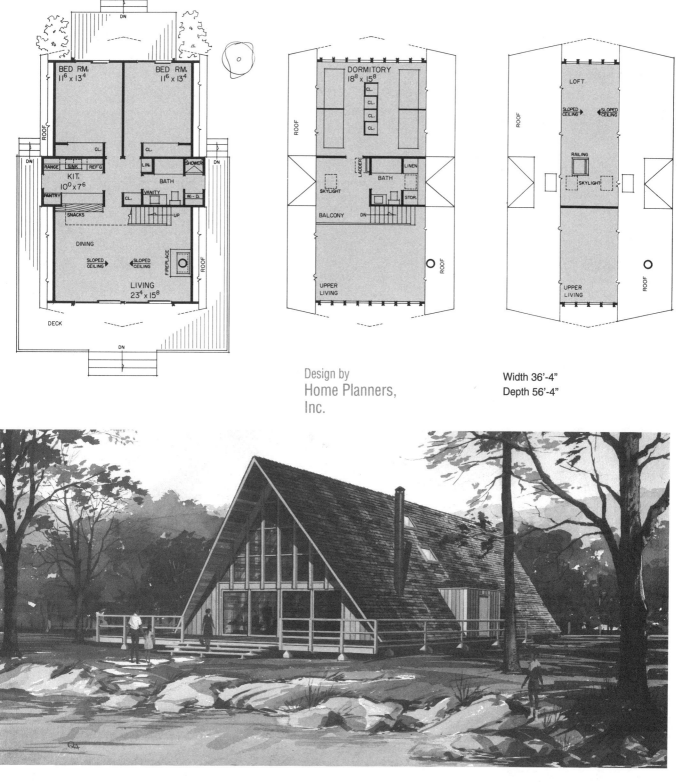

Design by
**Home Planners,
Inc.**

Width 36'-4"
Depth 56'-4"

● Three-level, A-frame living can be dramatic and, also, offer your family living patterns that will be a lot of fun all throughout the year. The ceiling of the living room soars upward to an apex of approximately twenty-four feet. Both the second floor and the upper level loft can look down into the living room below. The wall of glass permits a fine view of the outdoors from each of these levels. With all those sleeping facilities even the largest of families will have space left over for a few extra friends. Note two baths, efficient kitchen, snack bar and deck which are available to serve your everyday needs. A home to be enjoyed no matter what the occasion.

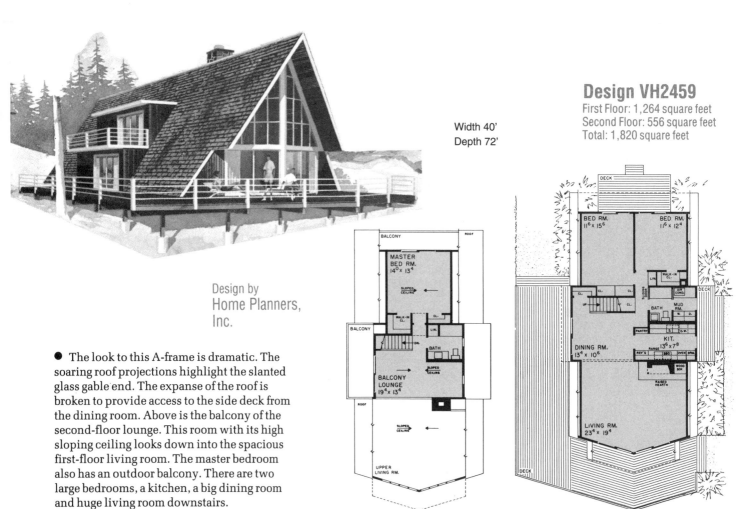

Design VH2459

Width 40'
Depth 72'

First Floor: 1,264 square feet
Second Floor: 556 square feet
Total: 1,820 square feet

Design by
Home Planners,
Inc.

● The look to this A-frame is dramatic. The soaring roof projections highlight the slanted glass gable end. The expanse of the roof is broken to provide access to the side deck from the dining room. Above is the balcony of the second-floor lounge. This room with its high sloping ceiling looks down into the spacious first-floor living room. The master bedroom also has an outdoor balcony. There are two large bedrooms, a kitchen, a big dining room and huge living room downstairs.

Design by
Home Planners,
Inc.

Width 44'
Depth 80'-2"

Design VH1432 First Floor: 1,512 square feet
Second Floor: 678 square feet; Total: 2,190 square feet

● Perhaps more than any other design in recent years the A-frame has captured the imagination of the prospective vacation home builder. There is a gala air about its shape that fosters a holiday spirit whether the house be a summer retreat or a structure for year 'round living. This particular A-frame offers a lot of living with five bedrooms, two baths, an efficient kitchen, a family/dining area, and outstanding storage. As in most designs of this type, the living room with its great height and large glass area is extremely dramatic at first sight.

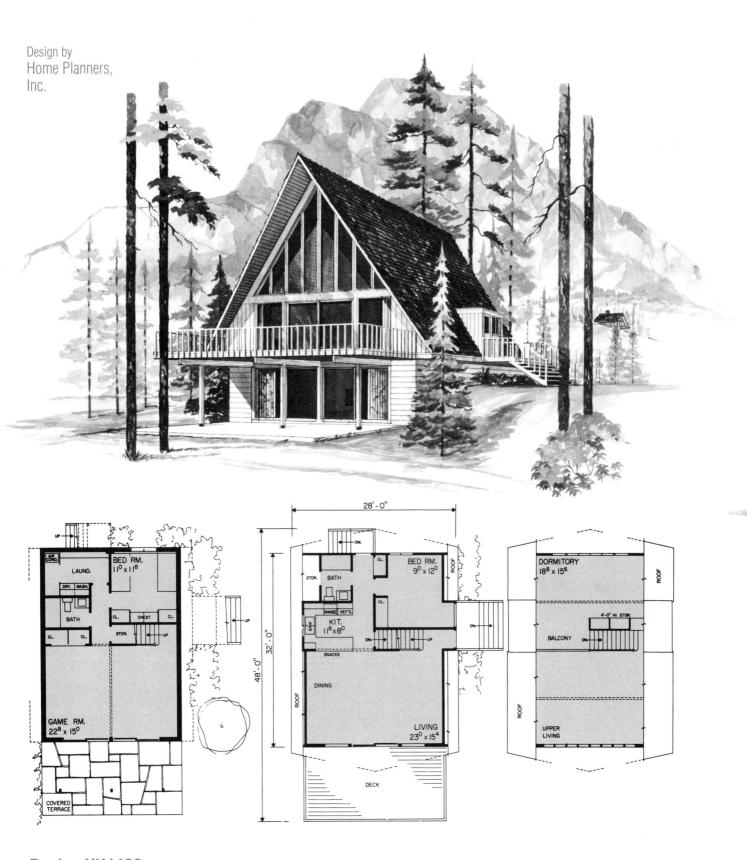

Design by
Home Planners,
Inc.

Design VH1499 Main Level: 896 square feet; Upper Level: 298 square feet; Lower Level: 896 square feet; Total: 2,090 square feet

● Three level living results in family living patterns which will foster a delightful feeling of informality. Upon arrival at this charming second home, each family member will enthusiastically welcome the change in environment – both indoors and out. Whether looking down into the living room from the dormitory balcony, or walking through the sliding doors onto the huge deck, or participating in some family activity in the game room, everyone will count the hours spent here as relaxing ones. Study the plan carefully. Note the sleeping facilities on each of the three levels. Two bedrooms and a dormitory in all to sleep the family and friends comfortably. There are two full baths, a separate laundry room and plenty of storage. Don't miss the efficient U-shaped kitchen.

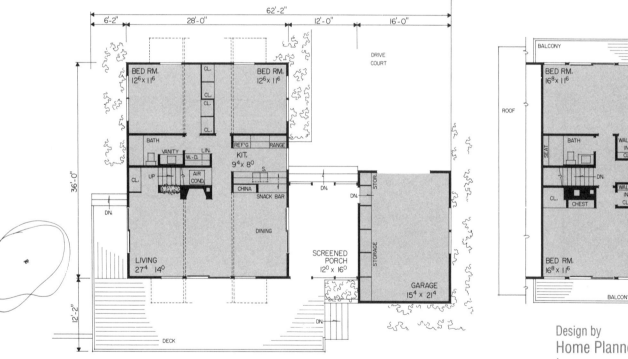

Design by
Home Planners,
Inc.

Design VH1422 First Floor: 1,008 square feet; Second Floor: 624 square feet; Total: 1,632 square feet

● The chalet influence takes over on this design. If you have a big family, the four bedrooms of this vacation home will force you to take the second look. Notice the balcony off of each bedroom on the second floor and the

fact that each bedroom has a walk-in closet. The first floor highlights many features highly desirable in the year-round home. Among these are the open-stairway with planter, the fireplace, the china cabinet and snack bar,

the bathroom vanity and the efficient kitchen which will be free of unnecessary thru traffic. Outdoor living will be enjoyed on the two outdoor balconies, the deck and even the screened-in porch between house and **garage**.

Design VH1475

First Floor: 1,120 square feet
Second Floor: 522 square feet
Lower Level: 616 square feet
Total: 2,258 square feet

● Built to accommodate
the slopes, this hillside
design with an exposed
lower level meets winter
vacation needs without a
second thought. The cov-
ered lower terrace is the
ideal entrance to a ski
lounge with raised-hearth
fireplace and walk-in ski
storage area. The main floor
holds sloped-ceilinged dining and living areas (with
another raised hearth here),
a kitchen with a patio, two
bedrooms and a full bath.
Enjoy the view from the
balcony lounge on the
second floor where there
are two more bedrooms
and another full bath.

Design by
Home Planners,
Inc.

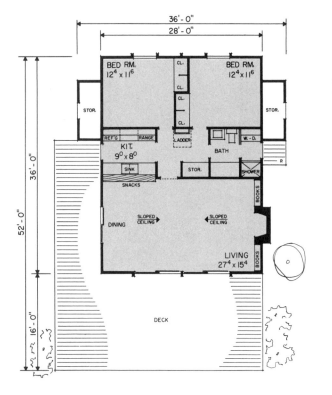

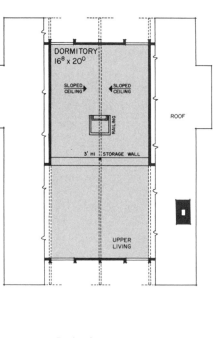

Design by
Home Planners,
Inc.

Design VH1472 First Floor: 1,008 square feet; Second Floor: 546 square feet; Total: 1,554 square feet

● Wherever perched, this smart leisure-time home will surely make your visits memorable ones. The large living area with its sloped ceiling, dramatic expanses of glass and attractive fireplace will certainly offer the proper atmosphere for quiet relaxation. Keeping house will be no chore for the weekend homemaker. The kitchen is compact and efficient. There is plenty of storage space for all the necessary recreational equipment. There is a full bath and even a stall shower accessible from the outside for use by the swimmers. A ladder leads to the second floor sloped ceiling dormitory which overlooks the living/dining area. Ideal for the younger generation.

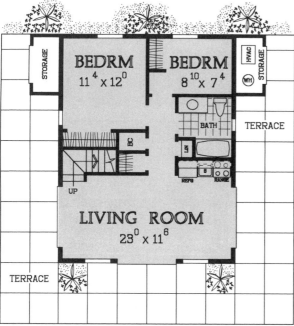

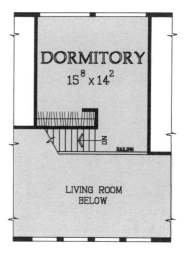

Width 32'
Depth 30'

Design VH3658

First Floor: 960 square feet
Second Floor: 302 square feet
Total: 1,262 square feet

L **D**

● This chalet-type vacation home with its steep, overhanging roof, will catch the eye of even the most casual onlooker. It is designed to be completely livable whether the season be for swimming or skiing. The dormitory on the upper level will sleep many vacationers, while the two bedrooms on the first floor provide the more convenient and conventional sleeping facilities. The upper level overlooks the beam-ceilinged living and dining area. With a wraparound terrace and plenty of storage space, what more could you ask for?

Design by
Home Planners,
Inc.

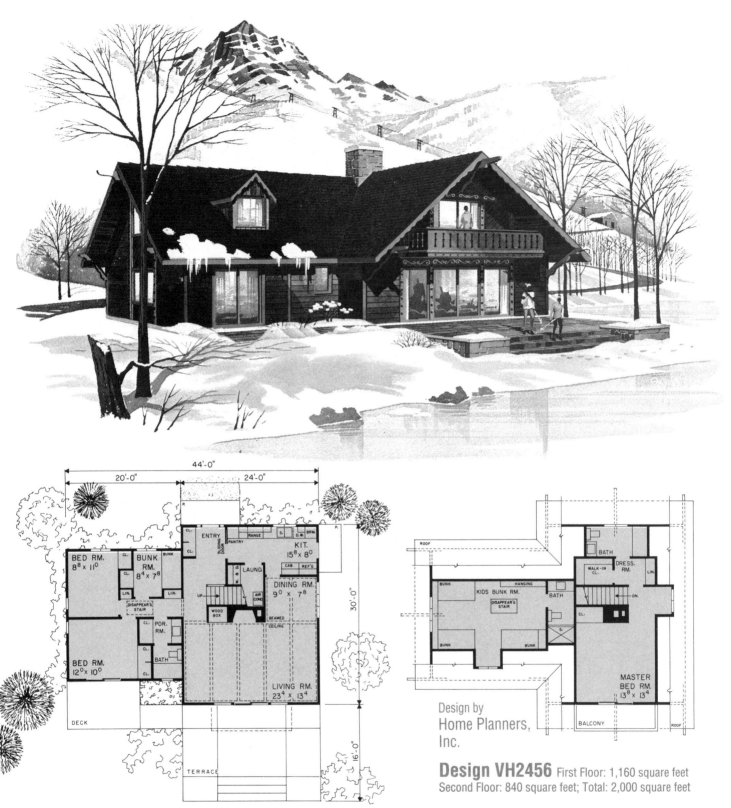

Design by
Home Planners, Inc.

Design VH2456 First Floor: 1,160 square feet
Second Floor: 840 square feet; Total: 2,000 square feet

● Here's how your Swiss chalet adaptation may look in the winter. Certainly an appealing design whatever the season. A delightful haven for skiers, fishermen and hunters alike. As for sleeping facilities, you'll really be able to pack 'em in. The first floor has two bedrooms plus a room which will take a double bunk. Across the hall is the compartment bath. A disappearing stair unit leads to the children's bunk room. The placement of single bunks or cots will permit the sleeping of three or four more. A bath with stall shower is nearby. The master bedroom suite is complete with walk-in closet, dressing room and private bath and opens onto the balcony. There is plenty of space in the L-shaped living-dining area with wood box and fireplace to accommodate the whole gang.

● It will not make any difference where you locate this chalet-type second home. The atmosphere it creates will be one for true leisure living. To guarantee sheer enjoyment you wouldn't even have to be situated close to the water. And little wonder with such an array of features as: the big deck, the fine porch and the two balconies. For complete livability there are four bedrooms, two full baths, an outstanding U-shaped kitchen, a large living area with a raised hearth fireplace and a super-abundance of closet and storage facilities. Of particular interest is the direct access from outdoors to the first floor bath with its stall shower.

Design VH2412

First Floor: 1,120 square feet
Second Floor: 664 square feet
Total: 1,784 square feet

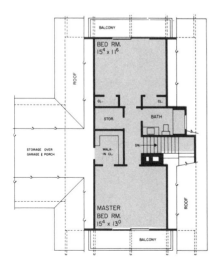

Design by
Home Planners,
Inc.

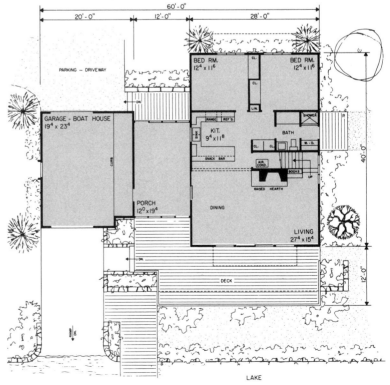

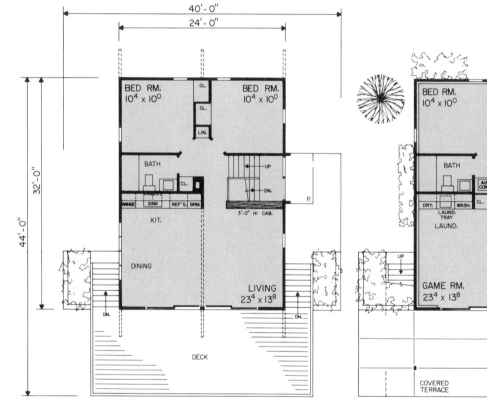

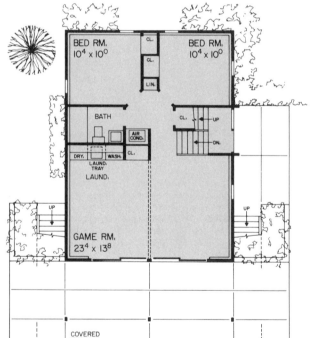

Labels on upper-level floor plan (left):

40'-0"
24'-0"
32'-0"
44'-0"

BED RM.
10⁴ x 10⁰

CL.
CL.
LIN.

BED RM.
10⁴ x 10⁰

BATH

UP
DN.

CL.

RANGE | SINK | REF'G. | BRM.

3'-0" HI CAB.

P.

KIT.

DINING

LIVING
23⁴ x 13⁸

DN.
DN.

DECK

Labels on lower-level floor plan (right):

BED RM.
10⁴ x 10⁰

CL.
LIN.

BED RM.
10⁴ x 10⁰

BATH

AIR COND.

CL.

UP
DN.

DRY. | WASH. | CL.

LAUND. TRAY

LAUND.

UP

UP

GAME RM.
23⁴ x 13⁸

COVERED TERRACE

Design VH2420 Upper Level: 768 square feet
Lower Level: 768 square feet; Total: 1,536 square feet

● Two-level living can be fun anytime. When it comes to two-level living at the lake, seashore or in the woods, the experience will be positively delightful. Two huge living areas include a lower-level game room with two bedrooms and a full bath nearby, and an upper-level living room with another two bedrooms, a full bath and a kitchen nearby.

Design by
Home Planners,
Inc.

Design VH1444

First Floor: 1,008 square feet
Second Floor: 624 square feet
Total: 1,632 square feet

● Everybody will have fun spending their vacations at this cottage. And why shouldn't they? The pleasant experiences of vacation living will be more than just sitting on the outdoor balconies of the second floor. They will include eating leisurely on the dining deck and lounging peacefully on the living deck. Further, they will encompass the relaxing hours spent before the cheerful fireplace in the living room on cool evenings.

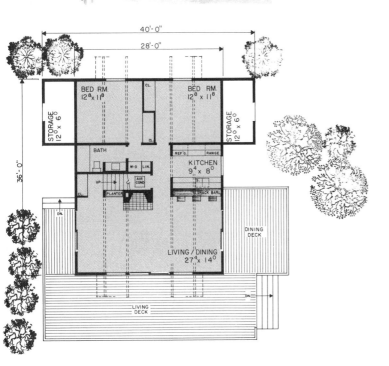

Design by
Home Planners,
Inc.

Design VH1482

First Floor: 1,008 square feet
Second Floor: 637 square feet
Total: 1,645 square feet

Design by
Home Planners,
Inc.

● Five bedrooms and a 27-foot living area! This darling chalet will take on the whole gang. A fireplace provides a warm glow and a snack bar in the kitchen means carefree dining. This plan also offers two full baths (one with access from outside and with a laundry area) and a second-floor master bedroom with a balcony overlooking the wood deck below.

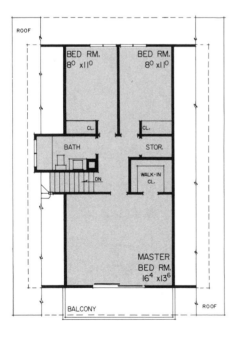

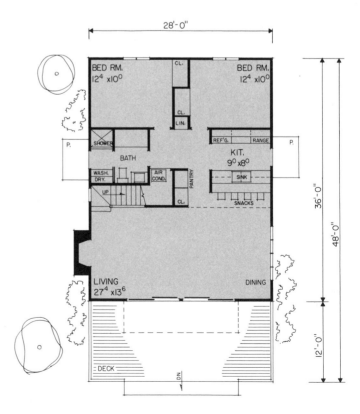

Design VH2427 First Floor: 784 square feet
Second Floor: 504 square feet; Total: 1,288 square feet

Design by
Home Planners,
Inc.

● Make your vacation dreams a reality with this fabulous chalet. A wood deck stretches the width of the house and finds the living room nearby. The kitchen utilizes a dining area and an efficient layout. A first-floor bedroom enjoys the use of a full hall bath. Upstairs, focus your attention on the master bedroom with its wall of closets and balcony. A dormitory sits across the hall from the master bedroom and leaves room for all the kids. Storage space abounds in this design—perfect for all of your seasonal storage needs.

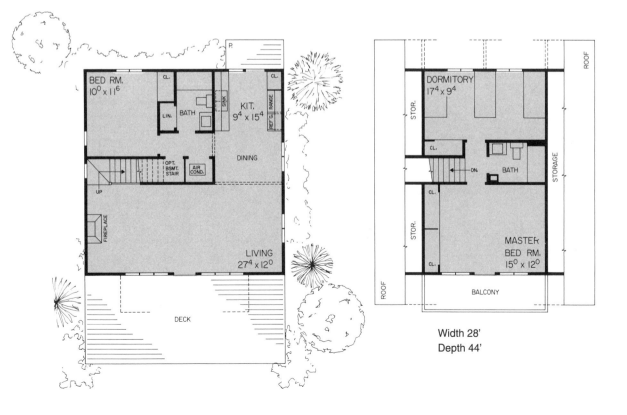

Width 28'
Depth 44'

Design VH2429

Main Level: 672 square feet
Upper Level: 672 square feet
Lower Level: 672 square feet
Total: 2,016 square feet

● Build your own mountain chalet with deck space galore to enjoy the outdoors in any season! Beamed ceilings throughout the main level and a raised-hearth fireplace with a wood box give this open area a feeling of coziness. You'll enjoy casual times in the lower-level ski lounge where another fireplace is located. Boots and wet outer wear can be shed upon entry to the wet hall which has easy access to the laundry room and a full bath. A work room on this level provides ample space for any project. Sleeping quarters are found on the upper level which has three bedrooms (two overlook the balcony) and two full baths.

Design by
Home Planners,
Inc.

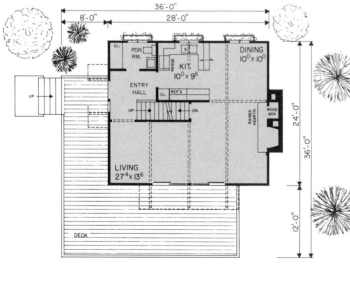

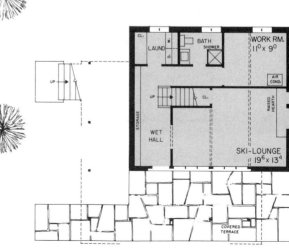

● Here is the epitome of private ski lodges. Or, if you live in an area where there is no snow, this will be a great chalet for just plain enjoying the surrounding green countryside. Whatever the environment, this retreat will serve its occupants to perfection. And little wonder. There are three levels of livability. There is plenty of space – from the lower level lounge, to the 35 foot living room, to the upper level dormitory. Note the two fireplaces, the fine kitchen, the excellent bath facilities and the outdoor decks and balconies.

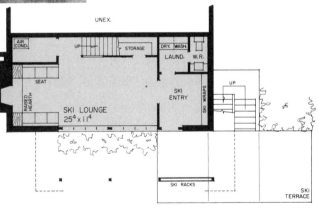

Design by
Home Planners,
Inc.

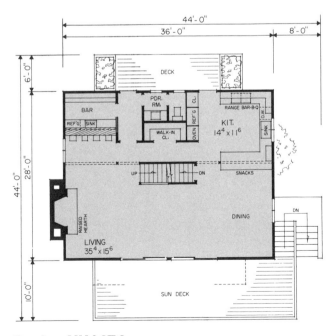

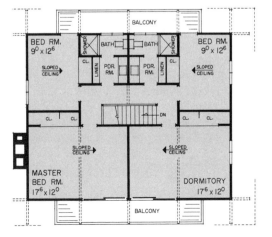

Design VH1474 Main Level: 1,008 square feet; Upper Level: 1,008 square feet; Lower Level: 594 square feet; Total: 2,610 square feet

Design VH2431

First Floor: 1,057 square feet
Second Floor: 406 square feet
Total: 1,463 square feet

● Dramatic use of glass and sweeping lines characterize a classic favorite—the A-frame. The sloped ceiling and exposed beams in the living room are gorgeous touches complemented by a wide deck for enjoying fresh air. The convenience of the central bath with attached powder room is accentuated by space here for a washer and dryer. The truly outstanding feature of this plan, however, is its magnificent master suite. There's a private balcony outside and a balcony lounge inside—the scenery is splendid from every angle.

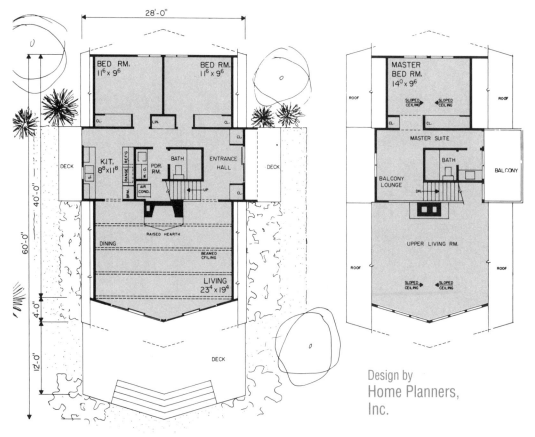

Design by
Home Planners,
Inc.

Contemporary Choices

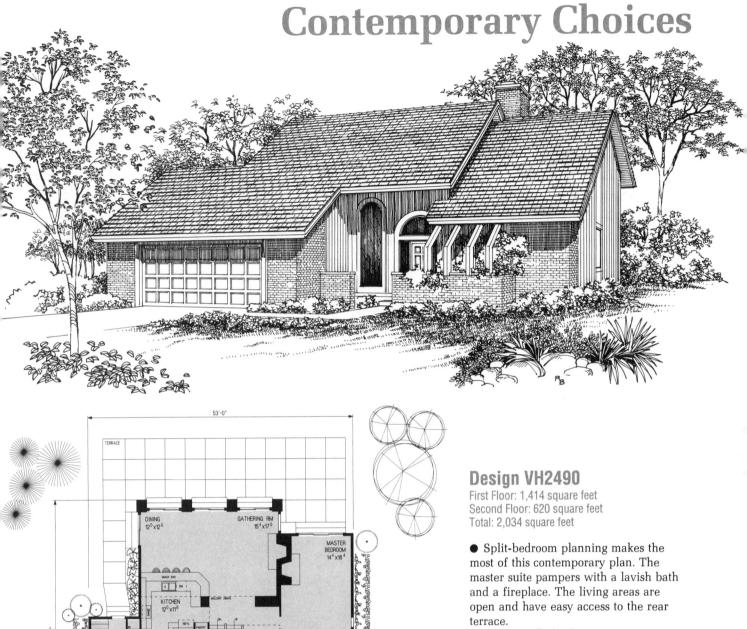

Design VH2490

First Floor: 1,414 square feet
Second Floor: 620 square feet
Total: 2,034 square feet

● Split-bedroom planning makes the most of this contemporary plan. The master suite pampers with a lavish bath and a fireplace. The living areas are open and have easy access to the rear terrace.

Design by
Home Planners,
Inc.

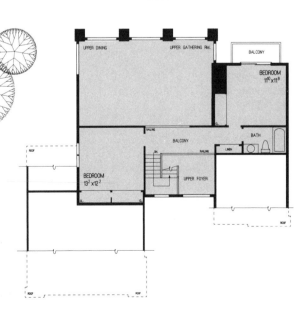

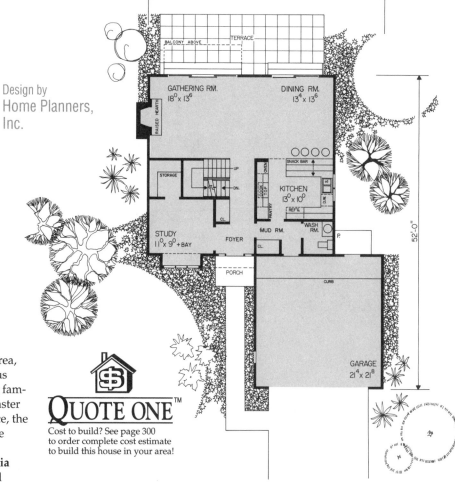

Design by
Home Planners,
Inc.

Design VH2711

First Floor: 975 square feet
Second Floor: 1,024 square feet
Total: 1,999 square feet

● Sleek, affordable style. The large dining area, kitchen, mudroom off the garage and spacious bedroom are key selling points for the young family. Also notice the private balcony off the master suite, the cozy study with lots of storage space, the terrace to the rear of the house and the sizable snack bar for the kids—and adults.

California Engineered Plans and California Stock Plans are available for this home. Call 1-800-521-6797 for more information.

QUOTE ONE™

Cost to build? See page 300
to order complete cost estimate
to build this house in your area!

Design VH2488 First Floor: 1,113 square feet
Second Floor: 543 square feet; Total: 1,656 square feet

D

Design by
Home Planners,
Inc.

QUOTE ONE™
Cost to build? See page 300
to order complete cost estimate
to build this house in your area!

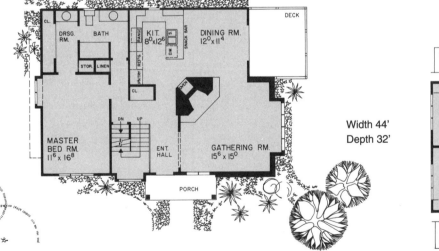

Width 44'
Depth 32'

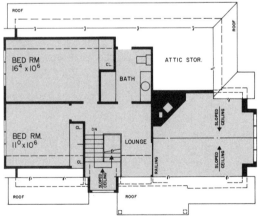

● Whether called upon to serve the young active family or used as an empty-nester home, this charming design will perform well. The upstairs, with its two sizable bedrooms, full bath and lounge area looking down into the gathering room, will ideally accommodate the younger members of the household. If functioning as a retirement home, the second floor caters to visiting family members and friends. Other uses for the second floor may include an office, a study, a sewing room, a music room, or a hobby room to name a few—the choices are many.

California Engineered Plans and California Stock Plans are available for this home. Call 1-800-521-6797 for more information.

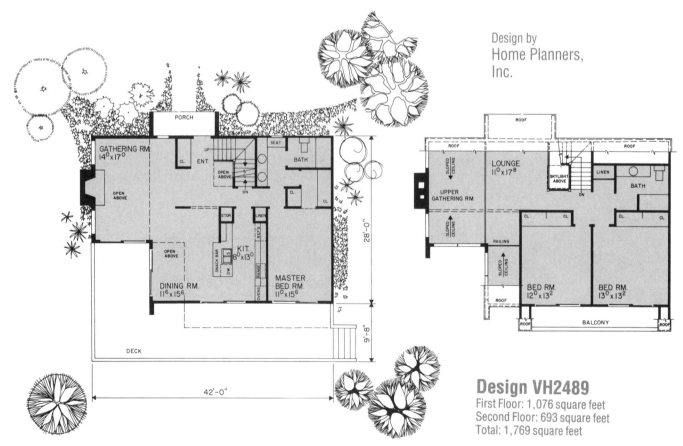

Design by
Home Planners,
Inc.

Design VH2489

First Floor: 1,076 square feet
Second Floor: 693 square feet
Total: 1,769 square feet

● Outdoors-oriented families will appreciate the dramatic sliding glass doors and the sweeping decks that make this contemporary perfect. The plan of the first floor features a spacious two-story gathering room with sloping ceiling, a large fireplace and access to the large deck which runs the full length of the house. Also having direct access to the deck is the dining room which is half-open to the second floor above. A snack bar divides the dining room from the compact kitchen. The master bedroom is outstanding with its private bath, walk-in closet and sliding glass door. The second floor is brightened by a skylight and houses two bedrooms, lounge and full bath.

Photos by Andrew D. Lautman

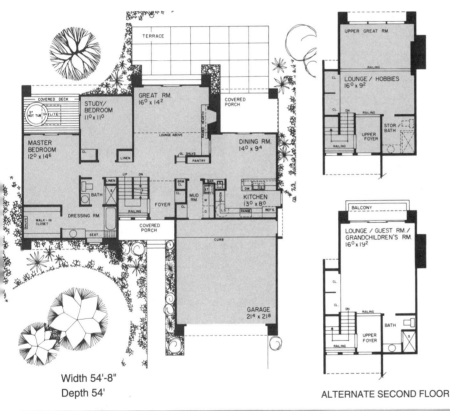

Width 54'-8"
Depth 54'

ALTERNATE SECOND FLOOR

Design VH2822

First Floor: 1,363 square feet
Second Floor: 351 square feet
Total: 1,714 square feet

● Tailor-made for small families and empty-nesters, this is basically a one-level design with second-floor possibilities. The room upstairs (see alternate layouts) can be nearly anything you want it to be: lounge, guest room, play room for the kids or grandchildren, partitioned or open. Downstairs, a little space goes a long way. In less than 1,400 square feet is the great room with a fireplace, a separate dining room with an adjacent porch, a study/bedroom, and a sizable master suite.

California Engineered Plans and California Stock Plans are available for this home. Call 1-800-521-6797 for more information.

Design by
Home Planners,
Inc.

QUOTE ONE™
Cost to build? See page 300
to order complete cost estimate
to build this house in your area!

193

Design VH9614

First Floor: 1,345 square feet
Second Floor: 536 square feet
Total: 1,881 square feet

● An elegant exterior combines with a functional interior to offer an exciting design for the contemporary-minded. Notice the cheery sun room that captures the heat of the sun. The master suite and the great room both have access to this bright space through sliding glass doors. A U-shaped kitchen has a window garden, a breakfast bar and ample cabinet space. Note how the great-room ceiling, with exposed wood beams, slopes from the deck up to operable clerestory windows at the study/play area on the second level. Also notice the bonus storage space in the attic over the garage. Please specify basement or crawlspace foundation when ordering.

Design by
Donald A.
Gardner,
Architects, Inc.

FRONT

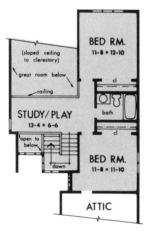

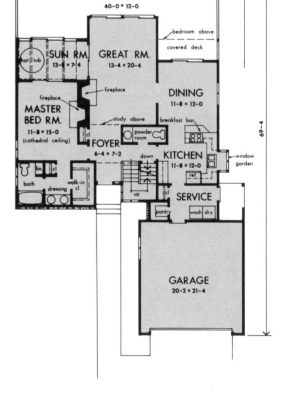

REAR

194

FRONT

Design VH9613

First Floor: 1,340 square feet
Second Floor: 504 square feet
Total: 1,844 square feet

● Because this home's sun room is a full two stories high, it acts as a solar collector when oriented to the south. Enjoying the benefits of this warmth are the dining room and great room on the first floor, and the master suite on the second floor. A spacious deck further extends the outdoor living potential. Special features to be found in this house include: a sloped ceiling with exposed wood beams and a fireplace in the great room; a cathedral ceiling, a fireplace, built-in shelves and ample closet space in the master bedroom; clerestory windows and a balcony overlook in the upstairs study; and convenient storage space in the attic over the garage. Please specify basement or crawlspace foundation when ordering.

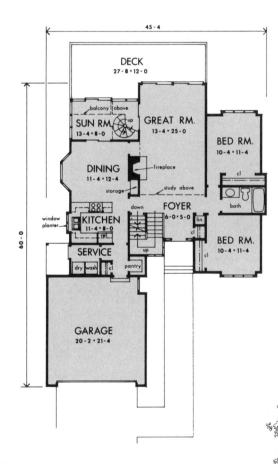

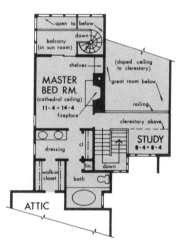

Design by
Donald A.
Gardner,
Architects, Inc.

REAR

195

Design VH8891

First Floor: 1,689 square feet
Second Floor: 534 square feet
Total: 2,223 square feet

● Interesting lattice detail, a combination of brick and shingle siding and rounded accent walls make this home unique in appearance. Inside, smaller front living and dining rooms are augmented by larger rear-oriented family and breakfast areas. A courtyard circled off the family room focuses the start of yard development and highlights

the forms of the house. The luxurious and stylish master bedroom suite has a very special bath with a platform tub divided from the glass-walled shower. Upstairs, two bedrooms and a loft share ample proportions and a hall bath. The two-car garage connects to the laundry/mudroom.

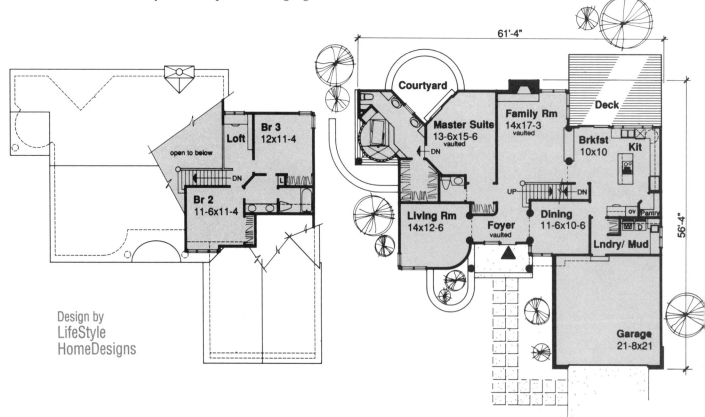

Design by
LifeStyle
HomeDesigns

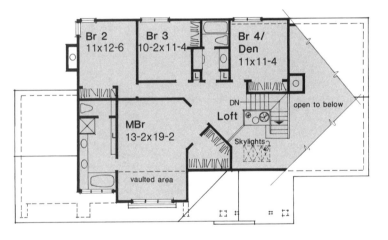

Br 2
11x12-6

Br 3
10-2x11-4

Br 4/
Den
11x11-4

DN

open to below

MBr
13-2x19-2

Loft

Skylights

vaulted area

Design by
LifeStyle
HomeDesigns

Design VH8899

First Floor: 1,290 square feet
Second Floor: 1,155 square feet
Total: 2,445 square feet

● A vaulted, skylit foyer with a dramatic staircase opens this plan. To the right, a gracious living room with a fireplace opens to a dining room. The full kitchen is conveniently located between the dining room and the breakfast room. The family room features a central hearth and built-in cabinets. A rear deck enhances outdoor livability. On the second floor, four bedrooms–or three and a den–include a spacious master suite. Its bath extends a separate shower and tub and dual lavatories.

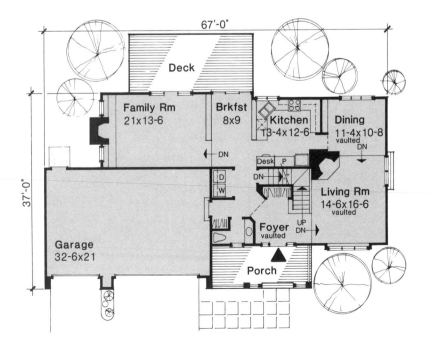

67'-0"

Deck

Family Rm
21x13-6

Brkfst
8x9

Kitchen
13-4x12-6

Dining
11-4x10-8
vaulted

DN

DN

Desk

P

37'-0"

D
W

DN

Living Rm
14-6x16-6
vaulted

Garage
32-6x21

Foyer
vaulted

UP
DN

Porch

Design VH9413

First Floor: 1,076 square feet
Second Floor: 819 square feet
Total: 1,895 square feet

● Consider this compact contemporary with a flair for the dramatic. The entry, den and great room feature impressive vaulted ceilings. Note that the great room has a floor that is sunken two steps; the den is accessed through French doors from the entry. An elegant master suite features a spa tub, large shower and walk-in closet. Don't miss the additional shop or storage area built out along one side of the garage.

Design by
Alan Mascord
Design Associates, Inc.

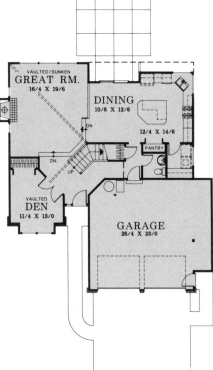

Design VH9505

First Floor: 960 square feet
Second Floor: 968 square feet
Total: 1,928 square feet

● Multi-level rooflines and a two-story foyer lend interest to this four-bedroom plan. The living room, with its stepped ceiling, serves as an elegant prelude to the dining room at the back of the house. A central kitchen services a bumped-out nook and a large family room with a fireplace. A powder room, with a window for natural light, rests across from the utility room. Access to the two-car garage is gained from this area. The master bedroom dominates the upstairs with a double-door entry, a stepped ceiling and a private bath with a spa tub. Three bedrooms—at the rear of the second floor—share a full hall bath. An open stairwell affords a grand view of the foyer below.

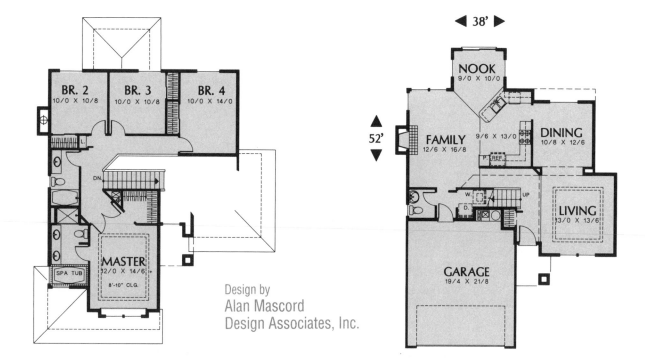

Design by
Alan Mascord
Design Associates, Inc.

Design VH4153 First Floor: 893 square feet
Second Floor: 549 square feet; Total: 1,442 square feet

L D

Design by
Home Planners,
Inc.

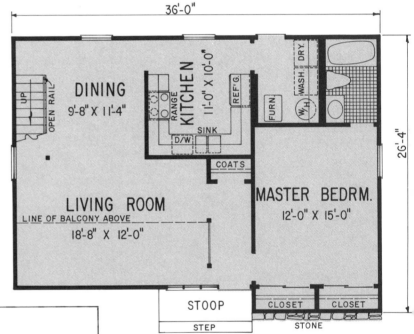

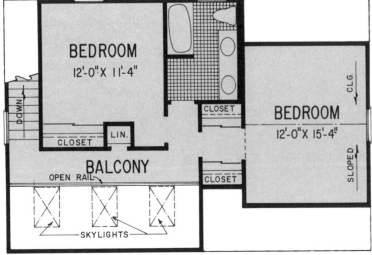

● The rectangular shape of this design will make it an economical and easy-to-build choice for those wary of high construction costs. The first floor benefits from the informality of open planning; the living room and dining room combine to make one large living space. The partitioned kitchen is conveniently adjacent yet keeps the cooking process out of the living area. Also downstairs is the master bedroom and bath. The second floor houses two large bedrooms, a full bath, and a balcony over the living room. Notice the skylights.

Design VH4210

Entry Level: 768 square feet
Upper Level: 288 square feet
Total: 1,056 square feet

● This unusual contemporary design has a refreshingly simple interior layout, with deck access at three points. Two bedrooms, one upstairs and one down, round out a floor plan that has an L-shaped kitchen with pantry, and a hearthwarmed living room. Two full baths are conveniently located near the bedrooms.

Design by
Home Planners,
Inc.

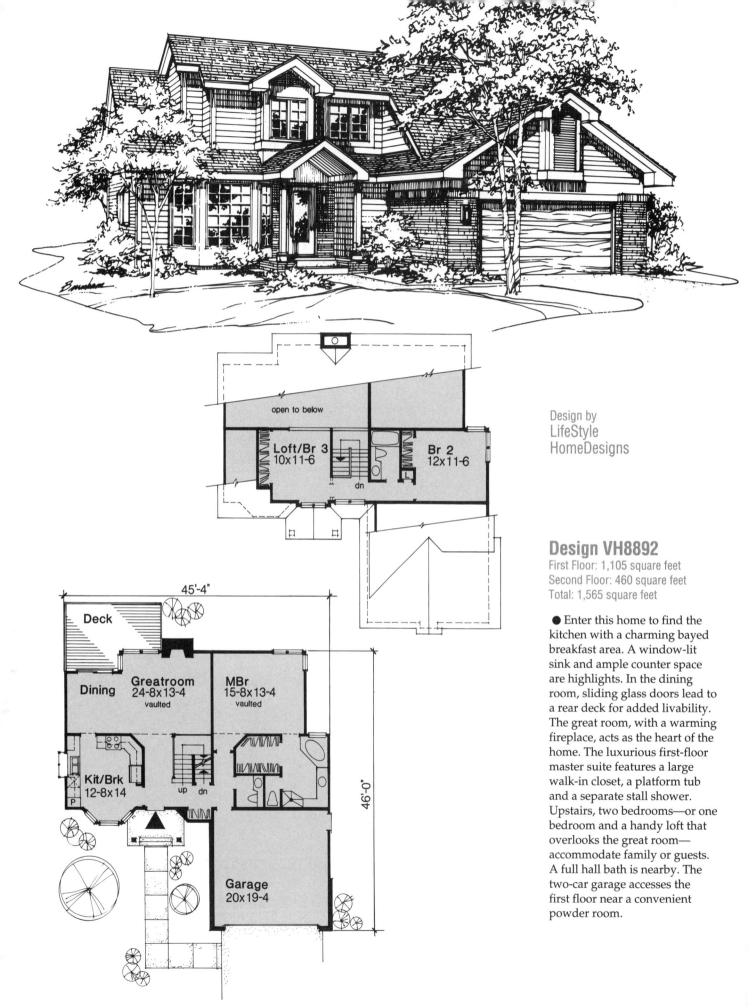

Design by
LifeStyle
HomeDesigns

Design VH8892

First Floor: 1,105 square feet
Second Floor: 460 square feet
Total: 1,565 square feet

● Enter this home to find the kitchen with a charming bayed breakfast area. A window-lit sink and ample counter space are highlights. In the dining room, sliding glass doors lead to a rear deck for added livability. The great room, with a warming fireplace, acts as the heart of the home. The luxurious first-floor master suite features a large walk-in closet, a platform tub and a separate stall shower. Upstairs, two bedrooms—or one bedroom and a handy loft that overlooks the great room— accommodate family or guests. A full hall bath is nearby. The two-car garage accesses the first floor near a convenient powder room.

Design VH8898

First Floor: 1,075 square feet
Second Floor: 816 square feet
Total: 1,891 square feet

● The vaulted entry area of this home will impress visitors. The great room features a vaulted ceiling shared with the dining room. The U-shaped kitchen serves the family room with a pass-through. A bay window and deck access make the family room extra special, as does a warming hearth. A utility room and a powder room lead to the two-car garage. Upstairs, three bedrooms include a master bedroom suite with an efficient, private bath and two closets. The secondary bedrooms share a full hall bath.

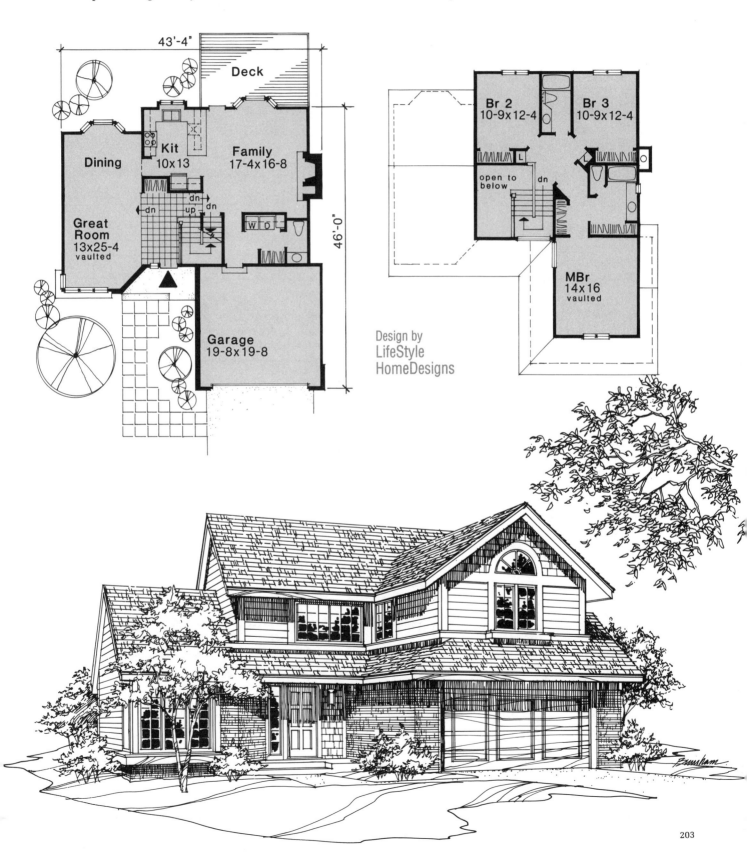

Design by
LifeStyle
HomeDesigns

Design VH2430

First Floor: 1,238 square feet
Second Floor: 648 square feet
Total: 1,886 square feet

● A retreat for all seasons, this chalet adaptation is as functional as it is attractive. A large terrace is overhung by a balcony off the second-floor master bedroom; a second balcony is found outside another bedroom on this floor. The first-floor living room and two bedrooms have ceilings with exposed beams for a country-casual look. The large kitchen with an attached dining area will handle a hungry crew well. The centrally located fireplace in the living room keeps everyone cozy. Conveniently located in the garage at the kitchen entrance is a lake bath.

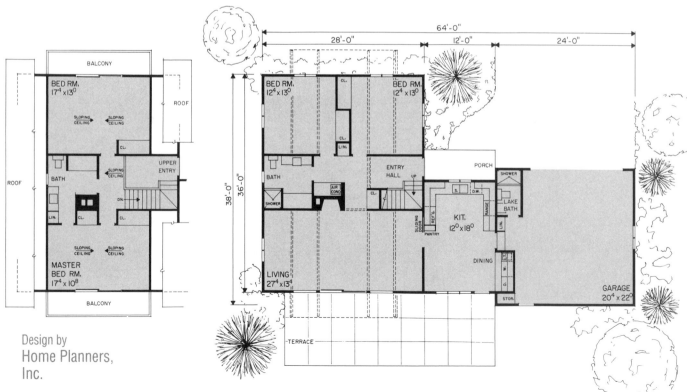

Design by
Home Planners,
Inc.

Design VH2422 First Floor: 1,056 square feet; Second Floor: 1,056 square feet; Total: 2,112 square feet

● The multi-family residence does not have to be restricted to the year 'round suburban living environment. If this type of housing is sound in the city, it may be particularly so in vacationland. This design offers plenty of space for two families. The soundproof wall assures the utmost in privacy from noise of the adjoining neighbor. Each unit offers three bedrooms, 1½ baths, a huge living area, an efficient kitchen and fine storage facilities. Sliding glass doors are features of two of the upstairs bedrooms. They lead to the balcony which looks down to the lower terrace. Development of a two family outdoor living area will be lots of fun for the two families to partake.

Design by
Home Planners,
Inc.

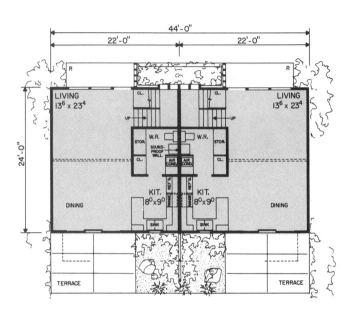

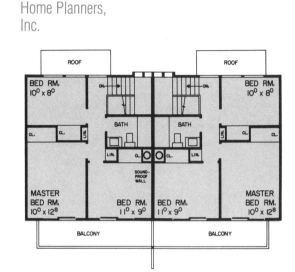

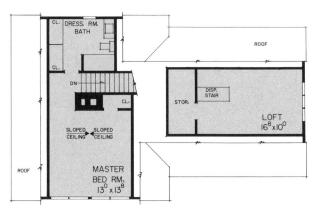

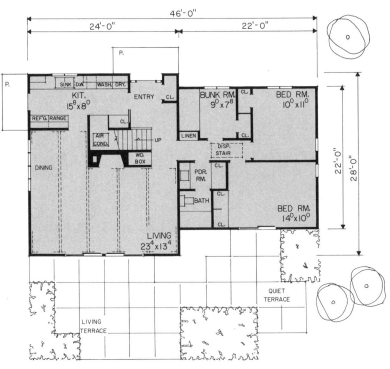

Design VH1478

First Floor: 1,156 square feet
Second Floor: 596 square feet
Total: 1,752 square feet

● This excellent vacation home features a beamed-ceilinged living room with a fireplace and an attached dining area. Two bedrooms and a bunk room accommodate visitors of all ages. Upstairs is the master bedroom with a private bath. A loft—accessed by disappearing stairs—holds storage space. Outdoor terraces make the perfect spots for picnics or lounging.

Design by
Home Planners,
Inc.

206

Design VH1427 First Floor: 1,008 square feet
Second Floor: 688 square feet; Total: 1,696 square feet

● Imagine yourself living in this outstanding vacation home. Whether located deep in the woods or along the shore line, you will forever be aware of your glorious surroundings. As you relax in your living room you will enjoy the massive, raised-hearth fireplace, the high-pitched beamed ceiling, the broad expanses of glass and the dramatic balcony looking down from above.

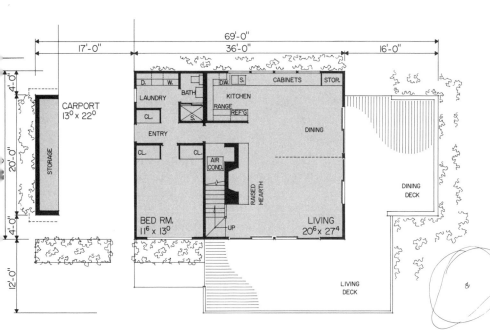

Design by
Home Planners,
Inc.

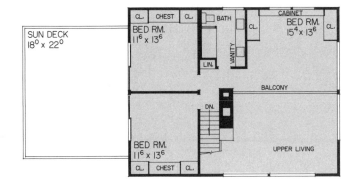

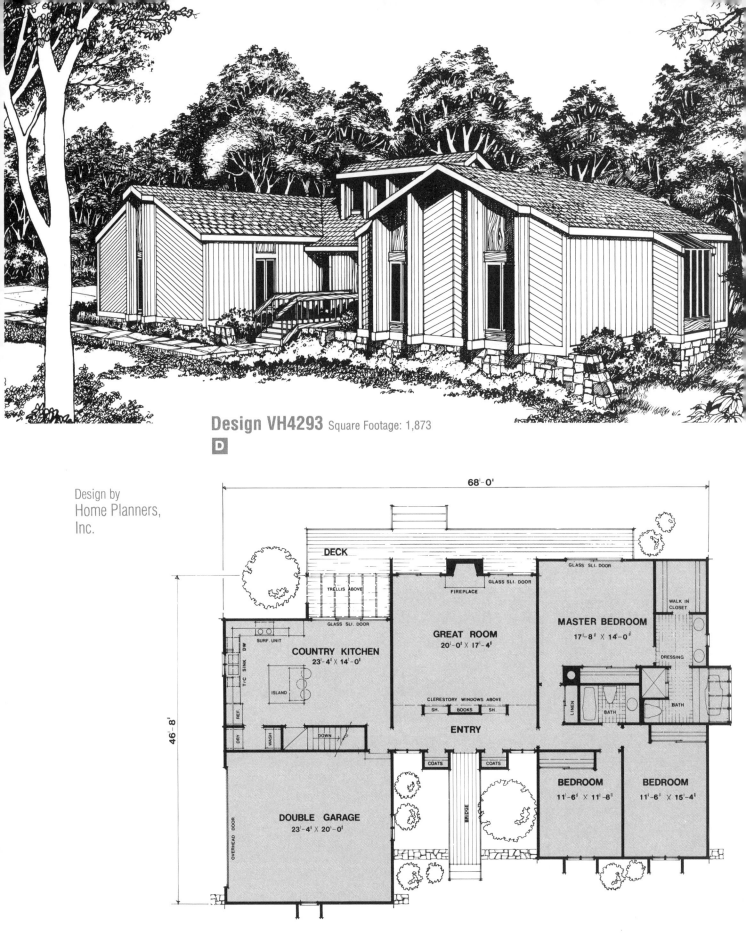

Design VH4293 Square Footage: 1,873

D

Design by
Home Planners,
Inc.

68'-0'

46'-8'

DECK

TRELLIS ABOVE

GLASS SLI. DOOR

FIREPLACE

GLASS SLI. DOOR

GLASS SLI. DOOR

WALK IN CLOSET

SURF. UNIT

T/C SINK DW

COUNTRY KITCHEN
23'-4' X 14'-0'

GREAT ROOM
20'-0' X 17'-4'

MASTER BEDROOM
17'-8" X 14'-0"

DRESSING

REF.

ISLAND

CLERESTORY WINDOWS ABOVE

SH.   BOOKS   SH.

LINEN

BATH

BATH

DRY

WASH

DOWN

ENTRY

COATS   COATS

BRIDGE

OVERHEAD DOOR

DOUBLE GARAGE
23'-4' X 20'-0'

BEDROOM
11'-6" X 11'-8"

BEDROOM
11'-6" X 15'-4"

● Simple lines and a balanced sense of proportion dominate the look of this compact design. The open great room (note clerestory windows), country kitchen with island work area, and master bedroom all overlook a rear deck. Two family bedrooms, to the front of the home, have access to a full bath.

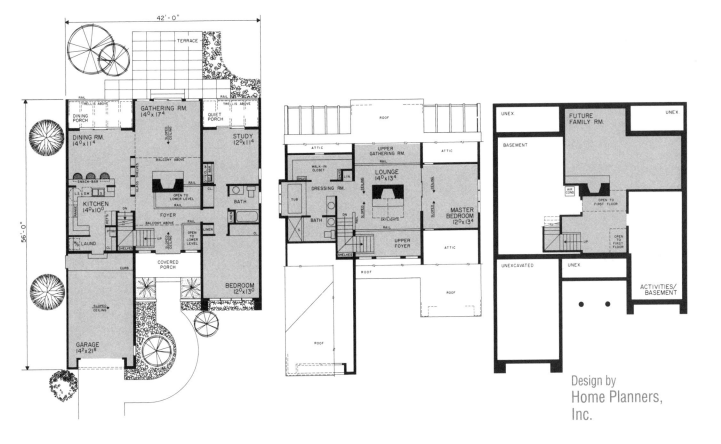

Design by
Home Planners,
Inc.

Design VH2887 First Floor: 1,338 square feet; Second Floor: 661 square feet
Total: 1,999 square feet; Finished Basement: 333 square feet

● This attractive, contemporary 1½-story will be the envy of many. First, examine the efficient kitchen. Not only does it offer a snack bar for those quick meals but also a large dining room. Notice the adjacent dining porch. The laundry and garage access are also adjacent to the kitchen. An exciting feature is the gathering room with fireplace. The first floor also offers a study with a wet bar and sliding glass doors that open to a private porch. This will make those quiet times cherishable. Adjacent to the study is a full bath followed by a bedroom. Upstairs a large master bedroom suite occupies the entire floor. It features a bath with an oversized tub and shower, a large walk-in closet with built-ins and an open lounge with fireplace. Both the lounge and master bedroom, along with the gathering room, have sloped ceilings. Develop the lower level for additional space.

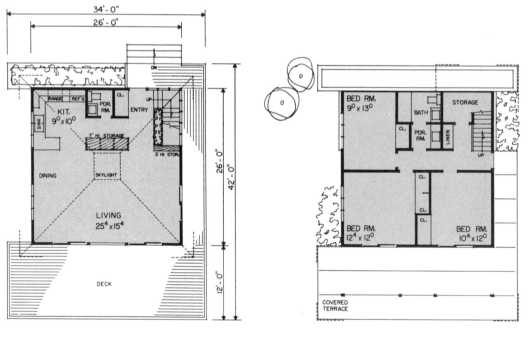

Design by
Home Planners,
Inc.

Design VH1468 Upper Level: 676 square feet; Lower Level: 676 square feet; Total: 1,352 square feet

● Vacation living patterns, because of the very nature of things, are different than the everyday living of the city or suburban America. However, they can be made to be even more delightfully so, when called upon to function in harmony with such a distinctive two-level design as this. The upper level is the pleasantly open and spacious living level. The ceilings are sloped and converge at the skylight. Outside the glass sliding doors is the large deck which looks down onto the surrounding countryside. The lower level is the sleeping level with three bedrooms and a full bath. The covered terrace is just outside two of the bedrooms through sliding glass doors.

● Finding sleeping space for the weekend gang that often shows up at the cottage, is frequently a major problem. Further, having adequate bath facilities presents an additional problem much of the time. This two-level design does a magnificent job in alleviating these problems to provide trouble-free leisure living. In addition to the four bedrooms, there are two bunk rooms! Two full baths, each with a stall shower and built-in vanity, are convenient to the bedrooms. A third bath is located on the lower level adjacent to the family room. The kitchen area provides plenty of space for eating. Observe the two-way fireplace in the living room plus a fireplace in the family room.

Design VH1434

Upper Level: 1,376 square feet
Lower Level: 576 square feet
Total: 1,952 square feet

Design by
Home Planners,
Inc.

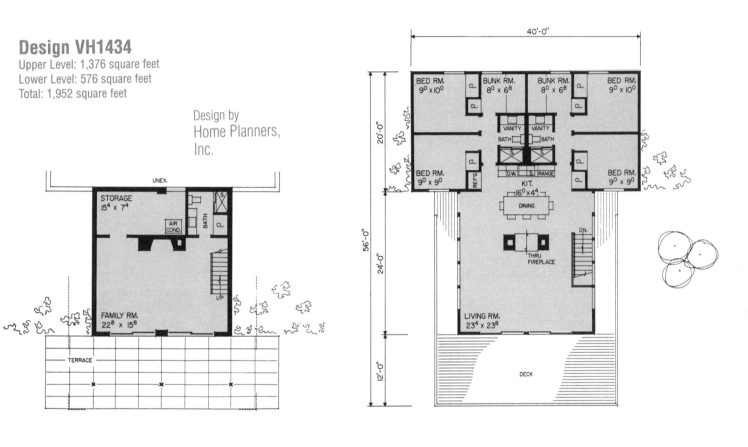

Design VH8889
Square Footage: 1,283

● This fine ranch home offers distinction with its circle-top window, shingle siding and stone enhancements. The vaulted great room focuses on a fireplace. The dining room shares views with this room. A pass-through from the kitchen assures ease in serving meals. A vaulted breakfast room enjoys access to a rear deck for added enjoyment. Three bedrooms include a master bedroom with a private bath. As a starter home or a retirement home, this design has it all!

Design by
LifeStyle
HomeDesigns

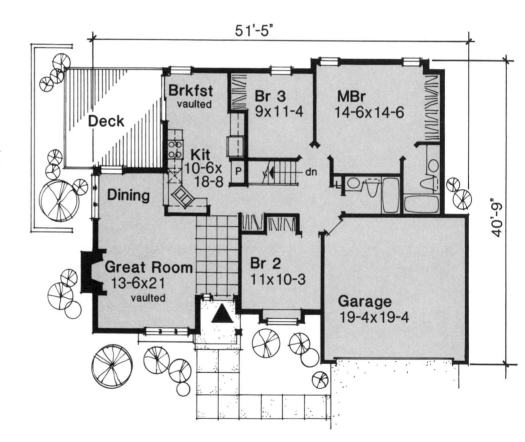

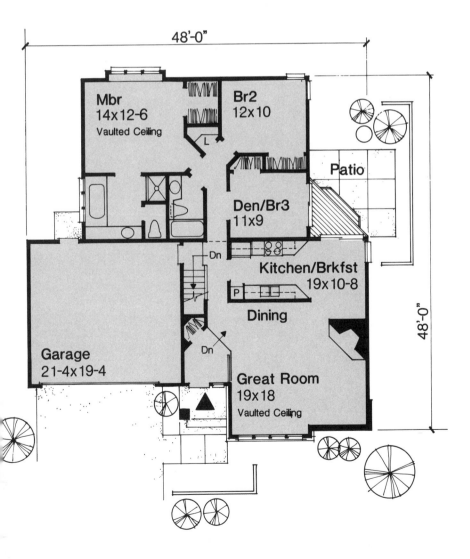

Mbr
14x12-6
Vaulted Ceiling

Br2
12x10

Patio

Den/Br3
11x9

Dn

Kitchen/Brkfst
19x10-8

P

Dining

Garage
21-4x19-4

Dn

Great Room
19x18
Vaulted Ceiling

48'-0"

48'-0"

Design by
LifeStyle
HomeDesigns

Design VH8893

Square Footage: 1,368

● Modern flair in this one-story home offers great curb appeal. Inside, flexible living patterns accommodate the growing family. The raised foyer leads to the vaulted great room. A fireplace and dining space make this a cozy space. The galley-style kitchen opens to a breakfast nook. Sliding glass doors here lead to a private patio. The sleeping zone in this home includes two secondary bedrooms—one could easily serve as a den. The master bedroom features a vaulted ceiling, bumped-out windows, a walk-in closet and a spacious bath.

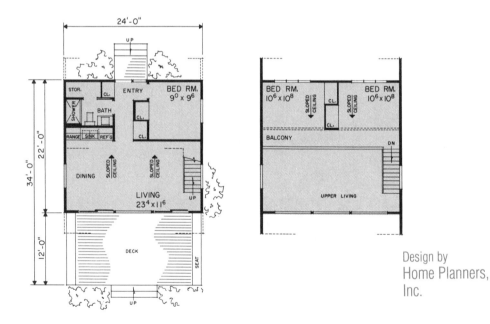

Design by
Home Planners,
Inc.

Design VH1464 First Floor: 528 square feet; Second Floor: 272 square feet; Total: 800 square feet

● A world of care will pass you by as you and your family enjoy all that this distinctive design and its setting have to offer. The economically built floor plan offers an abundance of vacation living potential. There are three bed-

rooms, fine storage facilities and sloped ceilings. There is a strip kitchen, a full bath, an appealing balcony, a generous living area and an outdoor deck. The use of glass, as in so many vacation homes, is most interesting.

While it carries an impressive design impact it is also practical. Study its use and how your family will function during their vacation times. Any location will be a perfect backdrop for this two-story vacation design.

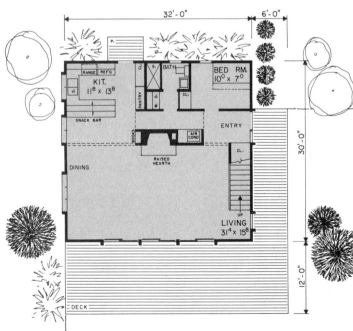

Design VH2464

First Floor: 960 square feet
Second Floor: 448 square feet
Total: 1,408 square feet

Design by
Home Planners,
Inc.

● Almost a perfect square (32 x 30 feet), this economically built leisure home has a wealth of features. The list is a long one and well might begin with that wood deck just outside the sliding glass doors of the 31 foot living area. And what an area it really is – 31 feet in length and with a sloped ceiling! The list of features continues with the U-shaped kitchen, the snack bar, the pantry and closet storage wall, the two full baths (one with stall shower), three bedrooms and raised hearth fireplace. Perhaps the favorite highlight will be the manner in which the second floor overlooks the first floor. The second floor balcony adds even a greater dimension of spaciousness and interior appeal. Don't miss side and rear entries. Observe coat closets placed nearby.

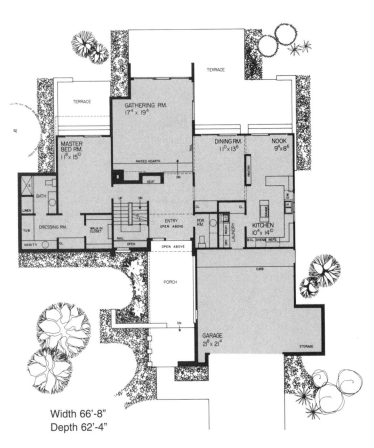

Width 66'-8"
Depth 62'-4"

Design by
Home Planners,
Inc.

Design VH2729

First Floor: 1,590 square feet
Second Floor: 756 square feet
Total: 2,346 square feet

L

● Entering this home will surely be a pleasure through the sheltered walk-way to the double front doors. And the pleasure and beauty does not stop there. The entry hall and sunken gathering room are open to the upstairs for added dimension.

There's even a built-in seat in the entry area. The kitchen-nook area is very efficient with its many built-ins and the adjacent laundry room. There is a fine indoor-outdoor living relationship in this design. Note the private terrace off the luxurious

master bedroom suite, a living terrace accessible from the gathering room, dining room and nook plus the balcony off the upstairs bedroom. Upstairs there is a total of two bedrooms, each having its own private bath and plenty of closets.

Design by
Home Planners,
Inc.

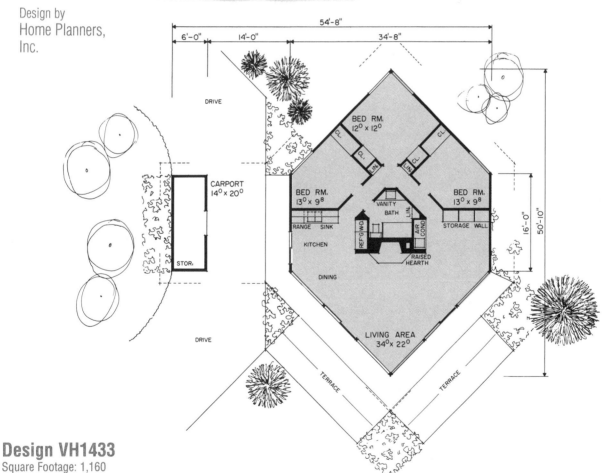

Design VH1433
Square Footage: 1,160

● This hexagonal vacation, or leisure-time, home surely will prove to be a delightful haven away from the conventions of everyday living. Like a breath of fresh air, its uniqueness will make the hours spent in and around this second home memorable ones, in-deed. The floor plan, in spite of its shape, reflects a wise and economical use of space. The spacious interior features a raised hearth fireplace, abundant storage facilities, a bathroom vanity and a combination washer-dryer space. Then, there is the attached car-port and its bulk storage area for recreational and garden equipment. The wide, overhanging roof provides for protection from the rays of the hot summer sun. This will be a great house from which to enjoy the beauty of the countryside.

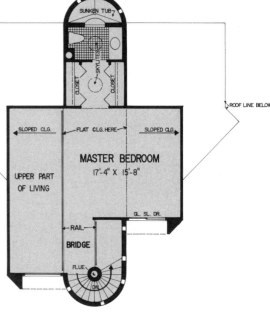

Design VH4125 Entry Level: 1,089 square feet
Upper Level: 508 square feet; Total: 1,597 square feet

Design by
Home Planners,
Inc.

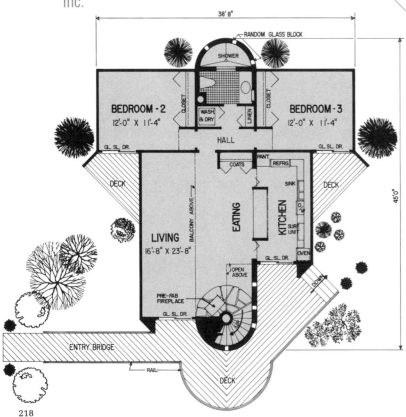

● Geometrical design elements are used to striking effect in this appealing contemporary. Several entrances lead into the open living and eating area. A pass-through to the kitchen saves steps in serving and cleaning up. Two rear bedrooms each have a private deck. A large circular tower encloses a spiral staircase leading up to the balcony master suite. Notice the semicircular sunken tub in the bath.

Design VH1460 Upper Level: 1,032 square feet; Lower Level: 1,067 square feet; Total: 2,099 square feet

Design by
Home Planners,
Inc.

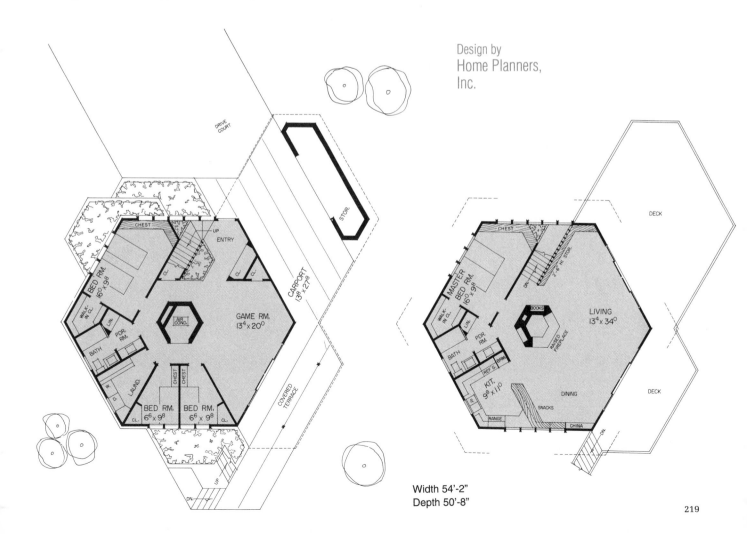

Width 54'-2"
Depth 50'-8"

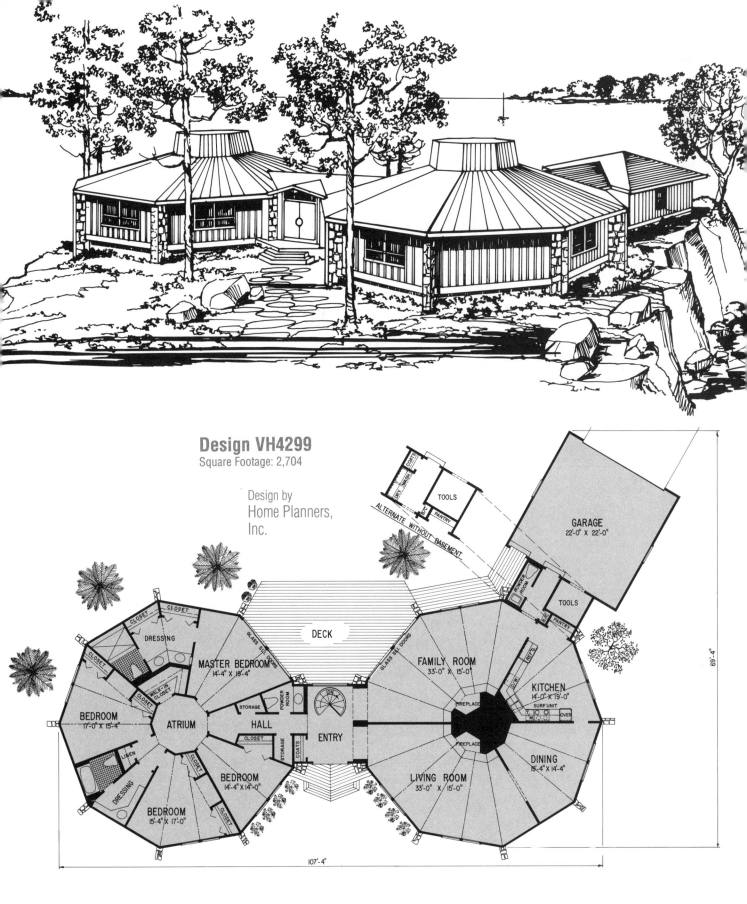

Design VH4299
Square Footage: 2,704

Design by
Home Planners,
Inc.

● Dramatic geometric design makes for a striking home both inside and out. To the right of the entry is the living area with its rooms flowing around the central fireplaces. The living room, dining room, and family room provide space for all activities. Convenient to all three rooms is a spacious kitchen. Across the entry hall is the sleeping wing with rooms radiating off of a central atrium. This area houses four large bedrooms, two baths, and plenty of closet space. Sliding glass doors in the master bedroom and family room open onto an enormous deck — perfect for sunning or enjoying the view.

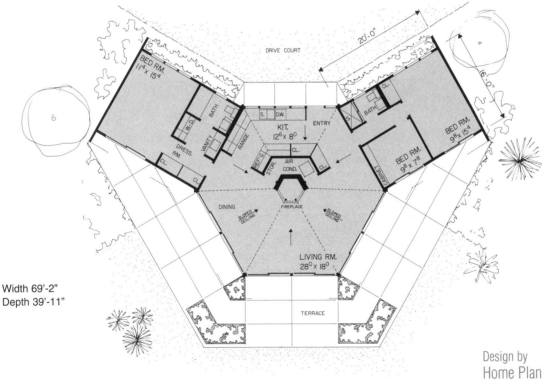

Width 69'-2"
Depth 39'-11"

Design by
Home Planners,
Inc.

Design VH1404
Square Footage: 1,336

● Here is an exciting design, unusual in character, yet fun to live in. This design with its frame exterior and large glass areas has as its dramatic focal point a hexagonal living area which gives way to interesting angles. The spacious living area features sliding glass doors through which traffic may pass to the terraces stretching across the entire length of the house. The wide overhanging roofs project over the terraces, thus providing partial protection from the weather. The sloping ceilings converge above the unique open fireplace. The sleeping areas are located in each wing from the hexagonal center. Three bedrooms in all to serve the family.

Width 66'-8"
Depth 38'-2"

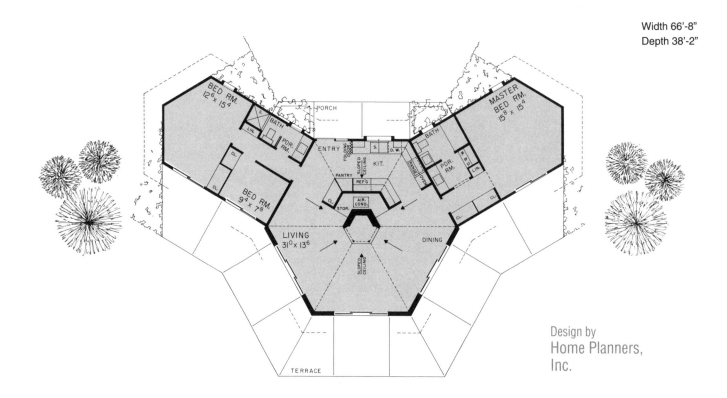

Design by
Home Planners,
Inc.

Design VH2461
Square Footage: 1,400

● If you have the urge to make your vacation home one that has a distinctive flair of individuality, this design is it. Not only will you love the unique exterior appeal of your new home, but you'll also love the exceptional living patterns offered by the interior. The basic living area is a hexagon. To this space-conscious geometric shape is added the sleeping wings with baths. The center of the living area has as its focal point a dramatic fireplace.

Design by
Home Planners,
Inc.

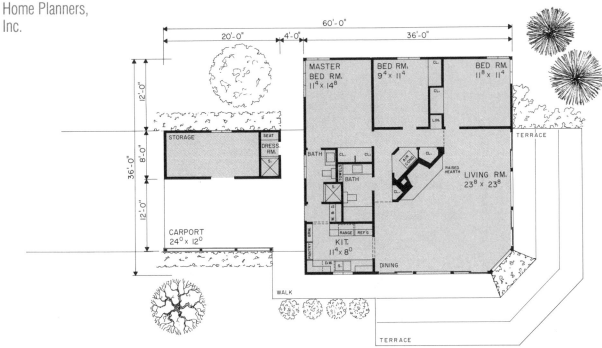

Design VH2457 Square Footage: 1,288

● Leisure living will indeed be graciously experienced in this hip-roofed second home. Except for the clipped corner, it is a perfect square measuring 36 x 36 feet. The 23 foot square living room enjoys a great view of the surrounding environment by virtue of the expanses of glass. The wide overhanging roof affords protection from the sun. The "open planning" adds to the spaciousness of the interior. The focal point is the raised hearth fireplace. The three bedrooms are serviced by two full baths which are also accessible to other areas. The kitchen, looking out upon the water, will be a delight to work in. Observe the carport, the big bulk storage room and the dressing room with its stall shower. This design has great planning for a leisure-time second home.

Design VH2416

Square Footage: 1,051

● The front exterior of this design is highlighted by the dramatic glass gable. The wide overhanging roof and the masses of masonry add their note of distinction to this three-bedroom second home. All the elements are present to permit perennial living. The raised-hearth fireplace, along with the wall of sliding glass doors, makes the living area an outstanding one. The kitchen features modern conveniences.

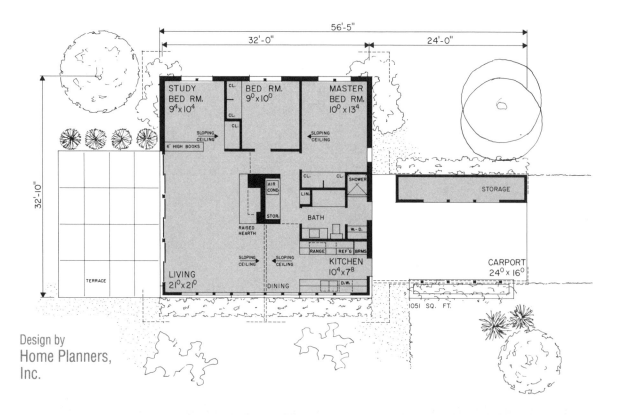

Design by
Home Planners,
Inc.

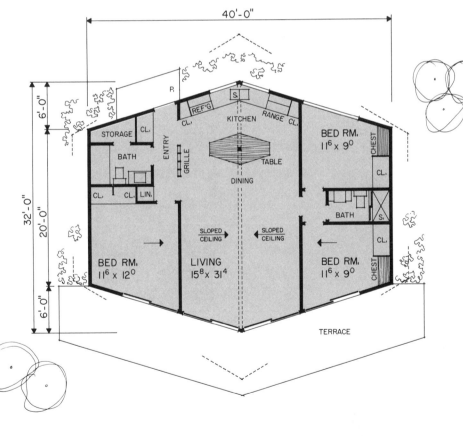

40'-0"

6'-0"

32'-0"

20'-0"

6'-0"

STORAGE

CL.

BATH

CL.

CL.

LIN.

ENTRY

GRILLE

P.

REF'G

S.

KITCHEN

RANGE

CL.

TABLE

DINING

BED RM.
11⁶ x 9⁰

CHEST

CL.

BATH

S.

CL.

BED RM.
11⁶ x 12⁰

SLOPED
CEILING

SLOPED
CEILING

LIVING
15⁸ x 31⁴

BED RM.
11⁶ x 9⁰

CHEST

TERRACE

Design VH1438
Square Footage: 1,040

● Vacations begin with this unique house. The angled terrace is echoed throughout the floor plan— with this orientation, no view is missed. The living room features a sloped ceiling and large dimensions. In the kitchen, a built-in table accommodates a feast. Three bedrooms sleep all. Two of these include built-in chests and well-balanced proportions. Another bedroom located on the other side of the house will make a nice master retreat. Two full baths and storage space round out the amenities.

Design by
Home Planners,
Inc.

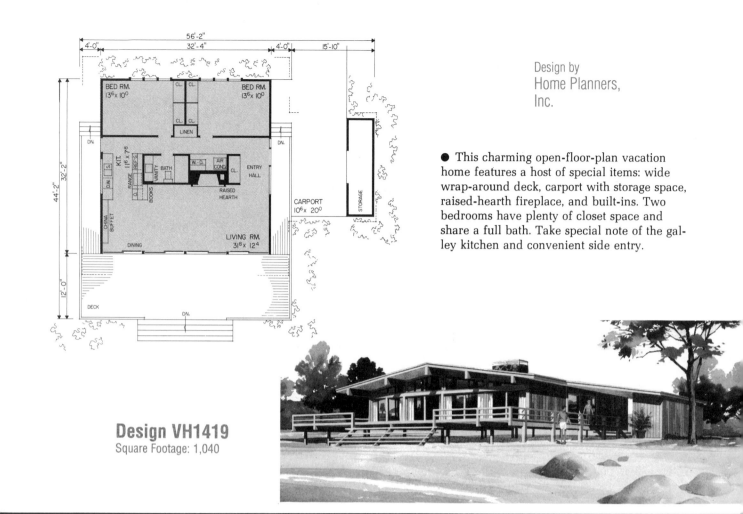

56'-2"
4'-0" · 32'-4" · 4'-0" · 15'-10"

BED RM. 13⁶ x 10⁰   BED RM. 13⁶ x 10⁰

CL. CL. CL. CL.

LINEN

KIT. 11⁶ x 7⁸
REF'G. · RANGE · W.-D. · AIR COND.
DW · VANITY · BATH · BOOKS · CL. · ENTRY HALL

CHINA BUFFET · RAISED HEARTH

DINING

LIVING RM. 31⁸ x 12⁴

DECK · DN.

CARPORT 10⁶ x 20⁰   STORAGE

44'-2" · 32'-2" · 12'-0"

DN. · DN.

Design by
Home Planners,
Inc.

● This charming open-floor-plan vacation home features a host of special items: wide wrap-around deck, carport with storage space, raised-hearth fireplace, and built-ins. Two bedrooms have plenty of closet space and share a full bath. Take special note of the galley kitchen and convenient side entry.

Design VH1419
Square Footage: 1,040

● A three-bedroom vacation home insures that everyone has a special get-away spot. This one boasts a true master suite with private bath. Also noteworthy are the laundry area in the central bath, wide front terrace, covered carport area, and abundant storage space.

Design by
Home Planners,
Inc.

BED RM. 13⁶ x 10⁰   MASTER BED RM. 13⁶ x 12⁰

SLOPED CEILING   SLOPED CEILING

CL. · CL. · LIN.   CL. · SL. DR. · BATH

BED RM. 10⁰ x 10⁸   BATH · SHOWER

CL. · CL. · LIN.   WASH. DRY. · CL. · ENTRY

AIR COND. · REF'G · KIT. 8⁰ x 11⁴ · SINK

STOR.   SLOPED CEILING   OVEN RANGE · DINING

CARPORT 11⁸ x 20⁰   STOR.   LIVING 27⁴ x 14⁰

1130 SQ. FT.   TERRACE   DN

Width 51'-4"
Depth 41'

Design VH2410
Square Footage: 1,130

Design VH1497
Square Footage: 1,292

● Here's another design whose general shape is most interesting and whose livability is truly refreshing. After a stay in this fine second home it will, indeed, be difficult to resume your daily routines back home. A spacious living room showcases a central fireplace and is near the angled kitchen. The master bedroom displays a pleasing layout with a walk-in closet and a private bath. With several sets of sliding glass doors, you will never be far from the great outdoors.

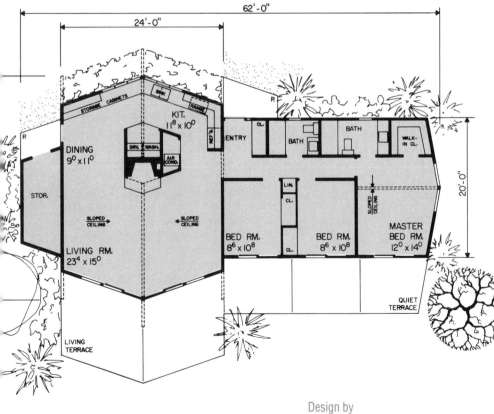

Design by
Home Planners,
Inc.

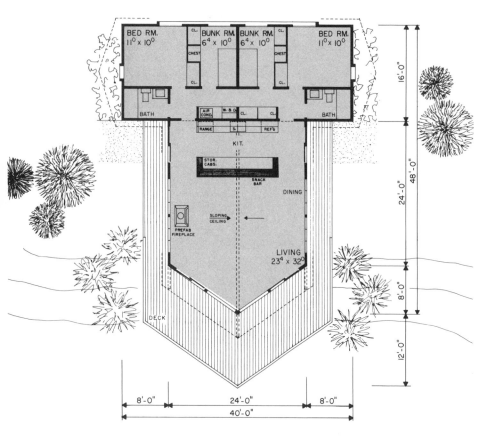

Design VH2439
Square Footage: 1,312

● Here is a wonderfully organized plan with an exterior that will command the attention of each and every passerby. Certainly the roof lines and the pointed glass gable-end wall will be noticed immediately. The delightful deck will be quickly noticed, too. Inside a visitor will be thrilled by the spaciousness of the huge living room. The ceilings slope upward to the exposed ridge beam. A free-standing fireplace will make its contribution to a cheerful atmosphere. The sleeping zone has two bedrooms, two bunk rooms, two full baths, two built-in chests and fine closet space.

Design by
Home Planners,
Inc.

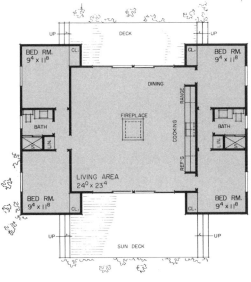

Design VH1440
Square Footage: 1,248

● Here's a clever design that separates the sleeping areas into two wings, each with its own bath. The living area radiates around a central fireplace and has two deck options — one to the front, the other to the rear. Kitchen chores are accomplished along one long wall of the living area.

Width 44'
Depth 44'

Design by
Home Planners,
Inc.

Design VH2418
Square Footage: 1,424

Design by
Home Planners,
Inc.

Width 52'
Depth 54'

● You'll search a long time before locating a vacation home that is any more exciting than this fascinating angular retreat. Whatever its setting, it will surely command attention and also provide its happy owners with a lifetime of carefree living. The soaring roof lines, the cedar shakes, the appealing glass areas and the sloping, beamed ceilings are distinctive features. Three quiet bedrooms share a full hall bath with dual lavatories.

Design VH1450 First Floor: 1,008 square feet; Second Floor: 476 square feet; Total: 1,484 square feet

● What leisure-time fun you, your family and friends will experience in this appealing and wonderfully planned design. And little wonder, for all the elements are present to guarantee vacation living patterns. Four good-sized bedrooms solve the problem of accommodating overnight weekend guests. A full bath on each floor is an important feature. In addition, there is a stall shower handy to the side entrance – just the right location to cater to the requirements of swimmers. The sweeping outdoor deck will be a favorite gathering spot. The living room is a full 27 feet long. It will be a great area to accommodate a crowd. Additional space on the screened-in porch.

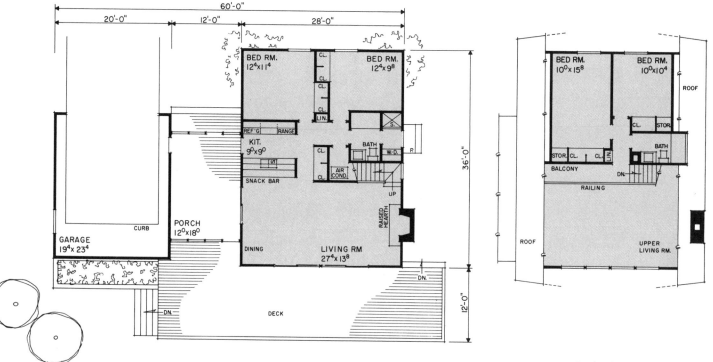

Design by
Home Planners,
Inc.

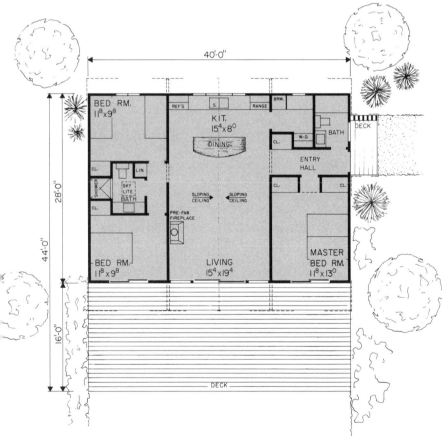

Design VH2428
Square Footage: 1,120

● This delightfully different vacation home will provide you with years of complete satisfaction. Your investment will deliver to you and your family a constant pride of ownership. As you sit upon the wood deck enjoying the view, at your back will be a distinctive exterior with an equally unique interior. A front-to-rear living area separates the children's bedrooms from the parents' master bedroom. There are two full baths—one with a tub, the other with a stall shower. The living area, with its glass gable, high sloping ceiling, free-standing fireplace and large built-in dining surface, is exciting, indeed. Notice the skylight in the children's bathroom.

Design by
Home Planners,
Inc.

Design VH8888
Square Footage: 1,850

● For all the room you need, this design takes precedence. A front den or office is highlighted by a massive brick fireplace and lots of bright windows. Use this space, too, to accommodate house guests. The living room also features a fireplace as well as a high ceiling. The gourmet kitchen enjoys an island and a sunny breakfast nook. The formal dining room opens to the rear deck and spa. Two bedrooms are situated on the left side of the plan. In the master bedroom suite, large proportions, deck access and a luxury bath are popular enhancements. A large walk-in closet and a linen closet assure you meet storage needs.

Design by
LifeStyle
HomeDesigns

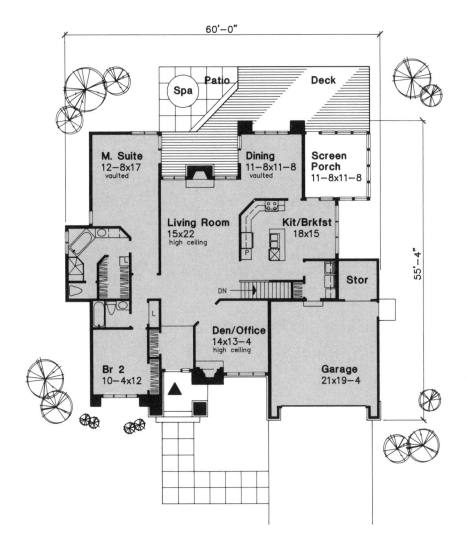

Design VH2824
Square Footage: 1,550

● Low-maintenance and economy in building are the outstanding exterior features of this sharp one-story design. It is sheathed in long-lasting cedar siding and trimmed with stone for an eye-appealing facade. Entrance to this home takes you through a charming garden courtyard then a covered walk to the front porch. The garage extending from the front of the house serves two purposes; to reduce lot size and to buffer the interior of the house from street noise. Sliding glass doors are featured in each of the main rooms for easy access to the outdoors. A sun porch is tucked between the study and gathering rooms. Optional non-basement details are included with the purchase of this design.

Design by
Home Planners, Inc.

OPTIONAL NON-BASEMENT

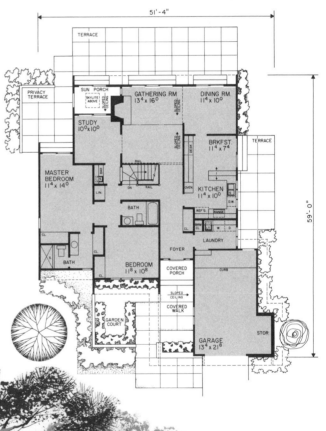

Design VH1471

Square Footage: 1,465

● A summer cottage which will surely play its part well. Although basically a two-bedroom house, its sleeping and living potential is much greater. The large screened porch offers a full measure of flexibility. It supplements the living room as an extra informal living area, while also permitting its use as a sleeping porch. Whatever its function, the screened porch certainly will be in constant use. Separating the living and dining rooms is the appealing raised hearth fireplace. A snack bar is handy to the kitchen which features a glass gable above the wall cabinets. This will be an efficient and cheerful place in which to work. A utility room houses the heating equipment and the combination washer-dryer. Sloping, beamed ceilings help maintain an aura of spaciousness throughout.

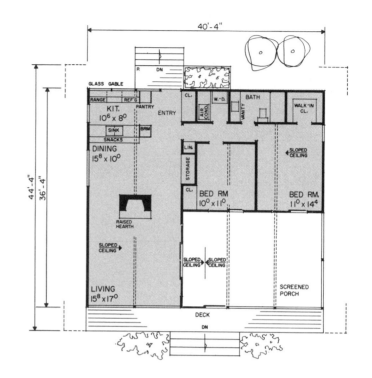

Design by
Home Planners,
Inc.

Design VH2432
Square Footage: 984

Design by
Home Planners,
Inc.

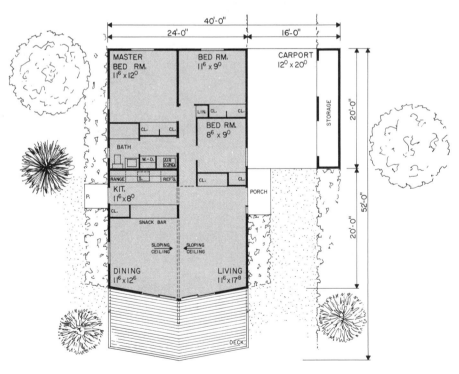

● Here is positive proof that even the most simple of floor plans can be long on livability and can be sheltered by a remarkably pleasing exterior. The 24 foot width of this second home is complemented by the 16 foot carport. The extension of the low-pitched roof to form the carport is a pleasing feature. The carport will double as a storage area for the boat while the storage wall will take care of all that fishing, boating, hunting and other recreational paraphernalia. The interior of this home is a model in the efficient use of space. None of it is wasted. There are plenty of closets; a fine, workable kitchen; a big counter snack bar; and sloping ceiling. You will cherish the hours spent on the wood deck. It is the ideal spot to sit back, relax and take in the beauty of the surroundings.

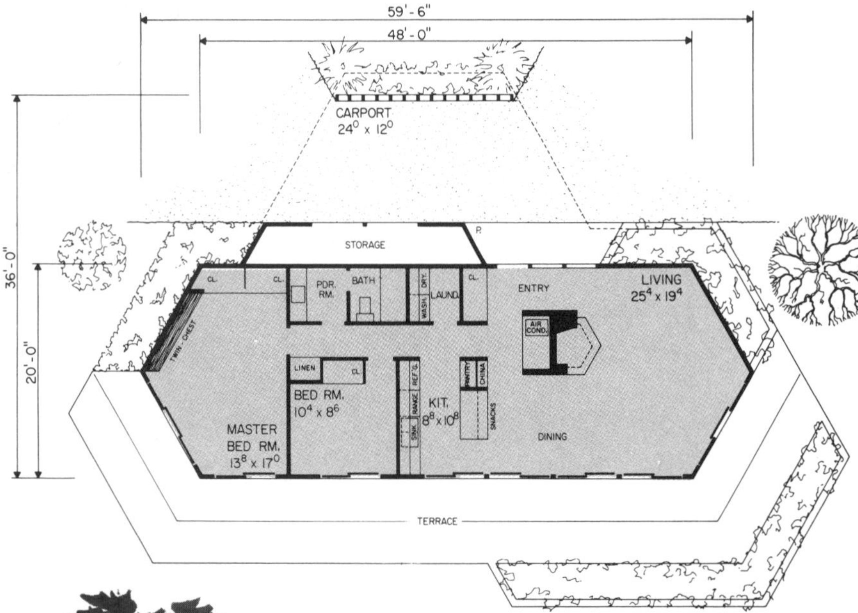

CARPORT
24⁰ x 12⁰

59'-6"
48'-0"
36'-0"
20'-0"

STORAGE

PDR. RM.
BATH
LAUND.
ENTRY

AIR COND.

LIVING
25⁴ x 19⁴

LINEN
BED RM.
10⁴ x 8⁶

RANGE
REF'G.
SINK

PANTRY
CHINA

KIT.
8⁸ x 10⁸
SNACK

MASTER
BED RM.
13⁸ x 17⁰

DINING

TERRACE

● Your setting for this refreshing six-sided home may differ tremendously from the picture below. But, whatever the character of the surroundings, the flair of distinction and the degree of livability will not change. This is truly a home away from home. As you welcome the new living patterns, you also will embrace the delightful change of pace. There are eight sets of sliding glass doors which facilitate passage in-and-out-of-doors.

Design VH2421
Square Footage: 1,075

Design by
Home Planners, Inc.

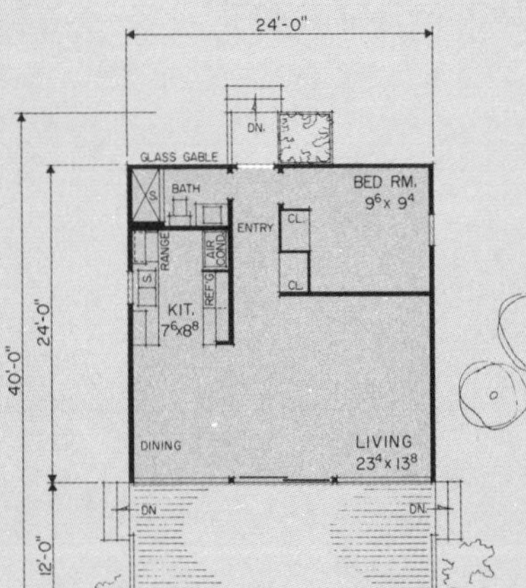

24'-0"
40'-0"
24'-0"
12'-0"

DN.

GLASS GABLE

BATH
RANGE
ENTRY
CL.

BED RM.
9⁶ x 9⁴

KIT.
7⁵ x 8⁸

DINING

LIVING
23⁴ x 13⁸

DN.
DN.

DECK

Design by
Home Planners, Inc.

Design VH1458 Square Footage: 576

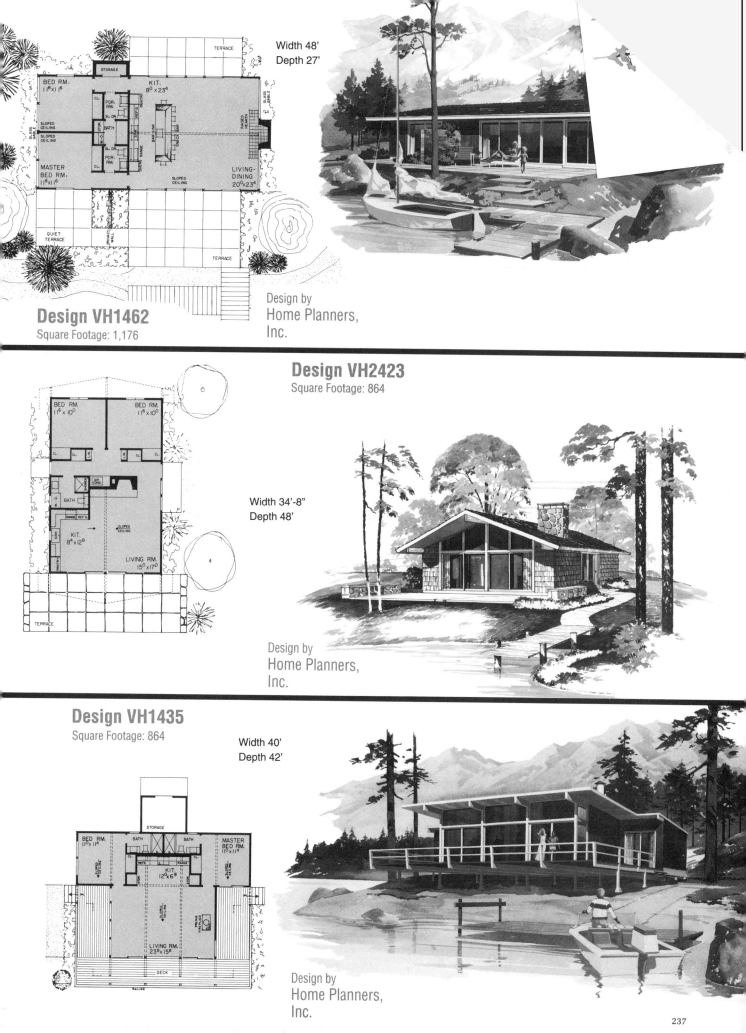

Width 48'
Depth 27'

Design VH1462
Square Footage: 1,176

Design by
Home Planners,
Inc.

Design VH2423
Square Footage: 864

Width 34'-8"
Depth 48'

Design by
Home Planners,
Inc.

Design VH1435
Square Footage: 864

Width 40'
Depth 42'

Design by
Home Planners,
Inc.

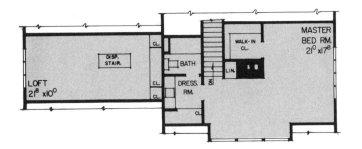

LOFT 21⁸ x10⁰	DISP. STAIR.	CL.	BATH	DRESS. RM.	CL.	CL.	CL.	WALK-IN CL.	LIN.	MASTER BED RM. 21⁰ x17⁸

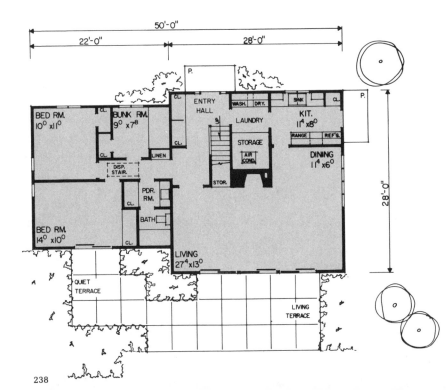

Design VH1481

First Floor: 1,268 square feet
Second Floor: 700 square feet
Total: 1,968 square feet

● Here is a vacation home that retains much of the form of traditional New England design. Modern window treatment has been added to provide a contemporary air. A large living room with a fireplace will accommodate all kinds of gatherings. An efficient kitchen serves the dining area. Two secondary bedrooms and a bunk room share a compartmented bath. Upstairs, a truly private master bedroom enjoys a bath with a dressing room. A loft furthers living potential.

Design by
Home Planners,
Inc.

Design VH1479
Square Footage: 1,360

68'-8"

20'-0"   6'-8"   32'-0"   10'-0"

32'-0"

40'-0"

BED RM.
9^6 x 10^4

BED RM.
9^6 x 9^4

P.

CL.   CL.

CL.   CL.

BATH

AIR COND.   LINEN

WALK-IN CL.

SLOPED CEILING   SLOPED CEILING

MASTER BED RM.
14^0 x 13^0

BATH

DECK

ENTRY HALL

SLID. DR.

SLOPED CEILING

RAISED HEARTH

SLOPED CEILING

W.R.

WASH. DRY.

AIR COND.

REF'G.   RANGE   CL.

P.

KIT.
10^0 x 9^6

SINK

SNACKS

LIVING
15^8 x 19^4

DINING
15^8 x 9^6

STORAGE
9^8 x 11^4

DECK

DECK

Design by
Home Planners,
Inc.

● This unique plan is basically two 20 x 32 foot rectangles connected by an entrance hall, or passage unit. A sweeping wood deck provides the common outdoor living area. The sleeping unit has three bedrooms and two full baths. The ceiling of the master bedroom slopes.

Design VH2434 Square Footage: 1,376

Design by
Home Planners,
Inc.

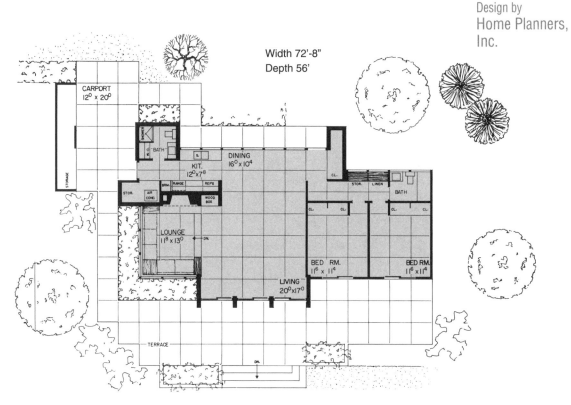

Width 72'-8"
Depth 56'

● It should be easy to visualize the fun and frolic you, your family, your guests and your neighbors will have in this home. The setting does not have to be near a bubbling brook, either. It can be almost any place where the pressures of urban life are far distant. The flat roof planes, the vertical brick piers, the massive chimney and the strategic glass areas are among the noteworthy elements of this design. Inside, there is space galore. The huge living-dining area flows down into the cozy, sunken lounge. The sleeping area of two bedrooms, a bath and good storage facilities is a zone by itself. The kitchen is efficient and has the bath and laundry equipment nearby. Imagine the spacious living area that runs from the front to the back of the house.

Design VH4015
Square Footage: 1,420

● The perfect vacation home combines open, informal living spaces with lots of sleeping space. Study this plan carefully. The spacious living room has a warming fireplace and sliding glass doors onto the deck. Convenient to the dining room, the efficient kitchen is carefully placed so as not to interfere with the living room. Notice the four spacious bedrooms — there's plenty of room for accommodating guests. Two of the bedrooms boast private porches.

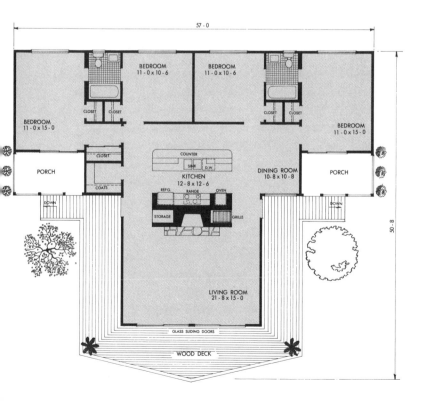

Design by
Home Planners,
Inc.

Design VH4114

Main Level: 852 square feet
Upper Level: 146 square feet
Total: 998 square feet

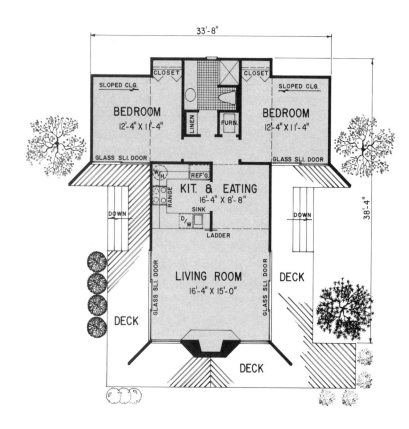

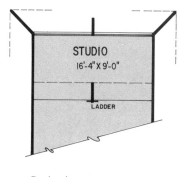

Design by
Home Planners,
Inc.

● This home was designed with the outdoors in mind. A large, wraparound deck provides ample space for sunning and relaxing. Huge windows and sliding glass doors open up the interior with lots of sunlight and great views — a must in a vacation home. Open planning makes for relaxed living patterns; the kitchen, living, and eating area flow together into one large working and living space. An upstairs loft provides added space for a lounge or an extra sleeping area.

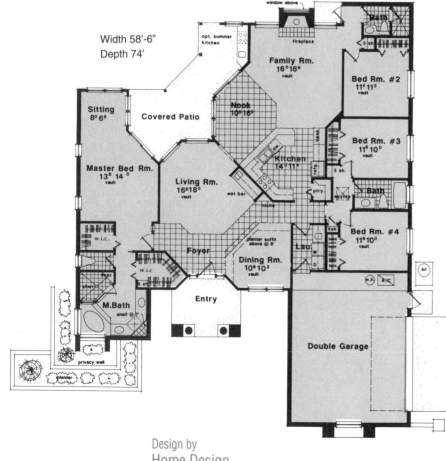

Width 58'-6"
Depth 74'

Design VH8645
Square Footage: 2,224

● Arches crowned by gentle, hipped rooflines provide an Italianate charm in this bright, spacious, family-oriented plan. A covered entry leads to the foyer that presents the angular, vaulted living and dining rooms. A wet bar in the living room enhances livability. A kitchen with V-shape counter includes a walk-in pantry and looks out over the breakfast nook and family room with a fireplace. The master suite features a sitting area, two walk-in closets and a full bath with garden tub. Two additional bedrooms share a full bath located between them. A fourth bedroom, with its own bath, opens off the family room and works perfectly as a guest room.

Design by
Home Design
Services, Inc.

243

Bedroom 2
11⁴ • 10⁰

Covered Patio

Breakfast

Master Bedroom
15⁰ • 13⁰

dw   desk

ref.

Kitchen

pan.

Family Room
17⁴ • 15⁰

W.I.C.

Lin

Bath

opt. fireplace

Lin

Bedroom 3
11⁴ • 10⁴

Living Room
11⁰ • 10⁸

Foyer

Utility

W

D

Dining
11⁰ • 10⁰

Bath

wh   opt.

Entry

ac

Double Garage

WIDTH 59'
DEPTH 55'-4"

Design by
Home Design
Services, Inc.

Design VH8644
Square Footage: 1,831

● A two-level entry, varying rooflines and multi-pane windows add to the spectacular street appeal of this three-bedroom home. To the right of the foyer is the dining room surrounded by elegant columns. Adjacent is the angular kitchen, which opens to the bayed breakfast nook. The elegant living room sits across the foyer from the dining room. The family room includes plans for an optional fireplace. The master bedroom is tucked in the back of the home and features a walk-in closet and a full bath with a dual vanity, spa tub and oversized shower. Two additional bedrooms—each with a large closet—share a full bath. Don't miss the covered patio that adds to outdoor livability.

Design VH8636
Square Footage: 2,010

● Not only does this house look exciting from the outside, with its contemporary use of glass, but upon entering this home, the excitement continues. The classic split living room and dining room sets this house apart from the rest. The family room, breakfast nook and kitchen all share the views to the rear yard. The efficient placement of the bedrooms creates privacy for family members. The master suite is ample, with a wonderful bath featuring a lounging tub, shower, private toilet room, double vanities and generous walk-in closet. Plans for this home include a choice of two exterior elevations.

Design by
Home Design
Services, Inc.

© HOME DESIGN SERVICES, INC.

R. BRADSHAW

← 65'-0" →

Design VH8608
Square Footage: 2,553

● A striking window ensemble gives this single-level home unrivalled street presence. The portico heralds a foyer which is flanked by the living and dining rooms and opens to the family room. A pass-through kitchen serves the dining room through a pocket door; nearby French doors provide access to the patio. The master bedroom is served by a walk-in closet and a dual-vanity bath. Two additional bedrooms are found in an opposite wing and flank a full bath. A pocket door off the breakfast area leads to a fourth bedroom which has its own full bath. Plans include two elevation choices!

69'-8"

Design by
Home Design
Services, Inc.

Floor plan labels:
Bedroom 4 — 11' · 11'
Bath
Breakfast
Patio
Bedroom 3 — 11' · 11'
Kitchen
Family Room — 20' · 17'
fireplace
Master Bedroom — 16' · 13'
Bath
w.i.c.
Bedroom 2 — 13' · 11'
Dining — 13' · 11'
Foyer
Living Room — 12' · 11'
Entry
Bath
desk
Double Garage

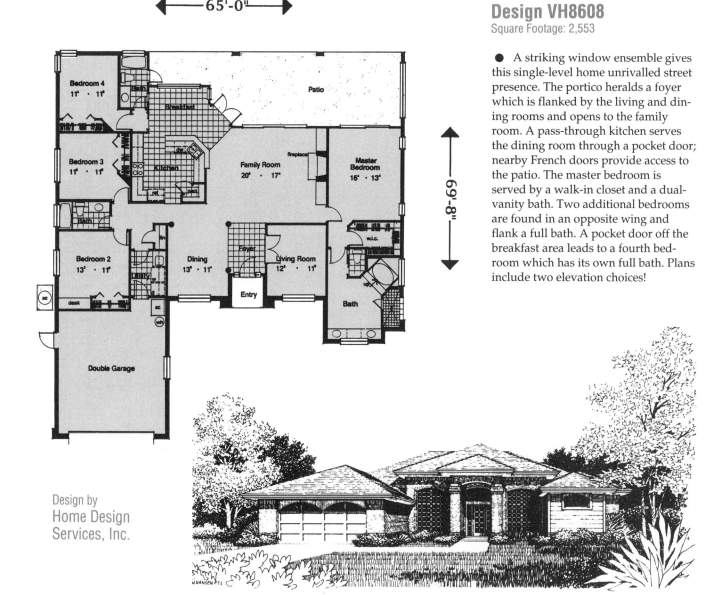

N. HANSEN PTL

246

Design VH8637

Square Footage: 2,089

● This four-bedroom, three-bath home offers the finest in modern amenities. The formal living spaces have a classic split design, perfect for quiet time and conversation. The unique design of the bedroom wing affords great flexibility for the family. Bedrooms 3 and 4 share their own bath while Bedroom 2 has a private bath with pool access, making it the perfect guest room. The huge family room, which opens up to the patio with twelve-foot, pocket sliding doors, has space for a fireplace and media equipment. The master suite, located just off the kitchen and nook, is private yet easily accessible. It has a double-door entry and a bed wall with glass above. The angled entry to the bath makes for a luxurious view of the corner tub. The step-down shower and private toilet room, walk-in linen closet, lavish vanity and closet make this a super bath!

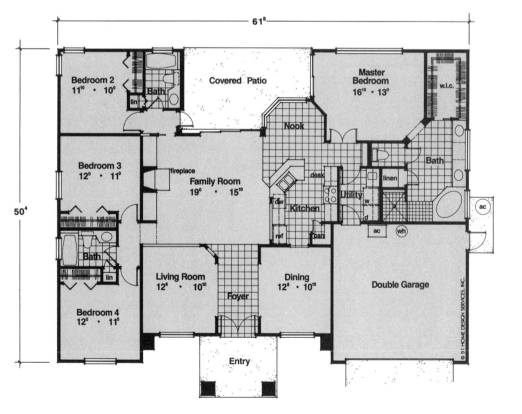

Design by
Home Design
Services, Inc.

247

Design VH8600
Square Footage: 2,041

● The striking facade of this house is only the beginning to a very livable design. A dramatic foyer with columns branches off into the living room on one side, the dining room on the other. A spacious family room graces the center of the house—a true focal point. Beyond the kitchen and breakfast nook you'll find the master bedroom with private access to the covered patio. Three family bedrooms occupy the other side of the house.

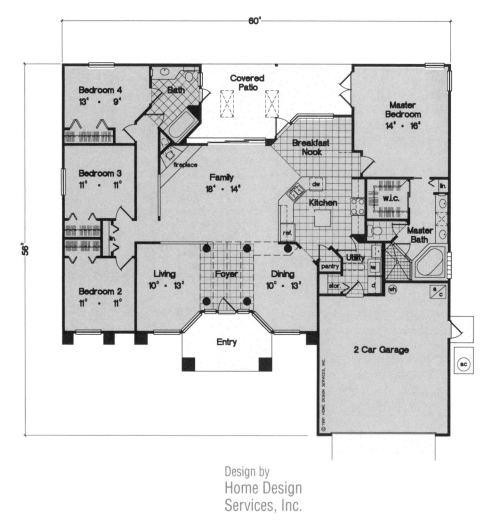

Design by
Home Design
Services, Inc.

Design by
Home Design
Services, Inc.

Design VH8604
Square Footage: 2,153

● Sophistication and elegance are the bywords of this four-bedroom, 2-bath home. Among the many special features are a dramatic foyer, a column-encircled dining room and twelve-foot ceilings. The kitchen is a true gourmet's delight and opens to a light-filled breakfast nook. The family room is enhanced by a barrel ceiling and a fireplace. Secondary bedrooms are separated from the master suite. Each contains a spacious closet; two contain corner windows. The master suite is luxurious with a walk-in closet, sliding glass doors to the rear porch and a bath with a double sink and a step-up tub.

Width 61'
Depth 67'-8"

Design VH8621
Square Footage: 2,480

● This Florida contemporary has been a best seller among families who insist on formal and casual living spaces. The master's retreat, with a bay sitting area, is secluded away from the family area for quiet and solitude. The master bath includes a sumptuous soaking tub, shower for two, His and Hers vanities and a huge walk-in closet. The secondary bedrooms share a split bath, designed for dual use as well as privacy. The kitchen, nook and family room all have magnificent views of the outdoor living space. Note the media wall in the family area—a must for today's sophisticated buyers.

Design by
Home Design
Services, Inc.

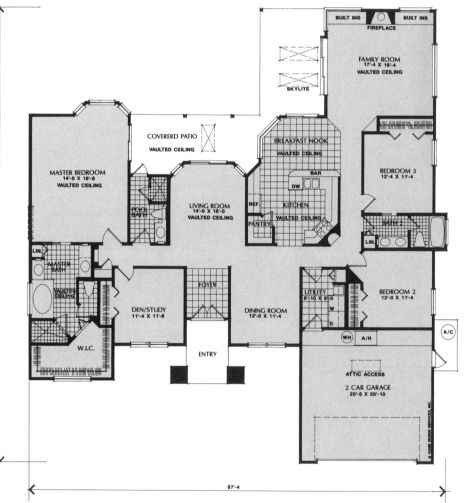

Design VH8601
Square Footage: 2,125

● A luxurious master suite is yours with this lovely plan—and it comes with two different options. Family bedrooms are on the opposite end of the home, separated from the master by the great room and kitchen/breakfast area. A formal dining room and den or study are to the front.

Design by
Home Design
Services, Inc.

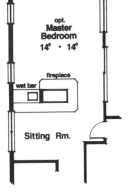

opt.
Master
Bedroom
14⁰ · 14⁰

fireplace

wet bar

Sitting Rm.

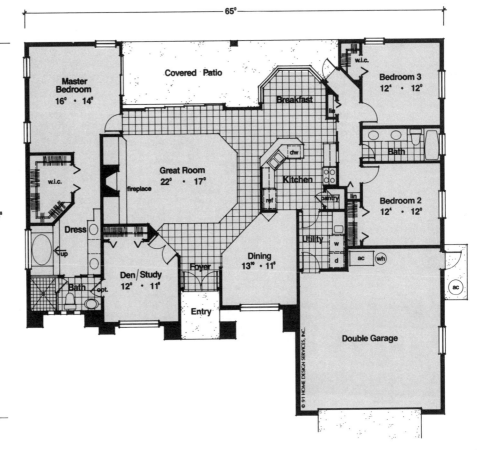

Design VH8617
Square Footage: 2,321

● Discreet placement of bedrooms provides for the utmost in privacy in this single-level plan. The dining and living rooms flank the foyer—note the columns that add drama to the living room. A volume-ceilinged family room includes a fireplace which is flanked by sliding doors leading to a covered rear patio. The master suite includes a walk-in closet and bath with a dual vanity and step-up corner spa tub set between columns. Two bedrooms and a full bath occupy the opposite wing, which is reached via a pocket door off the family wing. Blueprints for this design include three different elevations.

Design by
Home Design
Services, Inc.

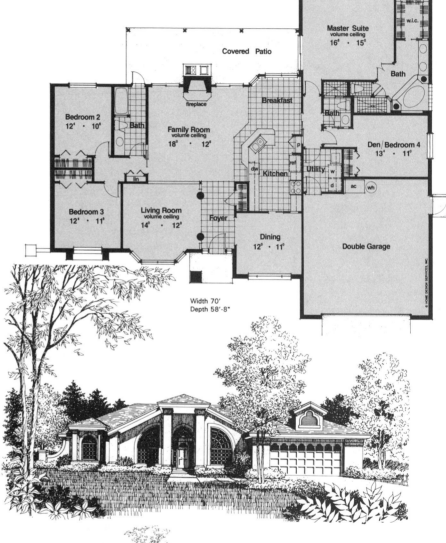

Covered Patio

Master Suite
volume ceiling
16⁸ · 15⁰

w.i.c.

Bath

Bedroom 2
12⁴ · 10⁸

Bath

Breakfast

Bath

fireplace

Family Room
volume ceiling
18⁰ · 12⁸

Den / Bedroom 4
13⁴ · 11⁰

Kitchen

Utility

dw

ref

p

w
d
ac
wh

lin

Bedroom 3
12⁴ · 11⁰

Living Room
volume ceiling
14⁰ · 12⁸

Foyer

Dining
12⁰ · 11⁰

Double Garage

Width 70'
Depth 58'-8"

252

68°

72°

Bedroom 4
12⁴ • 11⁰

Bedroom 3
11⁰ • 11⁰

summer
kitchen

fireplace

Bath

lin

Family Room
22⁰ • 15⁰

Kitchen

dw

ref

Breakfast

Covered Patio

Master
Bedroom
16⁰ • 14⁴

Living Room
18⁰ • 15⁰

w.i.c.

linen

Bath

w.i.c.

Bedroom 2
11⁰ • 11⁰

ac

wh

Pdr.

Utility

d   w

Double Garage

Dining
14⁰ • 11⁴

Foyer

Entry

Design by
Home Design
Services, Inc.

Design VH8619
Square Footage: 2,385

● This Florida classic has been an award winner, as well as a family favorite. Just looking at the flow of this plan will tell you why it has been a best seller. The formal living/dining area is the main impact as you enter this home. Tiered ceiling treatments add crisp contemporary flair to the ceilings. The double-door entry to the master's retreat leads you to a portico-style space, which adds privacy when the doors are opened. The mitered glass treatment in the large sleeping area provides unobstructed views of the outdoor living areas. The master bath is second to none in terms of amenities and intelligent use of space, right down to His and Hers walk-in closets. The secondary bedroom wing has everything for the large family. Note the "kids' door" which accesses the rear patio area from the hallway to the bedrooms and bath. A summer kitchen for outdoor entertaining is icing on the cake!

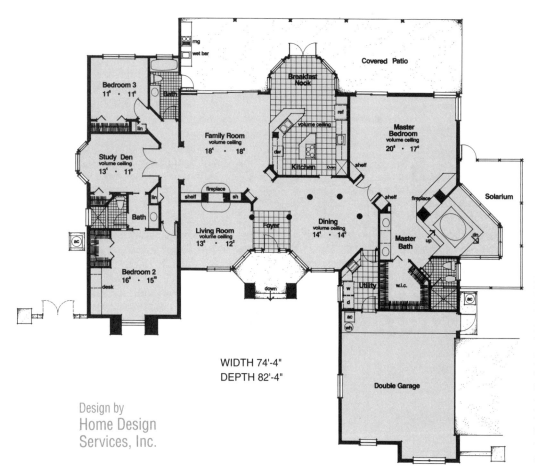

WIDTH 74'-4"
DEPTH 82'-4"

Design by
Home Design
Services, Inc.

Design VH8624
Square Footage: 2,987

● Classic columns, a tiled roof and beautiful arched windows herald a gracious interior for this fine home. Arched windows mark the entrance into the vaulted living room with a tiled fireplace. The dining room opens off the foyer with vaulted ceiling and lovely arched windows. The family room abounds with light from a wall of sliding glass doors that leads to the covered patio (note the wet bar and range that enhance outdoor living). The kitchen features a vaulted ceiling and unfolds into the roomy nook which boasts French doors onto the patio. The master bedroom also has patio access and shares a dual fireplace with the master bath. A solarium lights this space. A vaulted study/bedroom sits between two additional bedrooms—all share a full bath.

Design VH6644
Square Footage: 2,387

● This sunny design opens through double doors into the great room. A rounded dining area contributes a sense of the dramatic and is easily served by the roomy kitchen. A relaxing study also provides outdoor access. Two secondary bedrooms share a bath with dual lavatories. Each one enjoys ample closet space. In the master suite, a tiered ceiling and lots of windows gain attention. A luxury bath with a compartmented toilet, a garden tub, dual vanities and a separate shower also includes a walk-in closet. A bath with a stall shower serves the outdoor living areas.

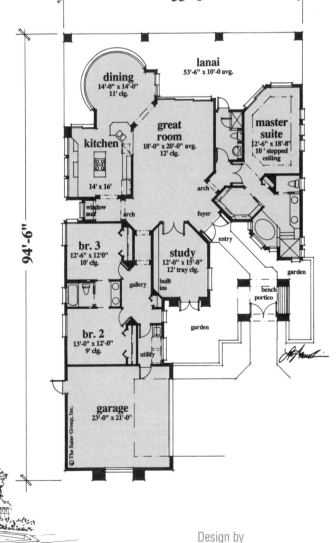

Design by
The Sater
Design Collection

© The Sater Group, Inc.

Design VH6612
Square Footage: 1,487

● Here's an offer too good to pass up! Two elevations and a wealth of modern livability is presented in this compact one-story home. Inside, a great room with a vaulted ceiling opens to the lanai, offering wonderful options for either formal or informal entertaining. Step out onto the lanai and savor the outdoors from the delightful kitchen with its bay-windowed breakfast nook. Two secondary bedrooms (each with its own walk-in closet) share a full bath. Finally, enjoy the lanai from the calming master suite and pampering bath featuring a corner tub, a separate shower and a large walk-in closet.

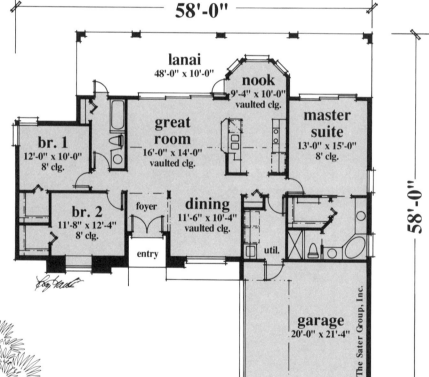

58'-0"

58'-0"

lanai
48'-0" x 10'-0"

nook
9'-4" x 10'-0"
vaulted clg.

master suite
13'-0" x 15'-0"
8' clg.

br. 1
12'-0" x 10'-0"
8' clg.

great room
16'-0" x 14'-0"
vaulted clg.

br. 2
11'-8" x 12'-4"
8' clg.

foyer

dining
11'-6" x 10'-4"
vaulted clg.

entry

util.

garage
20'-0" x 21'-4"

© The Sater Group, Inc.

© The Sater Group, Inc.

Design by
The Sater
Design Collection

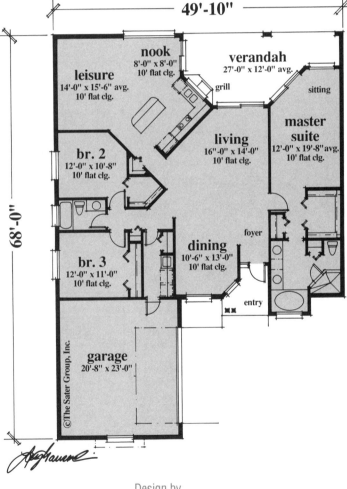

leisure
14'-0" x 15'-6" avg.
10' flat clg.

nook
8'-0" x 8'-0"
10' flat clg.

verandah
27'-0" x 12'-0" avg.

grill

sitting

living
16"-0" x 14'-0"
10' flat clg.

master suite
12'-0" x 19'-8"avg.
10' flat clg.

br. 2
12'-0" x 10'-8"
10' flat clg.

br. 3
12'-0" x 11'-0"
10' flat clg.

dining
10'-6" x 13'-0"
10' flat clg.

foyer

entry

garage
20'-8" x 23'-0"

©The Sater Group, Inc.

49'-10"

68'-0"

Design by
The Sater
Design Collection

Design VH6630 Square Footage: 1,953

● A clever floor plan distinguishes this three-
bedroom stucco Floridian. It features formal living
and dining rooms, plus an ample family room with
adjacent breakfast nook. The angled kitchen overlooks this casual gathering area and contains a pass-
through window to a patio counter. Secondary bedrooms are split from the master suite. They share a
full bath. The master contains patio access and features a grand bath with corner shower, whirlpool
tub and dual sinks. A handy utility room connects
the living space to the two-car garage.

Design VH6632
Square Footage: 2,562

● Design excellence is apparent in this one-story home. With open living and dining rooms, and a covered veranda, gatherings of all sorts are a breeze. The kitchen combines with a leisure room to provide a super casual living space. It is enhanced by an optional fireplace and T.V. niche. Two bedrooms—with ample closet space in each—are separated by a full hall bath. Right off the tiled foyer, a den meets work and school needs. In the master bedroom suite, plenty of wall space affords a variety of furniture arrangements. The master bath pleases with a double-bowl vanity, a compartmented toilet, a corner whirlpool tub and a large shower. A walk-in closet is also nearby.

Design by
The Sater
Design Collection

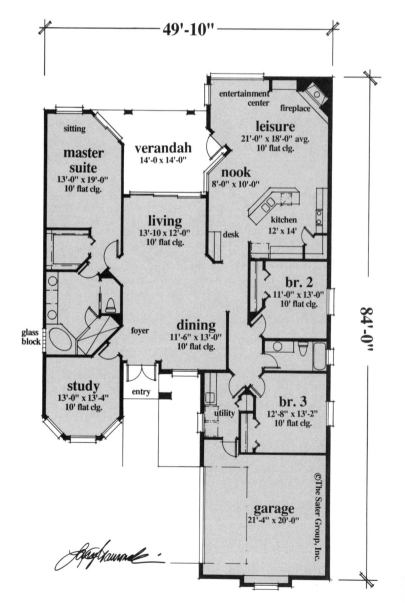

Design VH6629

Square Footage: 2,214

● Make yourself at home in this delightful one-story home. The dramatic entry—with an arched opening—leads to a comfortable interior. Volume ceilings highlight the main living areas which include a formal dining room and a great room with access to one of the verandas. In the turreted study, quiet time is assured with double doors closing off the rest of the house. Nearby, the master bedroom suite features a luxury bath with a double-bowl vanity, a bumped-out whirlpool tub and a compartmented stool and shower. The secondary bedrooms reside on the other side of the house and utilize a full bath that also accommodates outdoor living areas.

Design by
The Sater
Design Collection

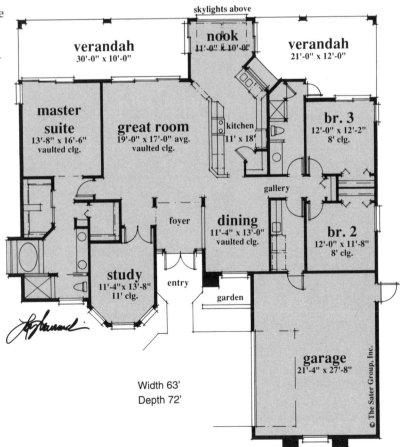

66'-8"

Design VH8620

Square Footage: 2,454

● This one-story sports many well-chosen, distinctive exterior details including a cameo window and hipped rooflines. The dining and living rooms flank the foyer. A tray ceiling in the living room adds further enhancement. The bayed breakfast area admits light softened by the patio. Secluded from the main house, the master bedroom comes with a tray ceiling and fireplace through to the master bath. A raised tub, double vanity and immense walk-in closet highlight the bath.

Design by
**Home Design
Services, Inc.**

Covered Patio

Bed Rm. #2
13⁰10⁸
10' flat ceiling

Master Bed Rm
17⁴13⁰
tray ceiling

Brkfst. Nook
11⁴8⁴

M. Bath
vaulted ceiling

Bath

Family Rm.
17⁰19⁰
vaulted ceiling

Kitchen
11⁰13⁴
vaulted ceiling

Bed Rm. #3
11⁴11⁸
10' flat ceiling

W.I.C.

Lau.

8' high wall

A/C

Bath

Foyer
8⁰10⁰
10' flat ceiling

Dining Rm.
10⁸13⁰
10' flat ceiling

Bed Rm. #4
11⁴13⁰
10' flat ceiling

Living Rm.
12⁴14⁸
tray ceiling

Entry

Double Garage

56'-8"

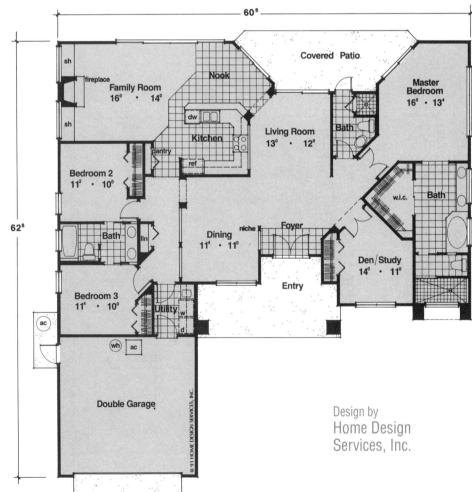

Family Room
16⁰ · 14⁰

Nook

Covered Patio

Master Bedroom
16⁰ · 13⁴

Kitchen

Living Room
13⁰ · 12⁰

Bath

Bedroom 2
11² · 10⁰

pantry

ref

Bath

Bath

w.i.c.

Dining
11⁴ · 11⁰

niche

Foyer

Den/Study
14⁰ · 11⁰

Bedroom 3
11⁴ · 10⁰

Utility

Entry

Double Garage

60⁸

62⁸

© 911 HOME DESIGN SERVICES, INC.

Design by
Home Design
Services, Inc.

Design VH8639
Square Footage: 2,149

● This impressive plan creates views which make this house look much larger than it really is. Upon entry into this three-bedroom, three-bath home, the formal living room overflows to outdoor living space. The formal dining room is designed with open wall areas for an air of spaciousness. A decorative arch leads to the family spaces of the home. The two bedrooms share a "pullman" bath, accessible only from the rooms themselves for total privacy. The kitchen/family room/nook area is large and inviting, with beautiful views of the outdoor living spaces. The master wing of the home is off the den/study and the pool bath. Double doors welcome you into the master suite with a glass bedwall and angled sliders to the patio. The efficient use of space makes the bath as functional as it is beautiful.

Design VH6631
Square Footage: 2,185

● Whether building in sunny climes or with contemporary styling in mind, this three-bedroom home offers the best in modern livability. The tiled foyer introduces a formal living zone consisting of a dining room and a living room with access to a covered veranda. The kitchen—with a large pantry—enjoys openness to a breakfast nook and a leisure room, also with access to the veranda. A split bedroom arrangement enhances the living patterns of the home. On the left is the master bedroom suite where a luxury bath and private passage to the lanai are sure to please. Two secondary bedrooms each enjoy ample closet space and a full bath. A utility area leads to the garage and completes the plan.

Design by
The Sater
Design Collection

verandah
33'-0" x 12'-0" avg.

leisure
15'-2" x 15'-6"
10' flat clg.

sitting

master
suite
13'-0" x 18'-10"
10' flat clg.

living
13'-10" x 15'-10"
10' flat clg.

nook
9'-0" x 9'-0"

kitchen

15' x 12'

desk

foyer

dining
10'-9" x 14'-0"
10' flat clg.

entry

br. 2
12'-0" x 11'-4"
10' flat clg.

br. 3
12'-0" x 11'-2"
8' flat clg.

garage
20'-8" x 20'-6"

© The Sater Group, Inc.

Width 49'-10"
Depth 68'

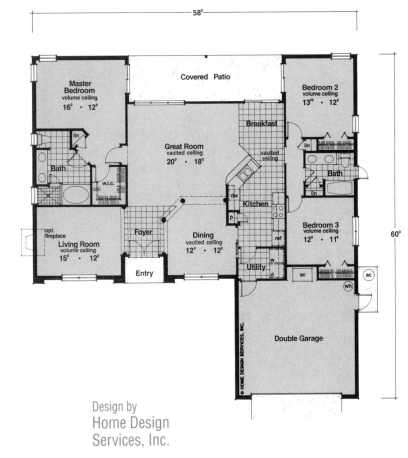

Covered Patio

Master Bedroom
volume ceiling
16⁰ · 12⁰

Bedroom 2
volume ceiling
13¹⁰ · 12⁰

Breakfast

Bath

lin

Great Room
vaulted ceiling
20⁰ · 18⁰

vaulted ceiling

lin

Bath

w.i.c.

Kitchen

dw

Bedroom 3
volume ceiling
12⁰ · 11⁸

opt. fireplace

Living Room
volume ceiling
15⁰ · 12⁰

Foyer

Dining
vaulted ceiling
12⁴ · 12⁰

p

ref

Entry

Utility

w
d

ac

ac

wh

Double Garage

58⁰

60⁰

Design by
Home Design
Services, Inc.

Design VH8662
Square Footage: 2,005

● A super floor plan makes this volume home that much more attractive. Inside you'll find a formal dining room—defined by columns—to the right and a living room—with an optional fireplace—to the left. Beyond this area is an expansive great room with a vaulted ceiling and openness to the kitchen and breakfast room. A covered patio in the back of the house enhances outdoor livability. Two secondary bedrooms complete the right side of the plan. Each features a volume ceiling, ample closet space and the use of a full hall bath with dual lavatories. The master bedroom enjoys its own bath with a whirlpool tub, separate shower, dual vanity and compartmented toilet.

263

Design VH6645
Square Footage: 2,473

● Luxurious living begins as soon as you step into the entryway of this home. With columns and a barrel-vaulted ceiling, it opens through double doors to the foyer and combined living and dining rooms. The octagonal kitchen serves this area with a pass-through counter. Two master suites characterize this plan as the perfect vacation retreat. Two guest rooms enjoy quiet locales and direct access to the master baths. Outdoor living areas include a master lanai and another that stretches around the back of the house. A pool bath is easily accessible from the lanai. A two-car garage and a utility room finish off the plan.

Design by
The Sater
Design Collection

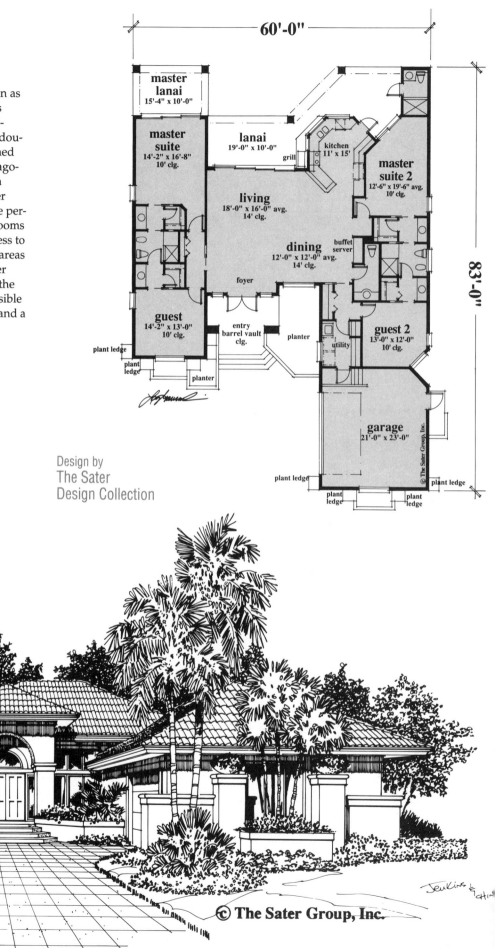

© The Sater Group, Inc.

Design VH8616
Square Footage: 2,294

● This plan makes the most of a picturesque lot, with the inclusion of a great view from the moment you enter. The floor plan boasts a formal living room/dining room layout—great for young families! The kids can enjoy the open family room, with the kitchen and breakfast nook nearby. The master's retreat has use of the den/guest room, as well as providing a lavish master bath.

Design by
Home Design Services, Inc.

WIDTH 61'-2"
DEPTH 70'-2"

Design VH8634
Square Footage: 1,869

Design by
Home Design Services, Inc.

● This open plan brings indoors and outdoors together beautifully with an undisturbed view of the rear yard. The secondary bedrooms feature a "kids" door off the hall for bathroom access from the patio and pool area. The super master suite features not only mitered glass for a great view of the pool area, but the bath is as sumptuous as it is practical. There is even a courtesy door off the toilet area accessing the den/study for the occasional guest. The fireplace and media center in the family room add fine finishing touches.

Width 61'-8"
Depth 55'

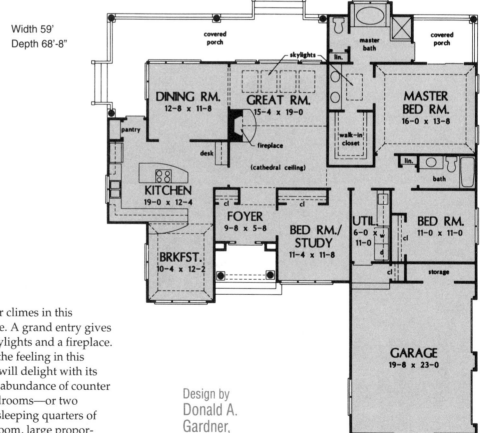

Width 59'
Depth 68'-8"

covered porch

covered porch

master bath

skylights

lin.

DINING RM.
12-8 x 11-8

GREAT RM.
15-4 x 19-0

MASTER BED RM.
16-0 x 13-8

pantry

desk

fireplace

walk-in closet

(cathedral ceiling)

lin.

bath

KITCHEN
19-0 x 12-4

cl

cl

FOYER
9-8 x 5-8

BED RM./
STUDY
11-4 x 11-8

UTIL.
6-0 x 11-0

BED RM.
11-0 x 11-0

BRKFST.
10-4 x 12-2

cl

storage

GARAGE
19-8 x 23-0

Design VH9737
Square Footage: 1,929

● Make the most of warmer climes in this striking three-bedroom home. A grand entry gives way to a great room with skylights and a fireplace. A cathedral ceiling furthers the feeling in this room. Adjacent, the kitchen will delight with its large island work space and abundance of counter and cabinet space. Three bedrooms—or two with a study—make up the sleeping quarters of this plan. In the master bedroom, large proportions include a private bath with dual lavs, a walk-in closet and a bumped-out garden tub.

Design by
Donald A.
Gardner,
Architects, Inc.

Design VH9740
Square Footage: 1,838

● This three-bedroom South-western design is enhanced by the use of arched windows and a dramatic arched entrance. An expansive great room features a cathedral ceiling and a fireplace with direct access to the patio and the dining room. An efficient U-shaped kitchen has plenty of counter space and easily serves both the dining and great rooms. A private master suite features a large walk-in closet and skylit bath with double vanity, whirlpool tub, and separate shower. Two additional bedrooms have generous closet space and share a full bath with double vanity.

Design by
Donald A.
Gardner,
Architects, Inc.

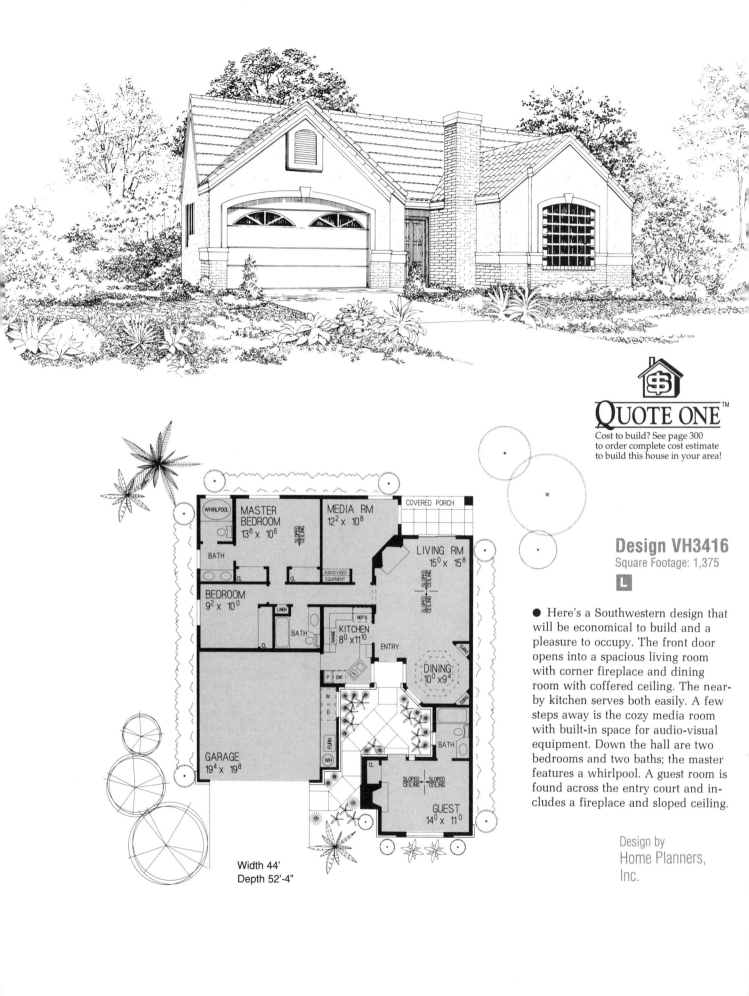

Width 44'
Depth 52'-4"

QUOTE ONE™
Cost to build? See page 300
to order complete cost estimate
to build this house in your area!

Design VH3416
Square Footage: 1,375

L

● Here's a Southwestern design that
will be economical to build and a
pleasure to occupy. The front door
opens into a spacious living room
with corner fireplace and dining
room with coffered ceiling. The nearby kitchen serves both easily. A few
steps away is the cozy media room
with built-in space for audio-visual
equipment. Down the hall are two
bedrooms and two baths; the master
features a whirlpool. A guest room is
found across the entry court and includes a fireplace and sloped ceiling.

Design by
Home Planners,
Inc.

Sater Group, Inc.

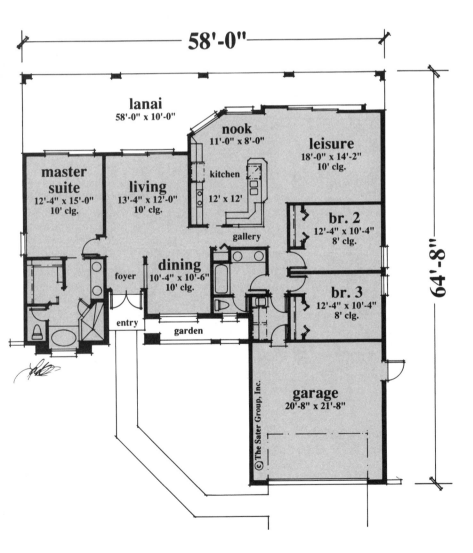

58'-0"

64'-8"

lanai
58'-0" x 10'-0"

nook
11'-0" x 8'-0"

leisure
18'-0" x 14'-2"
10' clg.

kitchen
12' x 12'

master suite
12'-4" x 15'-0"
10' clg.

living
13'-4" x 12'-0"
10' clg.

gallery

br. 2
12'-4" x 10'-4"
8' clg.

foyer

dining
10'-4" x 10'-6"
10' clg.

br. 3
12'-4" x 10'-4"
8' clg.

entry

garden

© The Sater Group, Inc.

garage
20'-8" x 21'-8"

Design VH6603
Square Footage: 1,784

● This one-story stucco home is filled with amenities. A raised entry features double doors that lead to the grand foyer. From the formal living room, large sliding glass doors open to the lanai, providing natural light and outdoor views. The dining room is separated from the foyer and living area by a half-wall and a column. The large kitchen, breakfast nook and leisure room round out the informal gathering areas. The secondary bedrooms are split from the master wing. The cozy master suite sports a large walk-in closet, a walk-in shower, a whirlpool tub and a private water closet.

Design by
The Sater
Design Collection

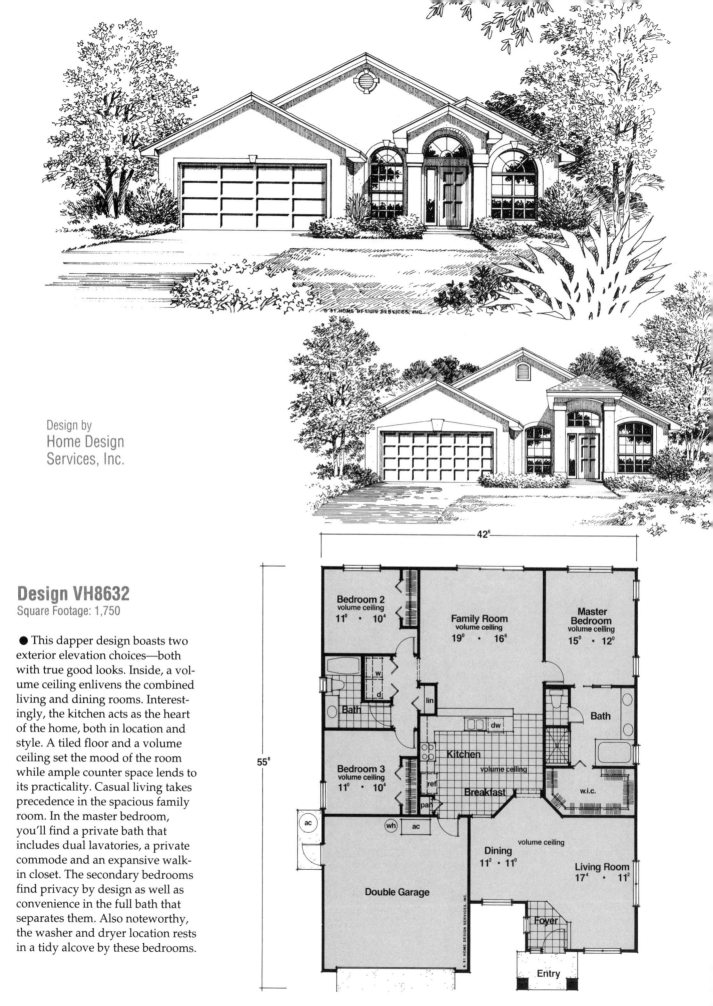

Design by
Home Design
Services, Inc.

Design VH8632
Square Footage: 1,750

● This dapper design boasts two exterior elevation choices—both with true good looks. Inside, a volume ceiling enlivens the combined living and dining rooms. Interestingly, the kitchen acts as the heart of the home, both in location and style. A tiled floor and a volume ceiling set the mood of the room while ample counter space lends to its practicality. Casual living takes precedence in the spacious family room. In the master bedroom, you'll find a private bath that includes dual lavatories, a private commode and an expansive walk-in closet. The secondary bedrooms find privacy by design as well as convenience in the full bath that separates them. Also noteworthy, the washer and dryer location rests in a tidy alcove by these bedrooms.

42⁶

55⁸

Bedroom 2
volume ceiling
11⁰ • 10⁴

Family Room
volume ceiling
19⁰ • 16⁶

Master Bedroom
volume ceiling
15⁰ • 12⁰

Bath

Bedroom 3
volume ceiling
11⁰ • 10⁴

Kitchen
volume ceiling

Bath

Breakfast

w.i.c.

dw

ref

pan

lin

w

d

ac

wh

ac

Double Garage

Dining
11² • 11⁰

volume ceiling

Living Room
17⁴ • 11²

Foyer

Entry

Design VH8631

Square Footage: 1,697

● Great great-room design! This exciting plan features a main gathering space bordered on the left by the formal dining area with decorative built-in wall for a custom touch. The unobstructed view of the rear outdoor space is maximized from the gathering space as well as the kitchen and breakfast room. The placement of secondary bedrooms toward the front of the home gives a sense of privacy. The master suite compares favorably to much larger homes, boasting a huge walk-in shower, private toilet and oversized vanity and closet. Space for a media center and fireplace are also allowed for in the design. The blueprints for this design include options for two different exteriors.

Dining

Design by
Home Design
Services, Inc.

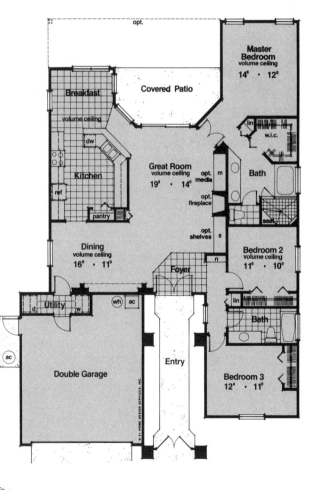

Width 45'
Depth 68'-4"

271

Design VH8611
Square Footage: 1,413

● An angled side entry to this home allows for a majestic, arched window that dominates its facade. The interior, though small in square footage, holds an interesting and efficient floor plan. Because the breakfast room is placed to the front of the plan, it benefits from two large, multipaned windows. The dining and family rooms form a single space enhanced by a volume ceiling and an optional fireplace, which is flanked by sets of optional double doors. Both the family room and master bedroom boast access

to the covered patio. A volume ceiling further enhances the master bedroom, which also has a dressing area, walk-in closet and full bath. The plans include options for a family room with corner fireplace, fireplace with French doors or a sliding glass door instead of a fireplace. The package includes plans for three different elevations!

Design by
Home Design
Services, Inc.

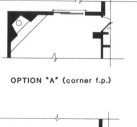

OPTION "A" (corner f.p.)

Stnd

Width 38'
Depth 58'

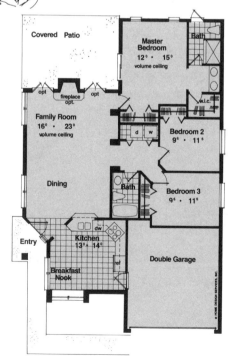

Covered Patio

Family Room
14⁰ · 12⁰
volume ceiling

Bedroom 2
13⁰ · 9⁰
volume ceiling

Breakfast

Bedroom 3
10⁰ · 9⁰
volume ceiling

Bath

Kitchen
14⁰ · 9⁰

Dining
11⁰ · 12⁰

w d

Bath

Foyer

Double Garage

Master Bedroom
13⁰ · 12⁰
volume ceiling

WIDTH 40'
DEPTH 48'

Design VH8610
Square Footage: 1,280

● This plan is ideal for the young family that needs a house that's small but smart. As in larger plans, this home boasts a private master's retreat with three closets and a private bath. The living area embraces the outdoor living space. The family eat-in kitchen design allows for efficient food preparation. Note the interior laundry closet included in the home. This plan comes with three options for Bedroom 2 and one option for the master bath. It also includes blueprints for three elevation choices!

Design by
Home Design
Services, Inc.

Design VH8612

Square Footage: 1,576

● Though modest in size, this home boasts an interior court-yard with solarium. The master suite surrounds the solarium and opens with double doors to the large open family room. The dining room shares a volume ceiling with this space and connects via a serving bar to the kitchen. Besides the fireplace in the family room, there is also a sliding glass door to a covered patio. Family bedrooms are to the rear of the plan. They share a full bath. Note the utility area just off the foyer and breakfast nook with bright multi-paned windows. Plans include three different elevation choices!

Design by
Home Design
Services, Inc.

WIDTH 40'
DEPTH 67'-8"

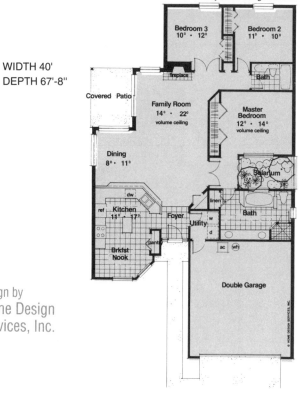

274

← 40'-0" →

Covered Patio

Master Bed Rm. 13⁰·17⁰ vault or 10' flat

Shelf @ 42"

Breakfast 11⁶·8⁶

Kitchen

shelf

Bath lin. wic

Family Rm. 14⁸·23⁰ vault or 10' flat

Dining Rm. vault or 10' flat

36" Pre-Fab Fireplace

Bed Rm. 2 13¹⁰·9⁶ vault or 10' flat

Living vault or 10' flat

Plant Shelf Abv.

Ba. **Foyer**

wh A/C W D A/C

Entry

Bed Rm. 3 13¹⁰·11⁰ vault or 10' flat

Double Garage

66'-8"

© HOME DESIGN SERVICES, INC.

Design VH8613
Square Footage: 1,872

● Vaulted ceilings throughout this home suggest the innovative touches that add interest in a single-level plan. Sidelight and overhead windows brighten a foyer that opens to the family and living rooms. A plant shelf spans the entry into the living room, which is united with the dining room under a high ceiling. A vaulted ceiling also augments the family room. Notice the two-way fireplace and access to a covered patio here. The kitchen is convenient to the dining room and to a bayed breakfast nook. The master bedroom also has a bay window plus a full bath with oversized shower. Two additional bedrooms share a full bath. Plans include two different elevation choices!

Design by
Home Design
Services, Inc.

Design VH3603

Width 70'
Depth 67'-4"

Design by
**Home Planners,
Inc.**

Design VH3602

QUOTE ONE™

Cost to build? See page 300
to order complete cost estimate
to build this house in your area!

Width 70'
Depth 67'-4"

Design VH3602/VH3603

Square footage: 2,312/2,520

L

● This lovely one-story home fits
right into sunny regions. Its stucco
exterior with easily accessed outdoor living areas makes it an all-time
favorite. Inside, the floor plan accommodates empty-nester lifestyles. There
is plenty of room for both formal and
informal entertaining: living room,
dining room, family room and morning room. A quiet office or den provides a getaway for quieter pursuits.
Sleeping areas are split with the master bedrooms and bath on one side and
a secondary bedroom and bath on the
other. Other special features include a
warming hearth in the family room, a
private porch off the den and a grand
rear deck. Design VH3603 provides a
three-bedroom option.

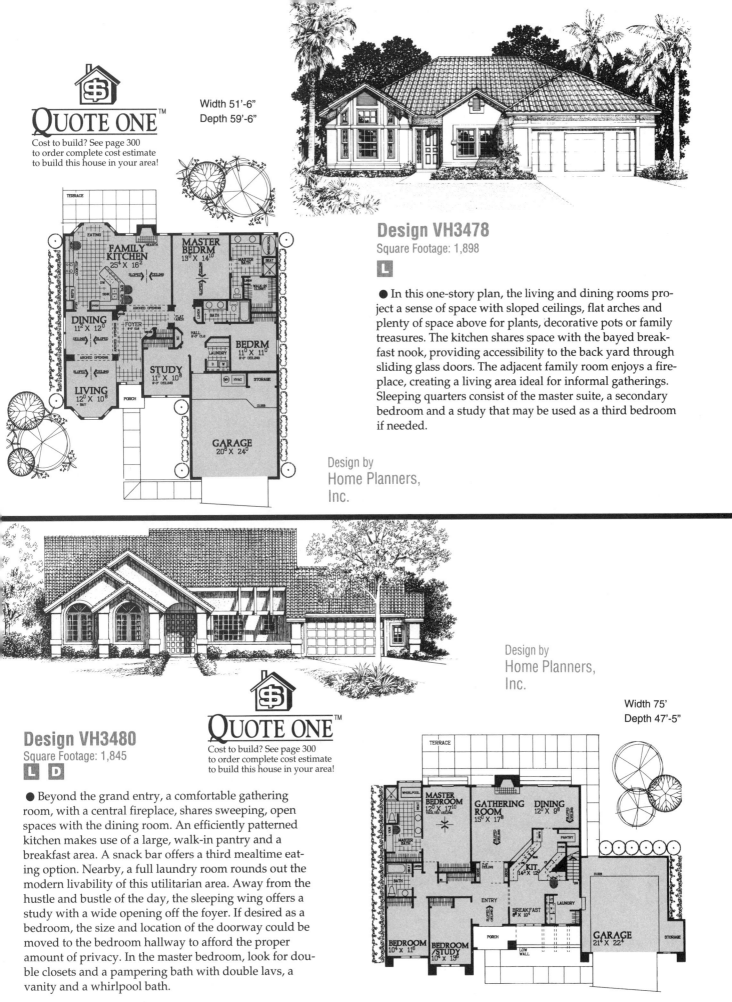

Quote One™

Cost to build? See page 300
to order complete cost estimate
to build this house in your area!

Width 51'-6"
Depth 59'-6"

Design VH3478

Square Footage: 1,898

L

● In this one-story plan, the living and dining rooms project a sense of space with sloped ceilings, flat arches and plenty of space above for plants, decorative pots or family treasures. The kitchen shares space with the bayed breakfast nook, providing accessibility to the back yard through sliding glass doors. The adjacent family room enjoys a fireplace, creating a living area ideal for informal gatherings. Sleeping quarters consist of the master suite, a secondary bedroom and a study that may be used as a third bedroom if needed.

Design by
Home Planners,
Inc.

Design by
Home Planners,
Inc.

Quote One™

Cost to build? See page 300
to order complete cost estimate
to build this house in your area!

Width 75'
Depth 47'-5"

Design VH3480

Square Footage: 1,845

L D

● Beyond the grand entry, a comfortable gathering room, with a central fireplace, shares sweeping, open spaces with the dining room. An efficiently patterned kitchen makes use of a large, walk-in pantry and a breakfast area. A snack bar offers a third mealtime eating option. Nearby, a full laundry room rounds out the modern livability of this utilitarian area. Away from the hustle and bustle of the day, the sleeping wing offers a study with a wide opening off the foyer. If desired as a bedroom, the size and location of the doorway could be moved to the bedroom hallway to afford the proper amount of privacy. In the master bedroom, look for double closets and a pampering bath with double lavs, a vanity and a whirlpool bath.

Design VH3563

First Floor: 1,023 square feet
Second Floor: 866 square feet
Total: 1,889 square feet

● Practical to build, this wonderful transitional plan combines the best of contemporary and traditional styling. Its stucco exterior is enhanced by arched windows and a recessed arched entry plus a lovely balcony off the second-floor master bedroom. A walled entry court extends the living room to the outside. The double front doors open to a foyer with a hall closet and a powder room. The service entrance is just to the right and accesses the two-car garage. The large living room adjoins directly to the dining room. The family room is set off behind the garage and features a sloped ceiling and a fireplace. Sleeping quarters consist of two secondary bedrooms with a shared bath and a generous master suite with a well-appointed bath.

Design by
Home Planners,
Inc.

Quote One™

Cost to build? See page 300
to order complete cost estimate
to build this house in your area!

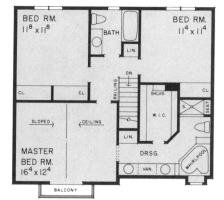

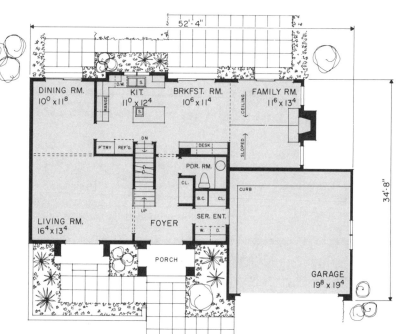

Width 36'
Depth 63'

Design VH3463

First Floor: 1,163 square feet
Second Floor: 1,077 square feet
Total: 2,240 square feet

L

Design by
Home Planners,
Inc.

● Fine family living takes off in this grand two-story plan. The tiled foyer leads to a stately living room with sliding glass doors to the back terrace and columns separating it from the dining room. Additional accents include a corner curios niche and access to a covered porch. For casual living, look no further than the family room/breakfast room combination. On the second floor, the master bedroom offers a fireplace.

Design VH3464

First Floor: 1,776 square feet
Second Floor: 876 square feet
Total: 2,652 square feet

L **D**

● A two-story foyer introduces an open formal area with a volume living room and a dining room. The kitchen sits to the rear of the plan and shares space with the breakfast room. The family room enjoys access to a terrace. The master bedroom offers a pampering bath. The sleeping accommodations are complete with three upstairs bedrooms.

Width 42'
Depth 72'-8"

Design by
Home Planners,
Inc.

Design VH3565

First Floor: 1,248 square feet
Second Floor: 1,012 square feet
Total: 2,260 square feet

L **D**

● Every detail of this plan speaks of modern design. The exterior is simple yet elegant, while interior floor planning is thorough yet efficient. The formal living and dining rooms are to the left of the home, separated by columns. The living room features a wall of windows and a fireplace. The kitchen with island cooktop is adjacent to the large family room with terrace access. A study with additional terrace access completes the first floor. The master bedroom features a balcony and a spectacular bath with whirlpool tub, shower with seat, separate vanities and a walk-in closet. Two family bedrooms share access to a full bath. Also notice the three-car garage.

QUOTE ONE™

Cost to build? See page 300 to order complete cost estimate to build this house in your area!

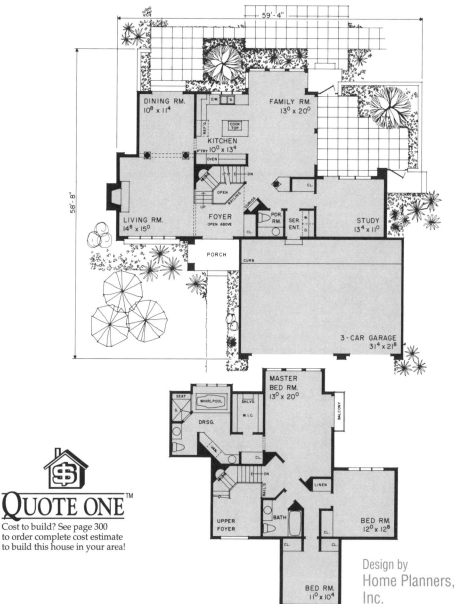

Design by
Home Planners,
Inc.

Design VH2843

Upper Level: 1,861 square feet
Lower Level: 1,181 square feet
Total: 3,042 square feet

L

54'-0"

40'-4"

TERRACE

FAMILY RM.
14⁰ x 21⁶

LOUNGE
11⁴ x 13⁶

STORAGE
10⁴ x 11²

BEDROOM
11⁰ x 11²

CL

MASTER BATH

CL

FURN

GARAGE
24⁰ x 19²

STOR

UP DN

FOYER

BATH

D W

LAUNDRY/
HOBBIES
14⁰ x 14⁰ BAY

PORCH

DECK

LIVING RM.
14⁰ x 21⁶

BEDROOM
11⁰ x 13⁶

CL

BEDROOM/
STUDY
11⁰ x 13⁶

CL

OPT. DOOR

OPEN THRU

DINING
12⁰ x 13⁶

CAB'T

OVEN

REF'D.

LIN.

BATH

CL

KITCHEN
15⁴ x 8⁰

RANGE

S DW

SNACK BAR

DESK

BATH

LINEN

UP DN

FOYER

PANTRY

BREAKFAST
15⁴ x 9⁶

DRESSING RM.

MASTER
BEDROOM
14⁰ x 16⁰

PORCH

● Bi-level living will be enjoyed to its fullest in this
Spanish styled design. There is a lot of room for the
various family activities. Informal living will take place
on the lower level in the family room and lounge. The
formal living and dining rooms, sharing a thru-fire-
place, are located on the upper level.

Design by
Home Planners,
Inc.

281

Design VH3561

First Floor: 1,006 square feet
Second Floor: 990 square feet
Total: 1,996 square feet

L **D**

● Great style demands an equally great floor plan—this home has both! The front-facing garage allows room for the home to be built on just about any size lot and keeps street noise to a minimum. Living areas are on the first floor and include a living room/dining combination and a conversation area just off the island kitchen. Note the fireplace in the

living area and the sliding glass doors to the rear terrace. You'll also enjoy the fact that the living room rises to two stories. Upstairs are three bedrooms including a master suite with a tray ceiling and a private bath. Here, amenities include a whirlpool tub, dual lavatories and a compartmented toilet and shower.

Design by
Home Planners, Inc.

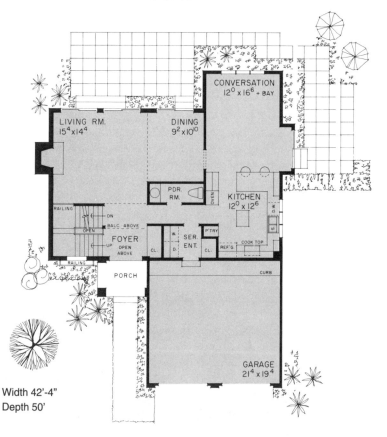

Width 42'-4"
Depth 50'

QUOTE ONE™

Cost to build? See page 300
to order complete cost estimate
to build this house in your area!

Design VH3558

First Floor: 2,328 square feet
Second Floor: 603 square feet
Total: 2,931 square feet

L D

Design by
Home Planners, Inc.

● This home will keep even the most active family from feeling cramped. A broad foyer opens to a living room that measures 24 feet across and features sliding glass doors to a rear terrace and a covered porch. Adjacent to the kitchen is a conversation area with additional access to the covered porch, a snack bar, fireplace and a window bay. A butler's pantry leads to the formal dining room. Placed conveniently on the first floor, the master suite features a roomy bath with a huge walk-in closet and dual vanities. Two large bedrooms are found on the second floor.

Width 69'-4"
Depth 66'

QUOTE ONE™

Cost to build? See page 300 to order complete cost estimate to build this house in your area!

Design VH6616 First Floor: 1,136 square feet
Second Floor: 636 square feet; Total: 1,772 square feet

● This two-story coastal design is sure to please with its warm character and decorative widow's walk. The covered entry—with its dramatic transom window—leads to a spacious great room highlighted by a warming fireplace. To the right, the dining room and kitchen combine to provide a delightful place for mealtimes inside or out, with access to a side deck through double doors. A study, a bedroom and a full bath complete the first floor. The luxurious master suite is located on the second floor for privacy and features an oversized walk-in closet. The pampering master bath enjoys a relaxing whirlpool tub, a double-bowl vanity and a compartmented toilet.

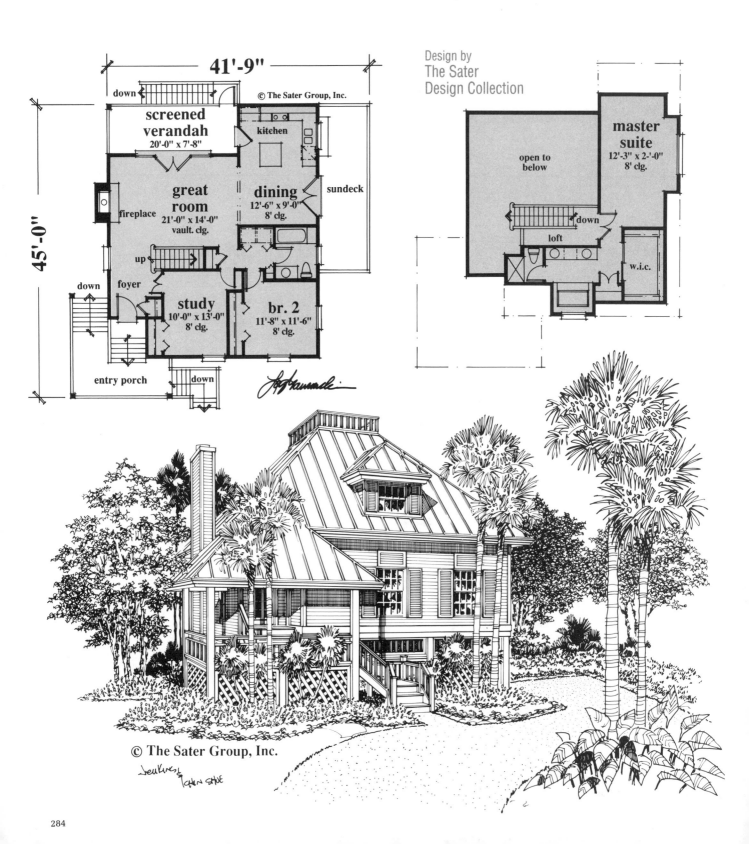

284

Design by
The Sater
Design Collection

Design VH6615

First Floor: 1,736 square feet; Second Floor: 640 square feet
Lower Level: 840 square feet; Total: 3,216 square feet

● Lattice panels, shutters, a balustrade and a metal roof add character to this delightful coastal home. Double doors flanking a fireplace open to the sun deck from the spacious great room sporting a vaulted ceiling. Access to the veranda is provided from this room also. An adjacent dining room provides views of the rear grounds and space for formal and informal entertaining. The glassed-in nook shares space with the L-shaped kitchen and a center work island. Bedrooms 2 and 3, a full bath and a utility room complete this floor. Upstairs, a sumptuous master suite awaits. Double doors extend to a private deck from the master bedroom. His and Hers walk-in closets lead the way to a grand master bath featuring an arched whirlpool tub, a double-bowl vanity and a separate shower.

Width 54'
Depth 44'

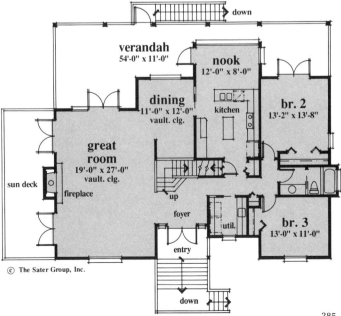

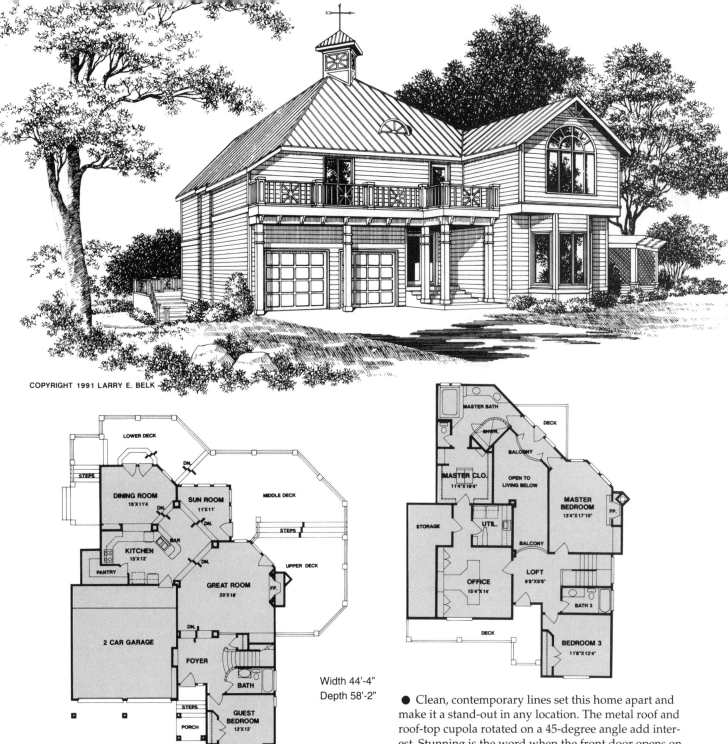

COPYRIGHT 1991 LARRY E. BELK

LOWER DECK

STEPS

DINING ROOM
15'X11'4

SUN ROOM
11'X11'

MIDDLE DECK

KITCHEN
15'X12'

BAR

PANTRY

STEPS

UPPER DECK

GREAT ROOM
20'X18'

FP

DN.

2 CAR GARAGE

FOYER

DN.

BATH

STEPS

PORCH

GUEST BEDROOM
12'X12'

MASTER BATH

SHWR.

DECK

BALCONY

MASTER CLO.
11'4"X10'4"

OPEN TO LIVING BELOW

STORAGE

UTIL.

MASTER BEDROOM
13'4"X17'10"

FP

BALCONY

OFFICE
15'4"X14'

LOFT
9'8"X9'8"

BATH 3

DECK

BEDROOM 3
11'8"X12'4"

Width 44'-4"
Depth 58'-2"

Design VH8001
First Floor: 1,309 square feet
Second Floor: 1,343 square feet
Total: 2,652 square feet

Design by
Larry E. Belk
Designs

● Clean, contemporary lines set this home apart and make it a stand-out in any location. The metal roof and roof-top cupola rotated on a 45-degree angle add interest. Stunning is the word when the front door opens on this home. Remote control transoms in the cupola open automatically to increase ventilation. The great room, sun room, dining room and kitchen are all adjacent to provide areas for entertaining. Originally designed for a sloping site, the home incorporates multiple levels inside. Additionally, there is access to a series of multi-level outside decks from the dining room, sun room and great room. All these areas have at least one glass wall overlooking the rear. The master bedroom and bath upstairs are bridged by a pipe rail balcony that provides access to a rear outside deck. The master suite includes a huge master closet. Additional storage and closet area is located off the hallway to the office. The open, spacious layout and emphasis on the views to the rear make this home a winner for harbor/marina, golf course, lake or wooded sites.

© The Sater Group, Inc.

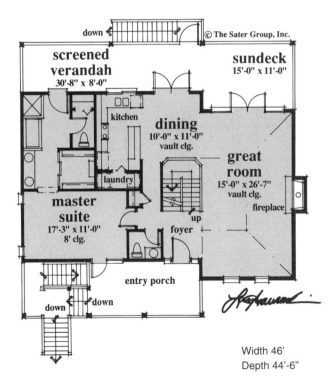

© The Sater Group, Inc.

screened verandah
30'-8" x 8'-0"

down

sundeck
15'-0" x 11'-0"

kitchen

dining
10'-0" x 11'-0"
vault clg.

great room
15'-0" x 26'-7"
vault clg.

fireplace

laundry

up

master suite
17'-3" x 11'-0"
8' clg.

foyer

down   down

entry porch

Width 46'
Depth 44'-6"

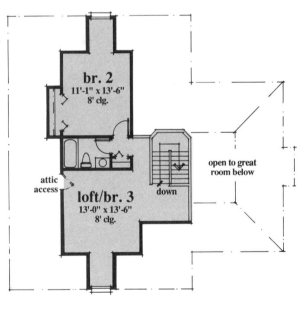

br. 2
11'-1" x 13'-6"
8' clg.

attic access

loft/br. 3
13'-0" x 13'-6"
8' clg.

down

open to great room below

Design by
The Sater
Design Collection

Design VH6617 First Floor: 1,189 square feet
Second Floor: 575 square feet; Total: 1,764 square feet

● An abundance of porches and a deck encourage year-round indoor/outdoor relationships in this classic two-story home. The spacious great room with its cozy fireplace and the adjacent dining room—both with access to the screened deck area—are perfect for formal or informal entertaining. An efficient kitchen and a nearby laundry room make chores easy. The private master suite offers access to the screened veranda and leads into a relaxing master bath complete with a walk-in closet, a tub and a separate shower, double-bowl lavs and a compartmented toilet. Bedroom 2 shares the second floor with a full bath and a loft which may be used as a third bedroom.

287

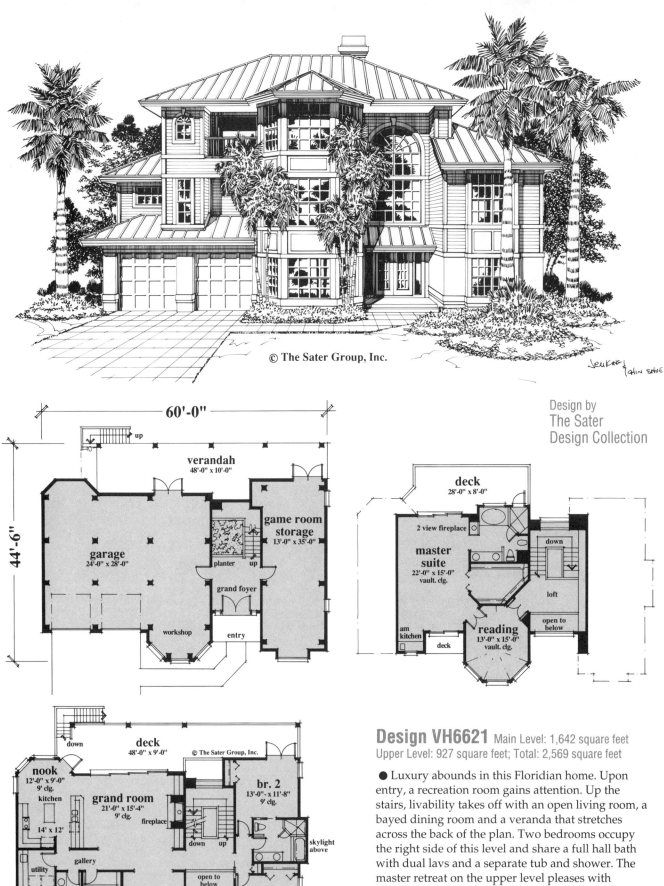

© The Sater Group, Inc.

Design by
The Sater Design Collection

60'-0"

44'-6"

verandah
48'-0" x 10'-0"

game room storage
13'-0" x 35'-0"

garage
24'-0" x 28'-0"

planter   up

grand foyer

workshop

entry

up

deck
28'-0" x 8'-0"

2 view fireplace

down

master suite
22'-0" x 15'-0"
vault. clg.

loft

open to below

am kitchen

deck

reading
13'-0" x 15'-0"
vault. clg.

down

deck
48'-0" x 9'-0"

© The Sater Group, Inc.

nook
12'-0" x 9'-0"
9' clg.

kitchen

grand room
21'-0" x 15'-4"
9' clg.

14' x 12'

fireplace

br. 2
13'-0" x 11'-8"
9' clg.

skylight above

gallery

utility

down   up

open to below

dining
13'-0" x 14'-0"
9' clg.

br. 3
13'-0" x 12'-0"
9' clg.

Design VH6621 Main Level: 1,642 square feet
Upper Level: 927 square feet; Total: 2,569 square feet

● Luxury abounds in this Floridian home. Upon entry, a recreation room gains attention. Up the stairs, livability takes off with an open living room, a bayed dining room and a veranda that stretches across the back of the plan. Two bedrooms occupy the right side of this level and share a full hall bath with dual lavs and a separate tub and shower. The master retreat on the upper level pleases with its own library, a morning kitchen, a large walk-in closet and a pampering bath with a double-bowl vanity, a compartmented toilet and bidet, a whirlpool tub and a shower that opens outside. A private deck allows outdoor enjoyments.

288

Photo by Oscar Thompson

Floor Plan Details

64'-0"

© The Sater Group, Inc.

45'-0"

screened verandah
50'-0" x 12'-0" avg.

grill

kitchen

nook

dining
11'-6" x 14'-0"
8'-6" clg.

18' x 14'

3 sided fireplace

wetbar

study
12'-8" x 13'-4"
vaulted clg.

grand room
17'-6" x 18'-0"
2 story clg.

br. 3
10'-4" x 15'-0"
8'-6" clg.

utility

elev.

foyer

entry

up   down

br. 2
12'-8" x 14'-0"
8'-6" clg.

down

balcony

Master Suite Floor Plan

spa

deck

3 sided fireplace

master suite
20'-0" x 16'-0"
vaulted clg.

open to grand room below

w.i.c.

elev.   gallery walkway

storage

open to below

down

Design by
The Sater
Design Collection

Design VH6620

First Floor: 2,066 square feet
Lower Level: 1,260 square feet
Second Floor: 810 square feet
Total: 4,136 square feet

● If entertaining's your passion, then this is the design for you. With a large, open floor plan and an array of amenities, every gathering will be a success. The foyer embraces living areas accented by a glass fireplace and a wet bar. The living and dining rooms each access a screened entertainment center for outside enjoyments. The gourmet kitchen delights with its openness to the rest of the house. A morning room here also adds a nice touch. Two bedrooms and a den radiate from the first-floor living areas. Upstairs—or use the elevator—is a masterful master suite. It contains a huge walk-in closet, a whirlpool tub and a private sun deck.

289

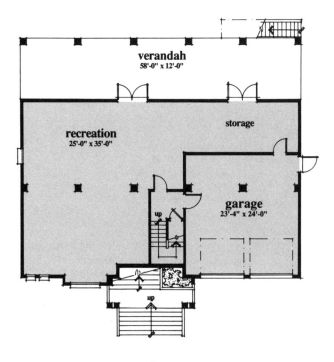

verandah
58'-0" x 12'-0"

recreation
25'-0" x 35'-0"

storage

garage
23'-4" x 24'-0"

up

up

Width 58'
Depth 54'

Design VH6622 Square Footage: 2,190

● A dramatic set of stairs leads to the entry of this home. The foyer leads to an expansive living room with a fireplace and built-in bookshelves. A lanai opens off this area and will assure outdoor enjoyments. For formal meals, a front-facing dining room offers a bumped-out bay. The kitchen serves this area easily as well as the breakfast room. A study and three bedrooms make up the rest of the floor plan. Two secondary bedrooms share a full hall bath. A utility area is also nearby. In the master suite, two walk-in closets and a full bath are appreciated features. In the bedroom, a set of French doors offers passage to the lanai.

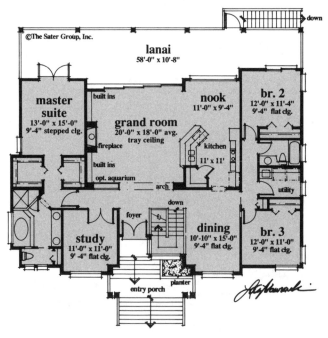

lanai
58'-0" x 10'-8"

master suite
13'-0" x 15'-0"
9'-4" stepped clg.

built ins

grand room
20'-0" x 18'-0" avg.
tray ceiling

fireplace

built ins

opt. aquarium

arch

nook
11'-0" x 9'-4"

br. 2
12'-0" x 11'-4"
9'-4" flat clg.

kitchen
11' x 11'

utility

foyer

down

study
11'-0" x 11'-0"
9'-4" flat clg.

dining
10'-10" x 15'-0"
9'-4" flat clg.

br. 3
12'-0" x 11'-4"
9'-4" flat clg.

entry porch   planter

down

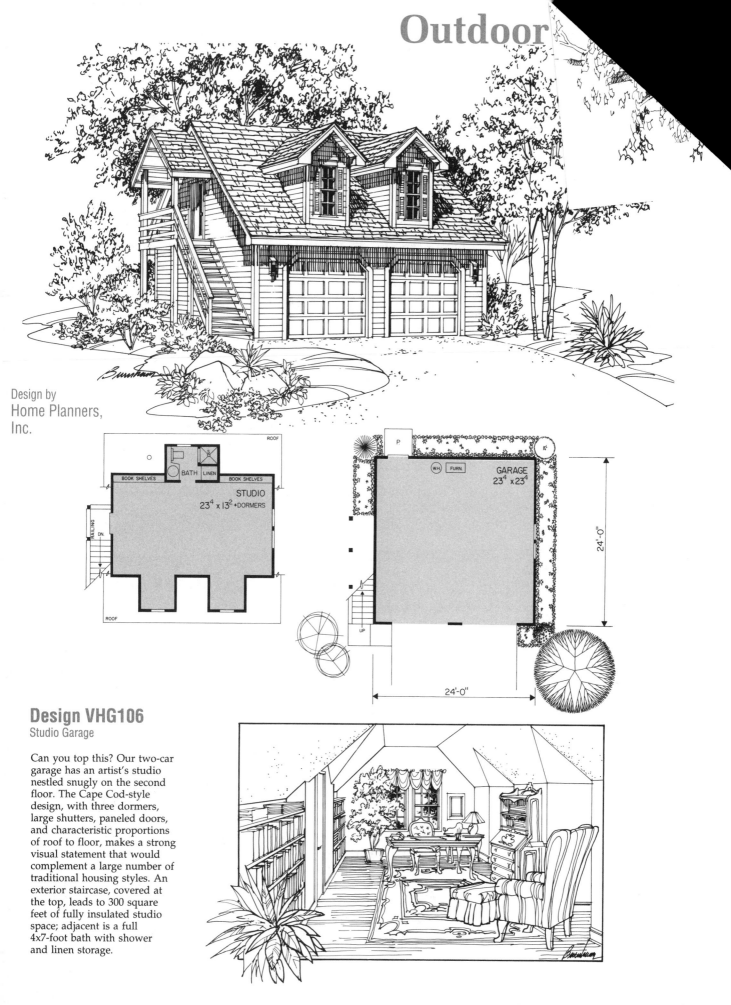

Design by
Home Planners,
Inc.

STUDIO
23⁴ x 13² +DORMERS

BOOK SHELVES   BATH   LINEN   BOOK SHELVES

RAILING   DN.

ROOF

ROOF

W.H.   FURN.   GARAGE
23⁴ x 23⁴

UP

24'-0"

24'-0"

Design VHG106
Studio Garage

Can you top this? Our two-car garage has an artist's studio nestled snugly on the second floor. The Cape Cod-style design, with three dormers, large shutters, paneled doors, and characteristic proportions of roof to floor, makes a strong visual statement that would complement a large number of traditional housing styles. An exterior staircase, covered at the top, leads to 300 square feet of fully insulated studio space; adjacent is a full 4x7-foot bath with shower and linen storage.

Design VHG206
3-Car Studio Garage

● This three-car traditional design is perfect for someone who needs extra space for an on-site office, a live-in relative or for the teen who wants a little independence close to home. The upstairs studio/loft offers a full bath, an efficiency kitchen, built-in bookshelves and three dormers to bathe the room in light. Use the downstairs area for three cars or two cars and lots of storage or work space.

Design by
Home Planners,
Inc.

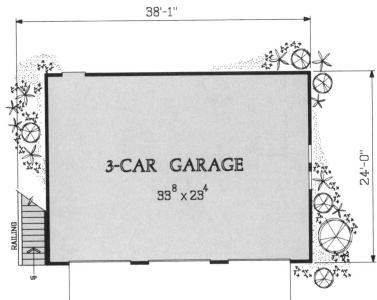

38'-1"

3-CAR GARAGE
$33^8 \times 23^4$

24'-0"

RAILING

UP

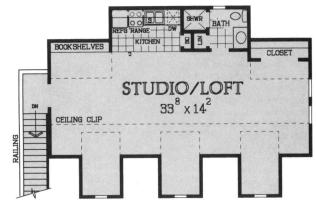

SHWR   BATH
REFG RANGE   DW
BOOKSHELVES   KITCHEN   CLOSET

STUDIO/LOFT
$33^8 \times 14^2$

DN

RAILING

CEILING CLIP

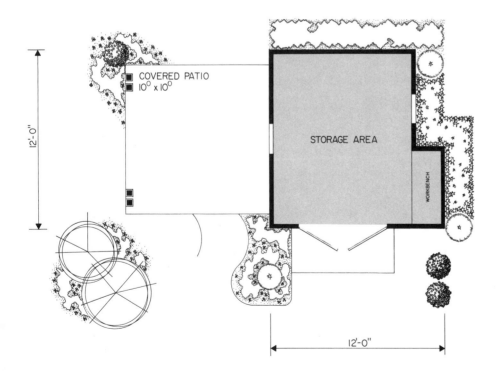

COVERED PATIO
10⁰ x 10⁰

STORAGE AREA

WORKBENCH

12'-0"

12'-0"

Design by
Home Planners,
Inc.

Design VHG107
Storage Shed With Patio

• Here's a hard-working
storage shed with a number
of bright touches. At 244
square feet, it's bigger than
most. A cupola, a birdhouse,
shutters and grooved ply-
wood siding add up to a traditional look that complements many popular housing
styles. It's a flexible design,
too, and could also be used
as a potting shed or a workshop. The nicest feature may
well be the covered patio.
After you cut the grass, just
stash the lawn mower, take
a seat and survey your
handiwork.

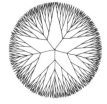

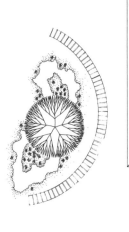

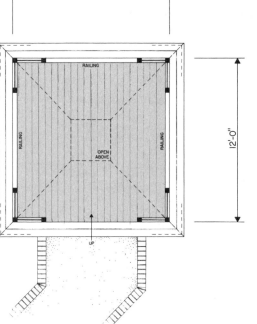

12'-0"

12'-0"

RAILING

RAILING

RAILING

RAILING

OPEN ABOVE

UP

Design by
Home Planners,
Inc.

Design VHG108
Neoclassic Gazebo

● Our gazebo is a prime spot for entertaining. At 144 square feet, it has as much surface space as the average family room. Plus, it's just under 17 ½ feet tall, which makes it the size of a typical one-story house. As a result, it's best suited for larger lots—at least a half acre. Boasting a number of neoclassic features—perfect proportions, columns, bases—it's also a good match with solid, traditional housing styles. The cupola is a homey touch that lets light in to the decking below. Cedar or redwood are the building materials of choice.

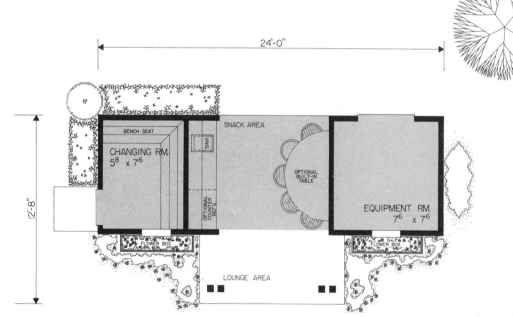

BENCH SEAT

CHANGING RM.
5⁸ x 7⁶

SINK

OPTIONAL COUNTER REF. G

SNACK AREA

OPTIONAL BUILT-IN TABLE

EQUIPMENT RM.
7⁶ x 7⁶

FLOWER BOX

FLOWER BOX

LOUNGE AREA

24'-0"

12'-8"

Design by
Home Planners,
Inc.

Design VHG110
Pool Cabana

● Imagine this charming structure perched adjacent to your back-yard swimming pool. Its exterior highlights such architectural features as hip and gable roofs, a decorative cupola, shuttered windows, flower boxes and horizontal wood and shingle siding. Its plan offers a spacious sheltered party/lounge area with counter, sink and refrigerator space. An optional built-in table could assure no rain-outs of those pool-side snacks. Flanking this practical breeze-way-type area are two rooms equal in size and utility. To the left is the changing room with a convenient bench. To the right is the equipment room for the handy storage of pool supplies and furniture. Surely a fine addition to the active family's back yard.

20'-0"

16'-0"

DECK

SUNROOM

WORK TABLE

UP

Design by
Home Planners,
Inc.

Design VHG109
Craft Cottage

● This little cottage is both functional and good-looking. Ample counter space and shelving provide plenty of room to spread out materials and tools. Plus, a vaulted ceiling opens up the whole area. Next to the work space is a cozy sunroom. French doors and several windows, including a circle-head version above the doors, bathe the room in sunlight, while overhangs offer adequate shading. To get maximum sun, a south facing for the sunroom is best; it will also provide soft, even illumination for the north-facing work area.

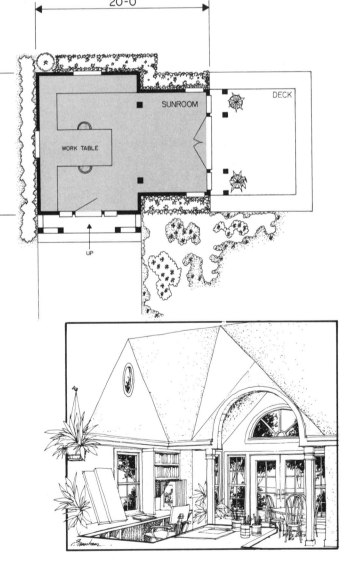

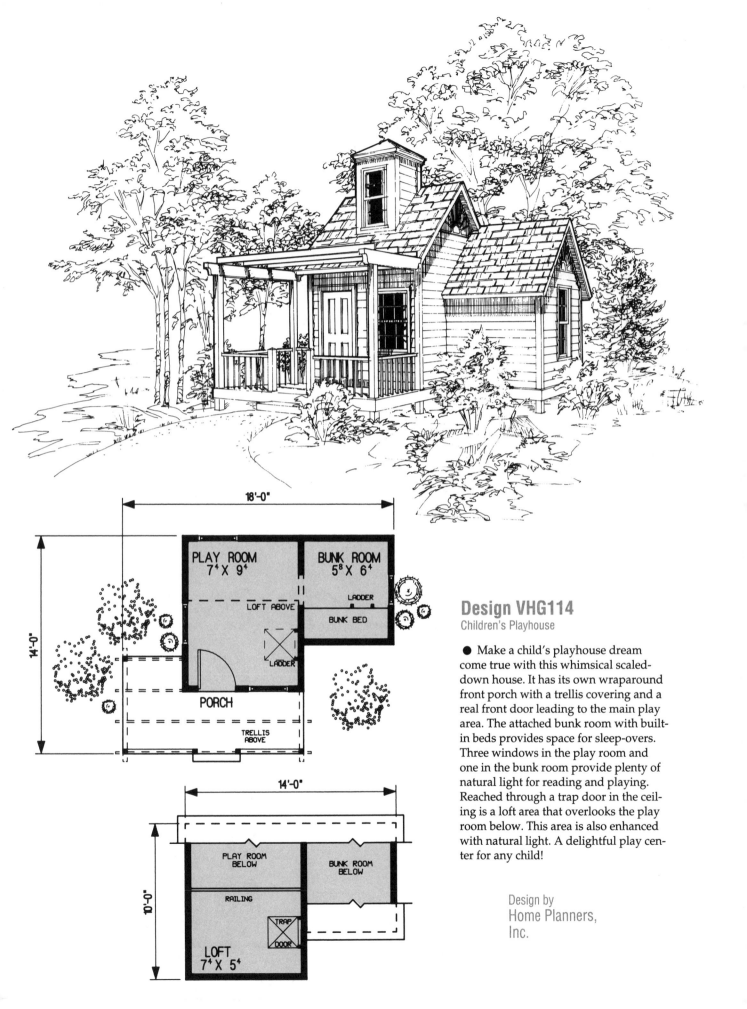

PLAY ROOM
7⁴ X 9⁴

BUNK ROOM
5⁸ X 6⁴

18'-0"

14'-0"

LOFT ABOVE

LADDER

BUNK BED

LADDER

PORCH

TRELLIS ABOVE

14'-0"

10'-0"

PLAY ROOM BELOW

BUNK ROOM BELOW

RAILING

TRAP DOOR

LOFT
7⁴ X 5⁴

Design VHG114
Children's Playhouse

● Make a child's playhouse dream come true with this whimsical scaled-down house. It has its own wraparound front porch with a trellis covering and a real front door leading to the main play area. The attached bunk room with built-in beds provides space for sleep-overs. Three windows in the play room and one in the bunk room provide plenty of natural light for reading and playing. Reached through a trap door in the ceiling is a loft area that overlooks the play room below. This area is also enhanced with natural light. A delightful play center for any child!

Design by
Home Planners,
Inc.

When You're Ready To Order . . .

Let Us Show You Our Home Blueprint Package.

Building a home? Planning a home? Our Blueprint Package has nearly everything you need to get the job done right, whether you're working on your own or with help from an architect, designer, builder or subcontractors. Each Blueprint Package is the result of many hours of work by licensed architects or professional designers.

QUALITY

Hundreds of hours of painstaking effort have gone into the development of your blueprint set. Each home has been quality-checked by professionals to insure accuracy and buildability.

VALUE

Because we sell in volume, you can buy professional-quality blueprints at a fraction of their development cost. With our plans, your dream home design costs only a few hundred dollars, not the thousands of dollars that custom architects charge.

SERVICE

Once you've chosen your favorite home plan, you'll receive fast, efficient service whether you choose to mail or fax your order to us or call us toll free at 1-800-521-6797.

SATISFACTION

Over 50 years of service to satisfied home plan buyers provide us unparalleled experience and knowledge in producing quality blueprints. What this means to you is satisfaction with our product and performance.

ORDER TOLL FREE 1-800-521-6797

After you've looked over our Blueprint Package and Important Extras on the following pages, simply mail the order form on page 309 or call toll free on our Blueprint Hotline: 1-800-521-6797. We're ready and eager to serve you.

Each set of blueprints is an interrelated collection of detail sheets which includes components such as floor plans, interior and exterior elevations, dimensions, cross-sections, diagrams and notations. These sheets show exactly how your house is to be built.

Among the sheets included may be:

Frontal Sheet
This artist's sketch of the exterior of the house gives you an idea of how the house will look when built and landscaped. Large ink-line floor plans show all levels of the house and provide an overview of your new home's livability, as well as a handy reference for deciding on furniture placement.

Foundation Plan
This sheet shows the foundation layout includ-

SAMPLE PACKAGE

ing support walls, excavated and unexcavated areas, if any, and foundation notes. If slab construction rather than basement, the plan shows footings and details for a monolithic slab. This page, or another in the set, may include a sample plot plan for locating your house on a building site.

Detailed Floor Plans

These plans show the layout of each floor of the house. Rooms and interior spaces are carefully dimensioned and keys are given for cross-section details provided later in the plans. The positions of electrical outlets and switches are shown.

House Cross-Sections

Large-scale views show sections or cut-aways of the foundation, interior walls, exterior walls, floors, stairways and roof details. Additional cross-sections may show important changes in floor, ceiling or roof heights or the relationship of one level to another. Extremely valuable for construction, these sections show exactly how the various parts of the house fit together.

Interior Elevations

Many of our drawings show the design and placement of kitchen and bathroom cabinets, laundry areas, fireplaces, bookcases and other built-ins. Little "extras," such as mantelpiece and wainscoting drawings, plus moulding sections, provide details that give your home that custom touch.

Exterior Elevations

These drawings show the front, rear and sides of your house and give necessary notes on exterior materials and finishes. Particular attention is given to cornice detail, brick and stone accents or other finish items that make your home unique.

Frontal Sheet

Foundation Plans

Detailed Floor Plans

Exterior Elevations

Interior Elevations

House Cross-Sections

*I*ntroducing nine important planning and construction aids

CUSTOM ENGINEERING

Our Custom Engineering Service Package provides an engineering seal for the structural elements of any Home Planners plan. This new Package provides complete calculations (except foundation engineering) from a registered professional, and offers many options invaluable to anyone planning to build. The Package includes: Structural framing plans for each horizontal framing area; Individual, certified truss designs; Specifications for all framing members; Calculation sheets detailing engineering problems and solutions concerning shear, bending, and deflections for all key framing members; Structural details for all key situations; Hanger and special connections specifications; Load and geometry information that may be used by a foundation design engineer and a Registered Professional Engineer's Seal for all of the above services. Home Planners also offers 3 Optional Engineering Services: Lateral load calculations and specifications for both wind and seismic considerations; Secondary Framing information for roofs, floors and walls; Light-gauge steel framing, providing details and cost comparisons for steel and wood.

SPECIFICATION OUTLINE

This valuable 16-page document is critical to building your house correctly. Designed to be filled in by you or your builder, this book lists 166 stages or items crucial to the building process. It provides a comprehensive review of the construction process and helps in making choices of materials. When combined with the blueprints, a signed contract, and a schedule, it becomes a legal document and record for the building of your home.

MATERIALS LIST

(Note: Because of the diversity of local building codes, our Materials List does not include mechanical materials.)

For many of the designs in our portfolio, we offer a customized materials take-off that is invaluable in planning and estimating the cost of your new home. This Materials List outlines the quantity, type and size of materials needed to build your house (with the exception of mechanical system items). Included are framing lumber, windows and doors, kitchen and bath cabinetry, rough and finish hardware, and much more. This handy list helps you or your builder cost out materials and serves as a reference sheet when you're compiling bids.

QUOTE ONE®

Summary Cost Report / Materials Cost Report

A new service for estimating the cost of building select designs, the Quote One® system is available in two separate stages: The Summary Cost Report and the Materials Cost Report.

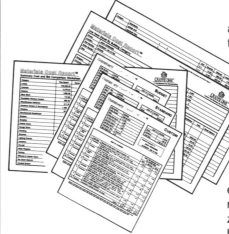

The Summary Cost Report is the first stage in the package and shows the total cost per square foot for your chosen home in your zip-code area and then breaks that cost down into ten categories showing the costs for building materials, labor and installation. The total cost for the report (which includes three grades: Budget, Standard and Custom) is just $19.95 for one home, and additionals are only $14.95. These reports allow you to evaluate your building budget and compare the costs of building a variety of homes in your area.

Make even more informed decisions about your home-building project with the second phase of our package, our Materials Cost Report. This tool is invaluable in planning and estimating the cost of your new home. The material and installation (labor and equipment) cost is shown for each of over 1,000 line items provided in the Materials List (Standard grade) which is included when you purchase this estimating tool. It allows you to determine building costs for your specific zip-code area and for your chosen home design. Space is allowed for additional estimates from contractors and subcontractors, such as for mechanical materials, which are not included in our packages. This invaluable tool is available for a price of $110 ($120 for a Schedule E plan) which includes a Materials List.

To order these invaluable reports, use the order form on page 309 or call 1-800-521-6797.

If you want to know more about techniques—and deal more confidently with subcontractors we offer these useful sheets. Each set is an excellent tool that will add to your understanding of these technical subjects.

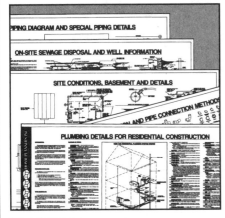

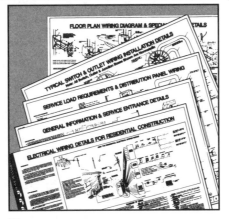

Plan-A-Home®

PLUMBING

The Blueprint Package includes locations for all the plumbing fixtures in your new house, including sinks, lavatories, tubs, showers, toilets, laundry trays and water heaters. However, if you want to know more about the complete plumbing system, these 24x36-inch detail sheets will prove very useful. Prepared to meet requirements of the National Plumbing Code, these six fact-filled sheets give general information on pipe schedules, fittings, sump-pump details, water-softener hookups, septic system details and much more. Color-coded sheets include a glossary of terms.

ELECTRICAL

The locations for every electrical switch, plug and outlet are shown in your Blueprint Package. However, these Electrical Details go further to take the mystery out of household electrical systems. Prepared to meet requirements of the National Electrical Code, these comprehensive 24x36-inch drawings come packed with helpful information, including wire sizing, switch-installation schematics, cable-routing details, appliance wattage, door-bell hookups, typical service panel circuitry and much more. Six sheets are bound together and color-coded for easy reference. A glossary of terms is also included.

Plan-A-Home® is an easy-to-use tool that helps you design a new home, arrange furniture in a new or existing home, or plan a remodeling project. Each package contains:

- **More than 700 reusable peel-off planning symbols** on a self-stick vinyl sheet, including walls, windows, doors, all types of furniture, kitchen components, bath fixtures and many more.

- **A reusable, transparent, 1/4-inch scale planning grid** that matches the scale of actual working drawings (1/4-inch equals 1 foot). This grid provides the basis for house layouts of up to 140x92 feet.

- **Tracing paper** and a protective sheet for copying or transferring your completed plan.

- **A felt-tip pen,** with water-soluble ink that wipes away quickly.

Plan-A-Home® lets you lay out areas as large as a 7,500 square foot, six-bedroom, seven-bath house.

CONSTRUCTION

The Blueprint Package contains everything an experienced builder needs to construct a particular house. However, it doesn't show all the ways that houses can be built, nor does it explain alternate construction methods. To help you understand how your house will be built—and offer additional techniques—this set of drawings depicts the materials and methods used to build foundations, fireplaces, walls, floors and roofs. Where appropriate, the drawings show acceptable alternatives. These six sheets will answer questions for the advanced do-it-yourselfer or home planner.

MECHANICAL

This package contains fundamental principles and useful data that will help you make informed decisions and communicate with subcontractors about heating and cooling systems. The 24x36-inch drawings contain instructions and samples that allow you to make simple load calculations and preliminary sizing and costing analysis. Covered are today's most commonly used systems from heat pumps to solar fuel systems. The package is packed full of illustrations and diagrams to help you visualize components and how they relate to one another.

To Order, Call Toll Free 1-800-521-6797

To add these important extras to your Blueprint Package, simply indicate your choices on the order form on page 309 or call us Toll Free 1-800-521-6797 and we'll tell you more about these exciting products.

 The Deck Blueprint Package

Many of the homes in this book can be enhanced with a professionally designed Home Planners' Deck Plan. Those home plans highlighted with a ▣ have a matching or corresponding deck plan available which includes a Deck Plan Frontal Sheet, Deck Framing and Floor Plans, Deck Elevations and a Deck Materials List. A Standard Deck Details Package, also available, provides all the how-to information necessary for building *any* deck. Our Complete Deck Building Package contains 1 set of Custom Deck Plans of your choice, plus 1 set of Standard Deck Building Details all for one low price. Our plans and details are carefully prepared in an easy-to-understand format that will guide you through every stage of your deck-building project. This page contains a sampling of 12 of the 25 different Deck layouts to match your favorite house. See page 304 for prices and ordering information.

SPLIT–LEVEL SUN DECK
Deck Plan D100

BI–LEVEL DECK WITH COVERED DINING
Deck Plan D101

WRAP–AROUND FAMILY DECK
Deck Plan D104

DECK FOR DINING AND VIEWS
Deck Plan D107

TREND–SETTER DECK
Deck Plan D110

TURN–OF–THE–CENTURY DECK
Deck Plan D111

WEEKEND ENTERTAINER DECK
Deck Plan D112

CENTER–VIEW DECK
Deck Plan D114

KITCHEN–EXTENDER DECK
Deck Plan D115

SPLIT–LEVEL ACTIVITY DECK
Deck Plan D117

TRI–LEVEL DECK WITH GRILL
Deck Plan D119

CONTEMPORARY LEISURE DECK
Deck Plan D120

⬛ The Landscape Blueprint Package

For the homes marked with an ⬛ in this book, Home Planners has created a front-yard landscape plan that matches or is complementary in design to the house plan. These comprehensive blueprint packages include a Frontal Sheet, Plan View, Regionalized Plant & Materials List, a sheet on Planting and Maintaining Your Landscape, Zone Maps and Plant Size and Description Guide. These plans will help you achieve professional results, adding value and enjoyment to your property for years to come. Each set of blueprints is a full 18" x 24" in size with clear, complete instructions and easy-to-read type. Six of the forty front-yard Landscape Plans to match your favorite house are shown below.

Regional Order Map

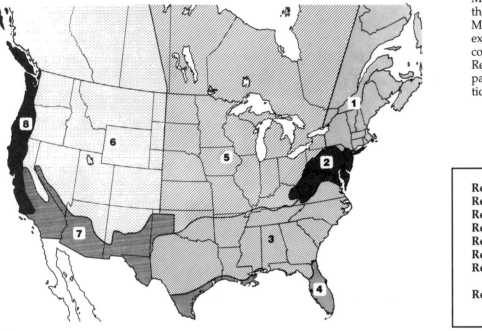

Most of the Landscape Plans shown on these pages are available with a Plant & Materials List adapted by horticultural experts to 8 different regions of the country. Please specify Geographic Region when ordering your plan. See page 304 for prices, ordering information and regional availability.

Region	1	Northeast
Region	2	Mid-Atlantic
Region	3	Deep South
Region	4	Florida & Gulf Coast
Region	5	Midwest
Region	6	Rocky Mountains
Region	7	Southern California & Desert Southwest
Region	8	Northern California & Pacific Northwest

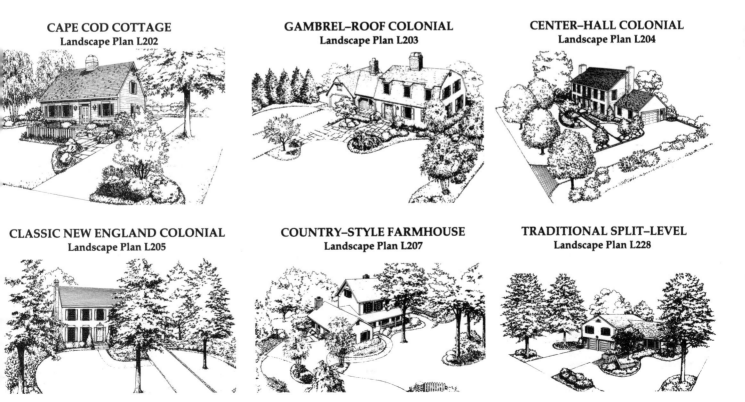

CAPE COD COTTAGE
Landscape Plan L202

GAMBREL–ROOF COLONIAL
Landscape Plan L203

CENTER–HALL COLONIAL
Landscape Plan L204

CLASSIC NEW ENGLAND COLONIAL
Landscape Plan L205

COUNTRY–STYLE FARMHOUSE
Landscape Plan L207

TRADITIONAL SPLIT–LEVEL
Landscape Plan L228

House Blueprint Price Schedule and Plans Index

These pages contain all the information you need to price your blueprints. In general, the larger and more complicated the house, the more it costs to design and thus the higher the price we must charge for the blueprints. Remember, however, that these prices are far less than you would normally pay for the services of a licensed architect or professional designer. Custom home designs and related architectural services often cost thousands of dollars, ranging from 5% to 15% of the cost of construction. By ordering our blueprints you are potentially saving enough money to afford a larger house, or to add those "extra" amenities such as a patio, deck, swimming pool or even an upgraded kitchen or luxurious master suite.

To use the Index below, refer to the design number listed in numerical order (a helpful page reference is also given). Note the price index letter and refer to the House Blueprint Price Schedule on page 305 for the cost of one, four or eight sets of blueprints or the cost of a reproducible sepia. Additional prices are shown for identical and reverse blueprint sets, as well as a very useful Materials List for some of the plans. Also note in the Index below those plans that have matching or complementary Deck Plans or Landscape Plans. Refer to the schedules on page 305 for prices of these plans. Some of our plans can be customized through Home Planners' Home Customizer® Service. These plans are indicated below with this symbol: ♠. See page 307 for information. Some plans are also part of our Quote One® estimating service and are indicated by this symbol: ☖ . See page 300 for more information.

To Order: Fill in and send the order form on page 309—or call toll free 1-800-521-6797 or 520-297-8200.

House Blueprint Price Schedule

(Prices guaranteed through December 31, 1997)

	1-set Study Package	4-set Building Package	8-set Building Package	1-set Reproducible Sepias	Home Customizer® Package
Schedule A	$300	$345	$405	$505	$555
Schedule B	$340	$385	$445	$565	$615
Schedule C	$380	$425	$485	$625	$675
Schedule D	$420	$465	$525	$685	$735
Schedule E	$540	$585	$645	$745	$795

Prices for 4- or 8-set Building Packages honored only at time of original order.

Additional Identical Blueprints in same order ....$50 per set
Reverse Blueprints (mirror image) ....$50 per set
Specification Outlines ....$10 each
Materials Lists (available only from those designers listed below):

- ▲ Home Planners Designs $50
- ≠ Larry Belk Designs $50
- • Design Traditions Designs $50
- ✳ Larry Garnett Designs $50
- † Design Basics Designs $75
- ✱ Alan Mascord Designs...$50
- ◆ Donald Gardner Designs $50
- ■ The Sater Design Collection.......................................$50

Materials Lists for "E" price plans are an additional $10.
Materials Lists are not available for California Engineering Service.

Deck Plans Price Schedule

CUSTOM DECK PLANS

Price Group	Q	R	S
1 Set Custom Plans	$25	$30	$35

Additional identical sets ....$10 each
Reverse sets (mirror image) ....$10 each

STANDARD DECK DETAILS
1 Set Generic Construction Details............................$14.95 each

COMPLETE DECK BUILDING PACKAGE

Price Group	Q	R	S
1 Set Custom Plans, plus 1 Set Standard Deck Details	$35	$40	$45

Landscape Plans Price Schedule

Price Group	X	Y	Z
1 set	$35	$45	$55
3 sets	$50	$60	$70
6 sets	$65	$75	$85

Additional Identical Sets ....$10 each
Reverse Sets (mirror image)..$10 each

DESIGN	PRICE	PAGE	CUSTOMIZABLE	QUOTE ONE®	DECK	DECK PRICE	LANDSCAPE	LANDSCAPE PRICE	REGIONS
▲ VH3480	B	277	■	🏠	D112	R	L238	Y	3,4,7,8
▲ VH3481	B	25	■	🏠			L200	X	1-3,5,6,8
▲ VH3495	C	143	■	🏠	D111	S	L200	X	1-3,5,6,8
▲ VH3496	B	129	■	🏠			L202	X	1-3,5,6,8
▲ VH3497	B	142	■	🏠					
▲ VH3507	B	106	■	🏠			L209	Y	1-6,8
▲ VH3558	C	238	■	🏠	D105	R	L203	Y	1-3,5,6,8
▲ VH3560	B	29	■	🏠			L234	Y	1-8
▲ VH3561	B	282	■	🏠	D110	R	L238	Y	3,4,7,8
▲ VH3563	B	278	■	🏠	D115	Q	L233	Y	3,4,7
▲ VH3565	C	280	■	🏠	D110	R	L233	Y	3,4,7
▲ VH3566	C	105	■	🏠	D111	S	L207	Z	1-6,8
▲ VH3569	B	28	■	🏠	D105	R	L238	Y	3,4,7,8
▲ VH3571	B	107	■	🏠	D115	Q	L202	X	1-3,5,6,8
▲ VH3600	C	7	■	🏠			L200	X	1-3,5,6,8
▲ VH3601	C	7	■	🏠			L200	X	1-3,5,6,8
▲ VH3602	C	276	■	🏠			L220	Y	1-3,5,6,8
▲ VH3603	C	276	■	🏠			L220	Y	1-3,5,6,8
▲ VH3609	C	112	■	🏠	D100	Q	L224	Y	1-3,5,6,8
▲ VH3615	B	113	■	🏠			L200	X	1-3,5,6,8
▲ VH3619	B	119	■	🏠	D111	S	L207	Z	1-6,8
▲ VH3620	B	112	■	🏠					
▲ VH3653	C	43	■	🏠	D111	S	L209	Y	1-6,8
▲ VH3658	B	179	■	🏠	D102	Q	L202	X	1-3,5,6,8
▲ VH4010	C	156							
▲ VH4012	A	158	■						
▲ VH4015	A	241	■						
▲ VH4027	B	157	■						
▲ VH4061	A	91	■	🏠	D115	Q			
▲ VH4113	B	152	■						
▲ VH4114	A	242	■						
▲ VH4115	B	153	■						
▲ VH4125	A	218	■						
▲ VH4134	B	150	■						
▲ VH4153	A	200			D115	Q	L202	X	1-3,5,6,8
▲ VH4210	A	201	■						
VH4293	B	208	■		D120	R			
VH4299	C	220	■						
VH6600	B	14							
VH6603	C	269							
■ VH6612	B	256		🏠					
■ VH6615	D	285		🏠					
VH6616	D	284							
VH6617	D	287							
VH6620	E	289							
■ VH6621	D	288		🏠					
■ VH6622	C	290		🏠					
VH6629	D	259							
VH6630	B	257							
VH6631	C	262							
VH6632	D	258							
VH6644	C	255							
VH6645	C	264							
† VH7213	B	21							
† VH7214	C	21							
† VH7215	C	64							
† VH7216	C	71							
† VH7217	D	65							
† VH7218	D	65							
† VH7219	E	61							
† VH7220	C	47							
† VH7221	C	20							
VH8001	C	286							
VH8023	D	51							
VH8044	D	50							
VH8045	D	50							
≠ VH8050	D	42		🏠					
VH8051	B	76							
VH8052	B	77							
VH8061	B	15							
≠ VH8063	B	16		🏠					
VH8064	B	26							
VH8065	C	51							
VH8066	C	37							
≠ VH8072	C	42		🏠					
VH8076	D	131							
VH8600	C	248							
VH8601	B	251							
VH8604	B	249							
VH8608	C	246							
VH8610	A	273							
VH8611	A	272							
VH8612	B	274							
VH8613	B	275							
VH8616	C	265							
VH8617	C	252							
VH8619	C	253							
VH8620	C	260							
VH8621	C	250							
VH8624	C	254							
VH8629	B	38							
VH8631	B	271							
VH8632	B	270							
VH8634	B	265							
VH8636	B	245							
VH8637	B	247							
VH8639	B	261							
VH8644	B	244							
VH8645	C	243							
VH8662	B	263							
VH8888	C	232	◆						
VH8889	A	212	◆						
VH8890	B	13	◆						
VH8891	C	196	◆						
VH8892	B	202	◆						
VH8893	B	213	◆						
VH8894	C	108	◆						
VH8898	C	203	◆						
VH8899	C	197	◆						
VH8901	A	117							

DESIGN	PRICE	PAGE	CUSTOMIZABLE	QUOTE ONE®	DECK	DECK PRICE	LANDSCAPE	LANDSCAPE PRICE	REGIONS
VH8978	A	127							
VH9044	B	135							
VH9045	B	115							
VH9094	B	114							
VH9096	C	134							
VH9117	B	137							
VH9123	B	79							
✽VH9131	C	136		🏠					
VH9132	A	137							
VH9133	A	119							
VH9150	B	116							
†VH9238	C	45		🏠					
†VH9256	B	22							
†VH9257	C	19							
†VH9259	D	60							
†VH9260	C	44							
†VH9273	C	69							
†VH9282	C	63							
†VH9293	D	68							
†VH9324	C	66							
†VH9328	C	18							
†VH9338	C	70							
†VH9339	C	34							
†VH9371	C	23							
†VH9378	E	61							
†VH9381	D	67							
✳VH9413	B	198							
✳VH9420	D	46							
✳VH9422	A	132							
✳VH9429	A	133							
✳VH9476	C	75							
✳VH9483	C	141							
✳VH9484	D	149							
✳VH9488	D	151							
✳VH9495	C	140							
✳VH9505	B	199							
✳VH9506	A	131							
✳VH9508	B	133							
✳VH9509	B	155							
✳VH9510	B	168							
✳VH9516	B	62							
✳VH9524	C	74							
✳VH9528	B	12							
✳VH9529	A	11							
✳VH9530	A	11							
✳VH9531	A	11							
✳VH9532	A	62							
✳VH9533	B	73							
✳VH9534	B	141							
✳VH9535	C	72		🏠					
✳VH9536	D	144							
✳VH9537	D	166							
✳VH9538	D	154							
✳VH9539	D	167							
◆VH9611	C	13							
◆VH9613	C	195							
◆VH9614	C	194							
◆VH9619	D	17							
◆VH9620	B	81							
◆VH9621	C	101		🏠					
◆VH9625	D	92							
◆VH9626	C	93		🏠					
◆VH9632	D	103		🏠					
◆VH9644	C	98							
◆VH9645	C	96		🏠					
◆VH9655	D	17							
◆VH9661	C	67		🏠					
◆VH9662	C	100		🏠					
◆VH9663	B	90							
◆VH9664	B	80		🏠					
◆VH9666	C	120		🏠					
◆VH9667	D	99		🏠					
◆VH9673	D	99		🏠					
◆VH9679	C	83							
◆VH9690	C	97		🏠					
◆VH9697	B	121							
◆VH9702	D	94		🏠					
◆VH9713	C	82							
◆VH9723	D	95		🏠					
◆VH9726	B	85							
◆VH9734	C	39		🏠					
◆VH9737	C	266							
◆VH9740	C	267							
◆VH9749	C	84							
•VH9813	C	126		🏠					
•VH9821	C	32		🏠					
VH9848	B	52							
VH9849	B	54							
•VH9853	B	33		🏠					
VH9854	C	130							
VH9855	D	36							
VH9861	D	104							
•VH9868	C	41							

DESIGN	PRICE	PAGE	CUSTOMIZABLE	QUOTE ONE®	DECK	DECK PRICE	LANDSCAPE	LANDSCAPE PRICE	REGIONS
VH9873	B	40							
VH9875	B	53							
VH9898	D	138							
VH9902	B	56							
VH9905	C	57							
VH9907	C	53							
VH9908	D	139							
•VH9914	B	31		🏠					
VH9948	C	55							
VH9949	B	35							
VH9950	C	30							
VHG106	$75	291							
VHG107	$50	293							
VHG108	$40	294							
VHG109	$50	296							
VHG110	$50	295							
VHG114	$40	297							
VHG206	$85	292							

Additional sets for VHG106-VHG206 are $10 each.

The Home Customizer®

"This house is perfect...if only the family room were two feet wider." Sound familiar? In response to the numerous requests for this type of modification, Home Planners has developed **The Home Customizer® Package**. This exclusive package offers our top-of-the-line materials to make it easy for anyone, anywhere to customize any Home Planners design to fit their needs.

Some of the changes you can make to any of our plans include:

- exterior elevation changes
- kitchen and bath modifications
- roof, wall and foundation changes
- room additions and more!

The Home Customizer® Package includes everything you need to make the necessary changes to your favorite design. The package includes:

- instruction book with examples
- architectural scale and clear work film
- erasable red marker and removable correction tape
- ¼"-scale furniture cutouts
- 1 set reproducible, erasable Sepias
- 1 set study blueprints for communicating changes to your design professional
- a copyright release letter so you can make copies as you need them
- referral list of drafting, architectural and engineering professionals in your region who are trained in modifying Home Planners designs efficiently and inexpensively

The price of the **Home Customizer® Package** ranges from $555 to $795, depending on the price schedule of the design you have chosen. **The Home Customizer® Package** will not only save you 25% to 75% of the cost of drawing the plans from scratch with a custom architect or engineer, it will also give you the flexibility to have your changes and modifications made by our referral network or by the professional of your choice.

Now it's even easier and more affordable to have the custom home you've always wanted.

New Custom Engineering Service

Through this exciting new service, you can now obtain an engineering seal for the structural elements of any Home Planners plan including complete calculations (minus foundation engineering) from a competent, registered professional. You'll receive a detailed analysis and engineering seal that will assist with the permit process, even in areas that normally require very specific calculations. For more complete information about this service, see page 300.

 For information about any of the above services or to order call 1-800-521-6797.

BLUEPRINTS ARE NOT RETURNABLE

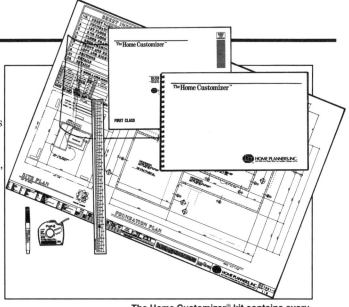

The Home Customizer® kit contains everything you'll need to make your home a one of a kind.

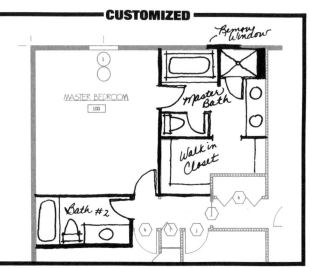

Making interior changes to the floor plan is simple and fun using the tools provided in The Home Customizer® kit!

Before You Order . . .

Before filling out the coupon at right or calling us on our Toll-Free Blueprint Hotline, you may want to learn more about our services and products. Here's some information you will find helpful.

Quick Turnaround

We process and ship every blueprint order from our office within 48 hours. Because of this quick turnaround, we won't send a formal notice acknowledging receipt of your order.

Our Exchange Policy

Since blueprints are printed in response to your order, we cannot honor requests for refunds. However, we will exchange your entire first order for an equal number of blueprints at a price of $50 for the first set and $10 for each additional set; $70 total exchange fee for 4 sets; $100 total exchange fee for 8 sets . . . *plus* the difference in cost if exchanging for a design in a higher price bracket or *less* the difference in cost if exchanging for a design in lower price bracket. One exchange is allowed within a year of purchase date. **(Sepias are not exchangeable.)** All sets from the first order must be returned before the exchange can take place. Please add $10 for postage and handling via ground service; $20 via Second Day Air; $30 via Next Day Air.

About Reverse Blueprints

If you want to build in reverse of the plan as shown, we will include an extra set of reverse blueprints (mirror image) for an additional fee of $50. Although lettering and dimensions will appear backward, reverses will be a useful aid if you decide to flop the plan.

Revising, Modifying and Customizing Plans

The wide variety of designs available in this publication allows you to select ideas and concepts for a home to fit your building site and match your family's needs, wants and budget. Like many homeowners who buy these plans, you and your builder, architect or engineer may want to make changes to them. Some minor changes may be made by your builder, but we recommend that most changes be made by a licensed architect or engineer. If you need to make alterations to a design that is customizable, you need only order our Home Customizer® Package to get you started. As set forth below, we cannot assume any responsibility for blueprints which have been changed, whether by you, your builder or by professionals selected by you or referred to you by us, because such individuals are outside our supervision and control.

Architectural and Engineering Seals

Some cities and states are now requiring that a licensed architect or engineer review and "seal" a blueprint, or officially approve it, prior to construction due to concerns over energy costs, safety and other factors. Prior to application for a building permit or the start of actual construction, we strongly advise that you consult your local building official who can tell you if such a review is required.

About the Designers

The architects and designers whose work appears in this publication are among America's leading residential designers. Each plan was designed to meet the requirements of a nationally recognized model building code in effect at the time and place the plan was drawn. Because national building codes change from time to time, plans may not comply with any such code at the time they are sold to a customer. In addition, building officials may not accept these plans as final construction documents of record as the plans may need to be modified and additional drawings and details added to suit local conditions and requirements. We strongly advise that purchasers consult a licensed architect or engineer, and their local building official, before starting any construction related to these plans.

Local Building Codes and Zoning Requirements

At the time of creation, our plans are drawn to specifications published by the Building Officials and Code Administrators (BOCA) International, Inc.; the Southern Building Code Congress (SBCCI) International, Inc.; the International Conference of Building Officials; or the Council of American Building Officials (CABO). Our plans are designed to meet or exceed national building standards. Because of the great differences in geography and climate throughout the United States and Canada, each state, county and municipality has its own building codes, zone requirements, ordinances and building regulations. Your plan may need to be modified to comply with local requirements regarding snow loads, energy codes, soil and seismic conditions and a wide range of other matters. In addition, you may need to obtain permits or inspections from local governments before and in the course of construction. Prior to using blueprints ordered from us, we strongly advise that you consult a licensed architect or engineer—and speak with your local building official—before applying for any permit or beginning construction. We authorize the use of our blueprints on the express condition that you strictly comply with all local building codes, zoning requirements and other applicable laws, regulations, ordinances and requirements. **Notice:** Plans for homes to be built in Nevada must be re-drawn by a Nevada-registered professional. Consult your building official for more information on this subject.

Foundation and Exterior Wall Changes

Most of our plans are drawn with either a full or partial basement foundation. Depending on your specific climate or regional building practices, you may wish to change this basement to a slab or crawlspace. Most professional contractors and builders can easily adapt your plans to alternate foundation types. Likewise, most can easily change 2x4 wall construction to 2x6, or vice versa.

Disclaimer

We and the designers we work with have put substantial care and effort into the creation of our blueprints. However, because we cannot provide on-site consultation, supervision and control over actual construction, and because of the great variance in local building requirements, building practices and soil, seismic, weather and other conditions, WE CANNOT MAKE ANY WARRANTY, EXPRESS OR IMPLIED, WITH RESPECT TO THE CONTENT OR USE OF OUR BLUEPRINTS, INCLUDING BUT NOT LIMITED TO ANY WARRANTY OF MERCHANTABILITY OR OF FITNESS FOR A PARTICULAR PURPOSE.

Terms and Conditions

The terms and conditions governing our license of blueprints to you are set forth in the material accompanying the blueprints. This material tells you how to return the blueprints if you do not agree to these terms and conditions.

How Many Blueprints Do You Need?

A single set of blueprints is sufficient to study a home in greater detail. However, if you are planning to obtain cost estimates from a contractor or subcontractors—or if you are planning to build immediately—you will need more sets. Because additional sets are cheaper when ordered in quantity with the original order, make sure you order enough blueprints to satisfy all requirements. The following checklist will help you determine how many you need:

_____ Owner

_____ Builder (generally requires at least three sets; one as a legal document, one to use during inspections, and at least one to give to subcontractors)

_____ Local Building Department (often requires two sets)

_____ Mortgage Lender (usually one set for a conventional loan; three sets for FHA or VA loans)

_____ TOTAL NUMBER OF SETS

HOME PLANNERS, A Division of Hanley-Wood, Inc.
3275 WEST INA ROAD
SUITE 110, TUCSON, ARIZONA 85741

E BASIC BLUEPRINT PACKAGE
h me the following (please refer to the Plans Index and Price Schedule in this section):

____ Set(s) of blueprints for plan number(s) _____. $_____
____ Set(s) of sepias for plan number(s) _____. $_____
____ Additional identical blueprints in same order @ $50 per set. $_____
____ Reverse blueprints @ $50 per set. $_____
____ Home Customizer® Package for plan number(s)_____ $_____

PORTANT EXTRAS Rush me the following:

____ Materials List: @ $50; $75 Design Basics.
Add $10 for Schedule E plans $_____
____ **Quote One®** Summary Cost Report @ $19.95 for 1, $14.95
for each additional, for plans _____. $_____
Building location: City_____Zip Code_____ $_____
____ **Quote One®** Materials Cost Report @ $110 Schedule A-D;
$120 Schedule E for plan, _____.
(Must be purchased with Blueprints sets.)
Building location: City_____Zip Code_____ $_____
____ Specification Outlines @ $10 each. $_____
____ Detail Sets @ $14.95 each; any two for $22.95; any three for $29.95;
all four for $39.95 (save $19.85)
❑ Plumbing ❑ Electrical ❑ Construction ❑ Mechanical
(These helpful details provide general construction
advice and are not specific to any single plan.) $_____
____ Plan-A-Home® @ $29.95 each. $_____

CK BLUEPRINTS

____ Set(s) of Deck Plan _____. $_____
____ Additional identical blueprints in same order @ $10 per set. $_____
____ Reverse blueprints @ $10 per set. $_____
____ Set of Standard Deck Details @ $14.95 per set. $_____
____ Set of Complete Building Package (Best Buy!) Includes
Custom Deck Plan _____
(See Index and Price Schedule)
Plus Standard Deck Details $_____

NDSCAPE BLUEPRINTS

____ Set(s) of Landscape Plan _____. $_____
____ Additional identical blueprints in same order @ $10 per set. $_____
____ Reverse blueprints @ $10 per set. $_____

ase indicate the appropriate region of the country for
nt & Material List. (See Map on page 303): Region _____

OSTAGE AND HANDLING	1-3 sets	4+ sets
LIVERY (Requires street address - No P.O. Boxes)		
egular Service (Allow 4-6 days delivery)	❑ $8.00	❑ $10.00
nd Day Air (Allow 2-3 days delivery)	❑ $12.00	❑ $20.00
ext Day Air (Allow 1 day delivery)	❑ $22.00	❑ $30.00
RTIFIED MAIL (Requires signature)		
no street address available. (Allow 4-6 days delivery)	❑ $10.00	❑ $14.00
VERSEAS DELIVERY	fax, phone or mail for quote	

NOTE: ALL DELIVERY TIMES ARE FROM DATE BLUEPRINT PACKAGE IS SHIPPED

OSTAGE (From shaded box above) $_____
UB-TOTAL $_____
ALES TAX (AZ 5%, CA & NY 8.25%, DC 5.75%,
6.25%, MI 6%, MN 6.5%) $_____
OTAL (Sub-total, and tax) $_____

OUR ADDRESS (please print)

ame _____

reet _____

ty _____State_____Zip _____

aytime telephone number (_____) _____

OR CREDIT CARD ORDERS ONLY Please fill in the information below:

redit card number _____

xp. Date: Month/Year _____

heck one ❑ Visa ❑ MasterCard ❑ Discover Card

gnature _____

ease check appropriate box: ❑ Licensed Builder-Contractor
❑ Homeowner

ORDER TOLL FREE!
1-800-521-6797 or
520-297-8200

Order Form Key
VH

O R D E R   F O R M

HOME PLANNERS, A Division of Hanley-Wood, Inc.
3275 WEST INA ROAD
SUITE 110, TUCSON, ARIZONA 85741

THE BASIC BLUEPRINT PACKAGE
Rush me the following (please refer to the Plans Index and Price Schedule in this section):

____ Set(s) of blueprints for plan number(s) _____. $_____
____ Set(s) of sepias for plan number(s) _____. $_____
____ Additional identical blueprints in same order @ $50 per set. $_____
____ Reverse blueprints @ $50 per set. $_____
____ Home Customizer® Package for plan number(s)_____ $_____

IMPORTANT EXTRAS Rush me the following:

____ Materials List: @ $50; $75 Design Basics.
Add $10 for Schedule E plans $_____
____ **Quote One®** Summary Cost Report @ $19.95 for 1, $14.95
for each additional, for plans _____. $_____
Building location: City_____Zip Code_____ $_____
____ **Quote One®** Materials Cost Report @ $110 Schedule A-D;
$120 Schedule E for plan, _____.
(Must be purchased with Blueprints sets.)
Building location: City_____Zip Code_____ $_____
____ Specification Outlines @ $10 each. $_____
____ Detail Sets @ $14.95 each; any two for $22.95; any three for $29.95;
all four for $39.95 (save $19.85)
❑ Plumbing ❑ Electrical ❑ Construction ❑ Mechanical
(These helpful details provide general construction
advice and are not specific to any single plan.) $_____
____ Plan-A-Home® @ $29.95 each. $_____

DECK BLUEPRINTS

____ Set(s) of Deck Plan _____. $_____
____ Additional identical blueprints in same order @ $10 per set. $_____
____ Reverse blueprints @ $10 per set. $_____
____ Set of Standard Deck Details @ $14.95 per set. $_____
____ Set of Complete Building Package (Best Buy!) Includes
Custom Deck Plan _____
(See Index and Price Schedule)
Plus Standard Deck Details $_____

LANDSCAPE BLUEPRINTS

____ Set(s) of Landscape Plan _____. $_____
____ Additional identical blueprints in same order @ $10 per set. $_____
____ Reverse blueprints @ $10 per set. $_____

Please indicate the appropriate region of the country for
Plant & Material List. (See Map on page 303): Region _____

POSTAGE AND HANDLING	1-3 sets	4+ sets
DELIVERY (Requires street address - No P.O. Boxes)		
•Regular Service (Allow 4-6 days delivery)	❑ $8.00	❑ $10.00
•2nd Day Air (Allow 2-3 days delivery)	❑ $12.00	❑ $20.00
•Next Day Air (Allow 1 day delivery)	❑ $22.00	❑ $30.00
CERTIFIED MAIL (Requires signature)		
If no street address available. (Allow 4-6 days delivery)	❑ $10.00	❑ $14.00
OVERSEAS DELIVERY	fax, phone or mail for quote	

NOTE: ALL DELIVERY TIMES ARE FROM DATE BLUEPRINT PACKAGE IS SHIPPED

POSTAGE (From shaded box above) $_____
SUB-TOTAL $_____
SALES TAX (AZ 5%, CA & NY 8.25%, DC 5.75%,
IL 6.25%, MI 6%, MN 6.5%) $_____
TOTAL (Sub-total, and tax) $_____

YOUR ADDRESS (please print)

Name _____

Street _____

City _____State_____Zip _____

Daytime telephone number (_____) _____

FOR CREDIT CARD ORDERS ONLY Please fill in the information below:

Credit card number _____

Exp. Date: Month/Year _____

Check one ❑ Visa ❑ MasterCard ❑ Discover Card

Signature _____

Please check appropriate box: ❑ Licensed Builder-Contractor
❑ Homeowner

ORDER TOLL FREE!
1-800-521-6797 or
520-297-8200

Order Form Key
VH

Helpful Books & Software

Home Planners wants your building experience to be as pleasant and trouble-free as possible. That's why we've expanded our library of Do-It-Yourself titles to help you along. In addition to our beautiful plans books, we've added books to guide you through specific projects as well as the construction process. In fact, these are titles that will be as useful after your dream home is built as they are right now.

COUNTRY
1 200 country designs from classic to contemporary by 7 winning designers. 224 pages $8.95

BUDGET-SMART
2 200 efficient plans from 7 top designers, that you can really afford to build! 224 pages $8.95

MOVE-UP
3 200 stylish designs for today's growing families from 9 hot designers. 224 pages $8.95 NEW!

NARROW-LOT
4 200 unique homes less than 60' wide from 7 designers. Up to 3,000 square feet. 224 pages $8.95

REGIONAL BEST
5 200 beautiful homes from across America by 7 regional designers. 224 pages $8.95 NEW!

EXPANDABLES
6 200 flexible plans that expand with your needs from 7 top designers. 240 pages $8.95 NEW!

BEST SELLERS
7 NEW! Our 50th Anniversary book with 200 of our very best designs in full color! 224 page $12.95

NEW ENGLAND
8 260 of the best in Colonial home design. Special interior design sections, too. 384 pages $14.95

AFFORDABLE
9 430 cost-saving plans specially selected for modest to medium building budgets. 320 pages $9.95

LUXURY
10 154 fine luxury plans-loaded with luscious amenities! 192 pages $14.95

ONE-STORY
11 448 designs for all lifestyles. 860 to 5,400 square feet. 384 pages $9.95 NEW!

TWO-STORY
12 460 designs for one-and-a-half and two stories. 1,245 to 7,275 square feet. 384 pages $9.95

VACATION
13 345 designs for recreation, retirement and leisure. 312 pages $8.95 NEW!

MULTI-LEVEL
14 312 designs for split-levels, bi-levels, multi-levels and walkouts. 224 pages $8.95 NEW!

OUTDOOR
15 42 unique outdoor projects. Gazebos, strombellas, bridges, sheds, playsets and more! 96 pages $7.95 NEW!

DECKS
16 25 outstanding single-, double- and multi-level decks you can build. 112 pages $7.95

ENCYCLOPEDIA
17 500 exceptional plans for all styles and budgets—the best book of its kind! 352 pages $9.95

MODERN & CLASSIC
18 341 impressive homes featuring the latest in contemporary design. 304 pages $9.95

TRADITIONAL
19 403 designs of classic beauty and elegance. 304 pages $9.95

VICTORIAN
20 160 striking Victorian and Farmhouse designs from three leading designers. 192 pages $12.95

SOUTHERN
21 207 homes rich in Southern styling and comfort. 240 pages $8.95 NEW!

WESTERN
22 215 designs that capture the spirit and diversity of the Western lifestyle. 208 pages $9.95

EMPTY-NESTER
23 200 exciting plans for empty-nesters, retirees and childless couples. 224 pages $8.95

STARTER
24 200 easy-to-build plans for starter and low-budget houses. 224 pages $8.95

Landscape Designs

FRONT & BACK
25 The first book of do-it-yourself landscapes. 40 front, 15 backyards. 208 pages $12.95

BACKYARDS
26 40 designs focused solely on creating your own specially themed backyard oasis. 160 pages $12.95

EASY CARE
27 NEW! 41 special landscapes designed for beauty and low maintenance. 160 pages $12.95

Design Software

BOOK & CD ROM
28 NEW! Both the Home Planners Gold book and matching Windows™ CD ROM with 3D floorplans. $24.95

3D HOME DESIGNER
29 Take home design to the next level. Windows™ compatible program automatically creates 3D views of any floor plan you draw. Includes bonus CD of 500 Designs. $49.95

Interior Design

HOME DECORATING
30 Special effects and creative ideas for all surfaces. Includes simple step-by-step diagrams. 96 pages $9.95

BATHROOMS
31 An innovative guide to organizing, remodeling and decorating your bathroom. 96 pages $8.95

KITCHENS
32 An imaginative guide to designing the perfect kitchen. Chock full of bright ideas to make your job easier. 176 pages $14.95

Planning Books & Quick Guides

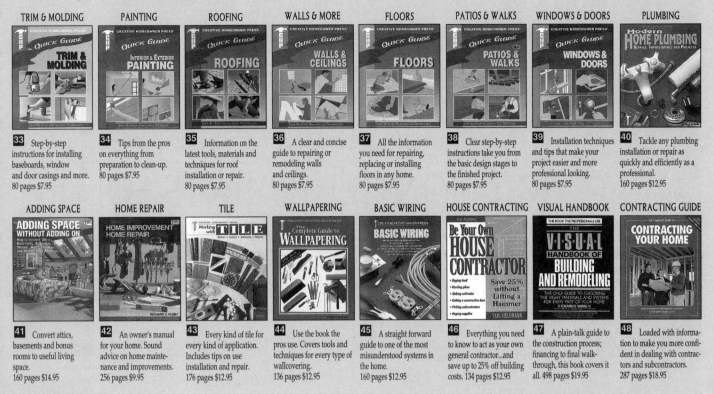

TRIM & MOLDING
33 Step-by-step instructions for installing baseboards, window and door casings and more. 80 pages $7.95

PAINTING
34 Tips from the pros on everything from preparation to clean-up. 80 pages $7.95

ROOFING
35 Information on the latest tools, materials and techniques for roof installation or repair. 80 pages $7.95

WALLS & MORE
36 A clear and concise guide to repairing or remodeling walls and ceilings. 80 pages $7.95

FLOORS
37 All the information you need for repairing, replacing or installing floors in any home. 80 pages $7.95

PATIOS & WALKS
38 Clear step-by-step instructions take you from the basic design stages to the finished project. 80 pages $7.95

WINDOWS & DOORS
39 Installation techniques and tips that make your project easier and more professional looking. 80 pages $7.95

PLUMBING
40 Tackle any plumbing installation or repair as quickly and efficiently as a professional. 160 pages $12.95

ADDING SPACE
41 Convert attics, basements and bonus rooms to useful living space. 160 pages $14.95

HOME REPAIR
42 An owner's manual for your home. Sound advice on home maintenance and improvements. 256 pages $9.95

TILE
43 Every kind of tile for every kind of application. Includes tips on use installation and repair. 176 pages $12.95

WALLPAPERING
44 Use the book the pros use. Covers tools and techniques for every type of wallcovering. 136 pages $12.95

BASIC WIRING
45 A straight forward guide to one of the most misunderstood systems in the home. 160 pages $12.95

HOUSE CONTRACTING
46 Everything you need to know to act as your own general contractor...and save up to 25% off building costs. 134 pages $12.95

VISUAL HANDBOOK
47 A plain-talk guide to the construction process; financing to final walk-through, this book covers it all. 498 pages $19.95

CONTRACTING GUIDE
48 Loaded with information to make you more confident in dealing with contractors and subcontractors. 287 pages $18.95

FRAMING

49 For those who want to take a more-hands on approach to their dream. 319 pages $19.95

Additional Books Order Form

To order your books, just check the box of the book numbered below and complete the coupon. We will process your order and ship it from our office within 48 hours. Send coupon and check (in U.S. funds).

YES! Please send me the books I've indicated:

☐ 1:FH $8.95	☐ 26:BYL $12.95
☐ 2:BS $8.95	☐ 27:ECL $12.95
☐ 3:MU $8.95	☐ 28:HPGC $24.95
☐ 4:NL $8.95	☐ 29:PLAN3D $49.95
☐ 5:AA $8.95	☐ 30:CDP $9.95
☐ 6:EX $8.95	☐ 31:CDB $8.95
☐ 7:HPG $12.95	☐ 32:CKI $14.95
☐ 8:NES $14.95	☐ 33:CGT $7.95
☐ 9:AH $9.95	☐ 34:CGP $7.95
☐ 10:LD2 . . . . . . $14.95	☐ 35:CGR $7.95
☐ 11:VO $9.95	☐ 36:CGC $7.95
☐ 12:VT $9.95	☐ 37:CGF $7.95
☐ 13:VH $8.95	☐ 38:CGW $7.95
☐ 14:VS $8.95	☐ 39:CGD $7.95
☐ 15:YG $7.95	☐ 40:CMP $12.95
☐ 16:DP $7.95	☐ 41:CAS $14.95
☐ 17:EN $9.95	☐ 42:CHR $9.95
☐ 18:EC $9.95	☐ 43:CWT $12.95
☐ 19:ET $9.95	☐ 44:CW $12.95
☐ 20:VDH $12.95	☐ 45:CBW $12.95
☐ 21:SH $8.95	☐ 46:SBC $12.95
☐ 22:WH $9.95	☐ 47:RVH $19.95
☐ 23:EP $8.95	☐ 48:BCC $18.95
☐ 24:ST $8.95	☐ 49:SRF $19.95
☐ 25:HL $12.95	

Canadian Customers
Order Toll-Free 1-800-561-4169

Additional Books Sub-Total $ _____
ADD Postage and Handling $ 3.00
Sales Tax: (AZ 5%, CA & NY 8.25%, DC 5.75%,
          IL 6.25%, MI 6%, MN 6.5%) $ _____
YOUR TOTAL (Sub-Total, Postage/Handling, Tax) $ _____

YOUR ADDRESS (Please print)

Name _____

Street _____

City _____ State _____ Zip _____

Phone (_____) _____ — _____

YOUR PAYMENT
Check one: ☐ Check ☐ Visa ☐ MasterCard ☐ Discover Card
Required credit card information:

Credit Card Number _____

Expiration Date (Month/Year) _____ / _____

Signature Required _____

Home Planners, A Division of Hanley-Wood, Inc.
3275 W Ina Road, Suite 110, Dept. BK, Tucson, AZ 85741

VH

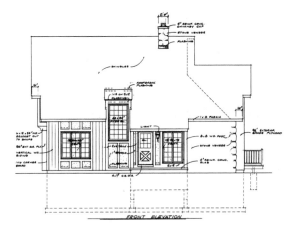

OVER 3 MILLION BLUEPRINTS SOLD

"We instructed our builder to follow the plans including all of the many details which make this house so elegant... Our home is a fine example of the results one can achieve by purchasing and following the plans which you offer... Everyone who has seen it has assured us that it belongs in 'a picture book.' I truly mean it when I say that my home 'is a DREAM HOUSE.'"

S.P.
Anderson, SC

"We have had a steady stream of visitors, many of whom tell us this is the most beautiful home they've seen. Everyone is amazed at the layout and remark on how unique it is. Our real estate attorney, who is a Chicago dweller and who deals with highly valued properties, told me this is the only suburban home he has seen that he would want to live in."

W. & P.S.
Flossmoor, IL

"Home Planners' blueprints saved us a great deal of money. I acted as the general contractor and we did a lot of the work ourselves. We probably built it for half the cost! We are thinking about more plans for another home. I purchased a competitor's book but my husband only wants your plans!"

K.M.
Grovetown, GA

"We are very happy with the product of our efforts. The neighbors and passersby appreciate what we have created. We have had many people stop by to discuss our house and kindly praise it as being the nicest house in our area of new construction. We have even had one person stop and make us an unsolicited offer to buy the house for much more than we have invested in it."

K. & L.S.
Bolingbrook, IL

"The traffic going past our house is unbelievable. On several occasions, we have heard that it is the 'prettiest house in Batavia.' Also, when meeting someone new and mentioning what street we live on, quite often we're told, 'Oh, you're the one in the yellow house with the wrap-around porch! I love it!'"

A.W.
Batavia, NY

"I have been involved in the building trades my entire life... Since building our home we have built two other homes for other families. Their plans from local professional architects were not nearly as good as yours. For that reason we are ordering additional plan books from you."

T.F.
Kingston, WA

"The blueprints we received from Home Planners were of excellent quality and provided us with exactly what we needed to get our successful home-building project underway. We appreciate Home Planners' invaluable role in our home-building effort."

T.A.
Concord, TN